WORKING WITH CLAY

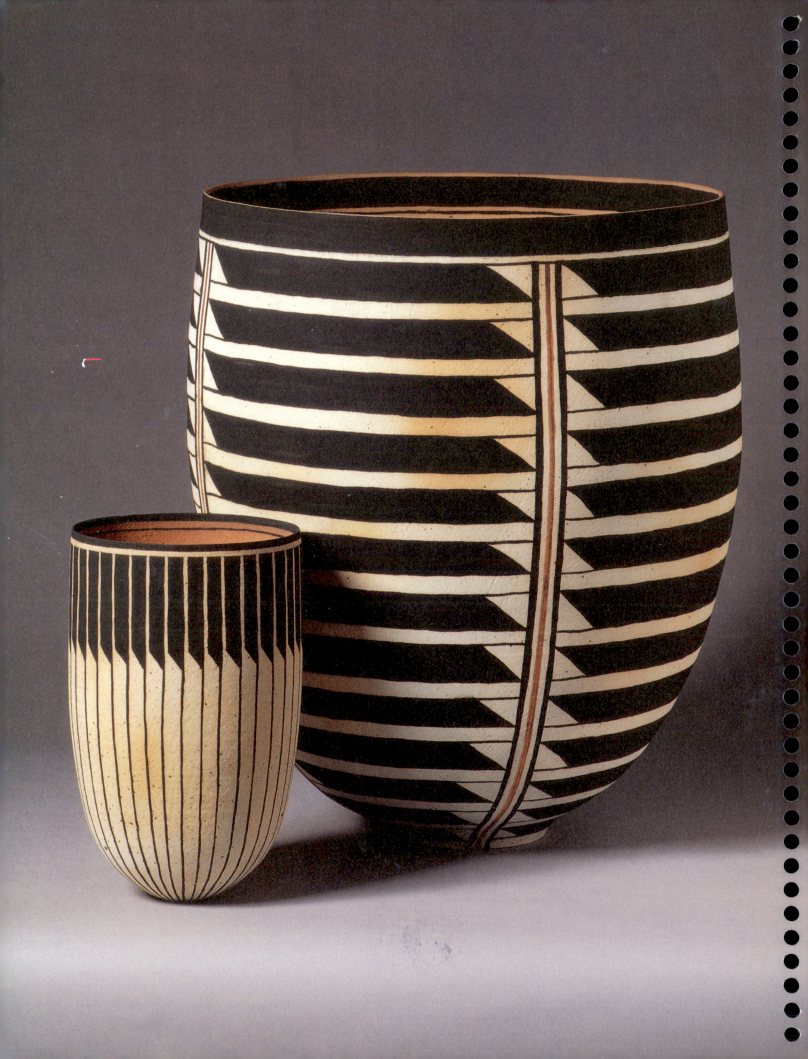

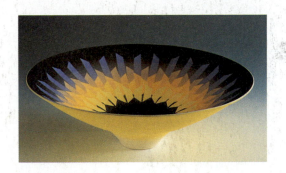

WORKING WITH CLAY

SECOND EDITION

Susan Peterson

Professor Emerita, Hunter College at the City University of New York

Jan Peterson

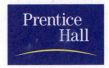

Prentice Hall

Published 2003 by Prentice Hall Inc.
A Division of Pearson Education
Upper Saddle River, New Jersey 07458

10 9 8 7 6 5 4 3 2 1

ISBN 0-13-098348-9

This book was designed and produced by
Laurence King Publishing Ltd,
71 Great Russell Street,
London WC1B 3BP
www.laurenceking.co.uk

Editor: Elisabeth Ingles
Designer: Karen Stafford
Cover Designer: Karen Stafford
Printed in China

FRONTISPIECE: Beate Andersen (Denmark), thrown vases, stoneware, matt glaze, handpainted decoration, c/10; 20 and 12½ ins. (52 and 32 cm) high

TITLE PAGE: Peter Lane's (UK) thrown unglazed porcelain bowl, 12½ ins. (32 cm) in diameter, is airbrushed with stains prepared by putting the color through a 200-mesh sieve to achieve the fineness for spraying. He bisque-fires, rubs down with wet and dry paper and repeats this process after the decoration and final firing in an electric kiln to c/10

FRONT COVER: Magdalene Odundo (UK), burnished earthenware sculpture, 16 x 8 ins. (40.5 x 20 cm)

BACK COVER: (left to right) Bryan Hiveley, *2000 Kiln Ritual*, glazed, 67 x 32 x 31 ins. (170 x 81 x 79 cm); Jill Bonovitz, porcelain vase, 6 ins. (15 cm) high; John McCuistion, Miró mask, c/10 reduction, acrylic paint, 13 x 10 x 6 ins. (33 x 25 x 15 cm)

CONTENTS PAGES Village potter, India, applying rice-paste decoration to bonfired local clay vessels, 24 ins. (61 cm) high
Floor vase by Susan Peterson
Lucy Lewis' (d. 1992) fine-line design painted with a yucca brush and natural ground hematite pigment on Acoma pueblo kaolin-type clay, bonfired; 10 ins. (25 cm) diameter
Detail of wall plaque by Robert Sperry (d. 1998), white engobe over black glaze, c/10 reduction, 36 x 36 ins. (91 x 91 cm)
Ernst Häusermann's pyramidal sculpture
Kirk Mangus, *Dead Soldier*
Robert Brady's 5 ft (152 cm) tall coil sculpture, engobe painted
Bruria Finkel, *Head*
Delft plate, Holland, c. 1600

CONTENTS

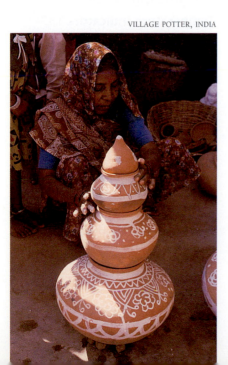

VILLAGE POTTER, INDIA

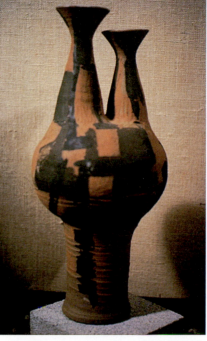

SUSAN PETERSON

3 Throwing on the Potter's Wheel 67

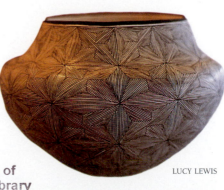

LUCY LEWIS

CONTENTS

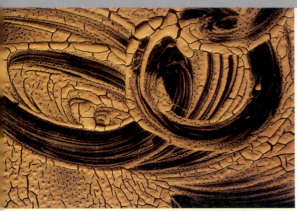

ROBERT SPERRY

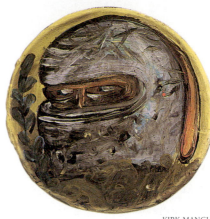

KIRK MANGUS

ERNST HAÜSERMANN

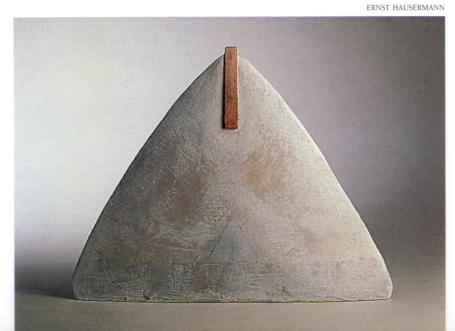

CONTENTS

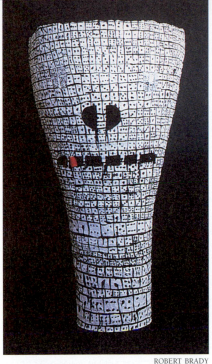

ROBERT BRADY

BRURIA FINKEL

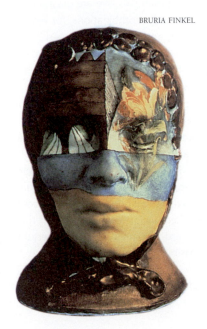

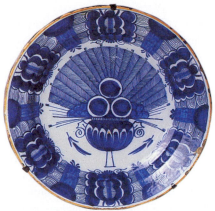

DELFT PLATE

Temperatures in the book are generally given in figures on the Orton Cone Scale. Refer to Compendium, page 195, for Fahrenheit and Centigrade equivalent temperatures for Orton (USA) and Seger (world) cones

PREFACE TO THE FIRST EDITION, 1998

I have written this book to inspire and to teach the beginner about working with clay through colorful photographs and anecdotal descriptions of the various processes involved. I also aim to appeal to the collector, who can make use of this analysis to gain an indepth perspective on historical and contemporary ceramics. The practical photographs are set off by copious illustrations of what can be achieved, from everyday items such as plates and bowls to international examples of the potter's art such as sculpture and site installations. Beginner students and all those who appreciate the art of ceramics will find many illuminating insights into this endlessly fascinating world.

My long career as a professor of ceramic art and a practicing potter has enabled me to pass on the benefits of my experience to students and aficionados at all levels. I have five books in print, apart from this one: *Shoji Hamada, A Potter's Way and Work*; *The Living Tradition of Maria Martinez*; *Lucy M. Lewis, American Indian Potter*; *The Craft and Art of Clay*; *Pottery by American Indian Women*. I have a video in circulation from film made at Hamada's studio in 1970 when I did the notes for his book, and a series of 54 videos on

ceramics, called "Wheels, Kilns, and Clay." Thanks are due to the many artists all over the world who have helped me with suggestions and by sending me their own examples. I am grateful to Laurence King, Lee Ripley Greenfield, Judy Rasmussen, Janet Pilch, and the staff at Calmann & King in London who package the book; to Elisabeth Ingles, my editor, and Karen Stafford, who designed the book; to Craig Smith, who photographed the process shots of me working in my studio, to Bud Therien at Prentice Hall, and to Overlook/Viking. I also acknowledge the help and encouragement of my three children, Jill Peterson Hoddick, Jan Sigrid Peterson, and Taäg Paul Peterson, plus five grandchildren, Annah Gerletti, Kayley Hoddick, Alexander and Calder Peterson, and Augustus John Gerletti. I would not have got so much done without assistants Nori Pao, Judith Schreibman, and Tony Mulanix.

Finally, a fond remembrance and deep gratitude to my deceased parents, Iva and Paul Harnly, and my late husband Robert Schwarz Jr.

SUSAN HARNLY PETERSON
Carefree, Arizona, June 1998

PREFACE TO THE SECOND EDITION, 2002

Since 1998 I have published five more books: the second edition of this one, *Working with Clay*; the third edition of *The Craft and Art of Clay*; *Contemporary Ceramics*; *Smashing Glazes*; and *Jun Kaneko* – quite an output! March 2002 sees the establishment of the Susan Harnly Peterson Ceramic Archive and Study Collection in the Ceramic Research Center of the Nelson Art Museum of Arizona State University. We hope many of you will add to this beginning.

I am grateful to all you artists over the globe who send me your images, invite me to lecture in your schools and conferences, and aid in countless other ways. Helpers on this edition include my children and grandchildren, and my assistants Lucy Horner and Jarilyn Mason (daughter of John and Vernita). K.C. O'Connell, my studio assistant, made the new clay and glaze tests. My friend and remarkable photographer Craig Smith took the process and test photos. I am grateful to the same team as before at Laurence King Publishing, London.

This edition has increased in length, to include modifications and new techniques. Much is changing in the ceramic world. I see fewer purely functional pots except in folk cultures – we all want to decorate and invent forms!

More use of prepared clay and commercial glazes is apparent, but there is a return to basics in building your own kilns, in old-fashioned firings such as wood, oil, raku, pit, salt, and to prospecting your own materials. We are grasping for ever larger scale, for mixed media combinations, for room- or building-sized installations, and there is a renewed emphasis on architectural and landscape collaborations. I am saddened that a number of the wonderful images you have submitted had to be left out because of lack of space.

There are more galleries, more museum exhibitions honoring ceramic material and artists, more books, more internet material, more websites, more serious collectors, and more opportunities for making a living as a ceramist.

My daughter Jan has helped greatly with this book; her process photos have appeared in previous books and she has always been involved with my work. Ceramics is a serious art and a lifelong journey. Begin at the beginning with this book, go upward and onward. Beginners can't do everything but need to know the possibilities. Good luck!

SUSAN HARNLY PETERSON, *Carefree, Arizona, March 2002*
e-mail: shpeterson@aol.com

nique and transformed it into Delft ware. The Persians also developed luster glazes, and the Italians found that metallic oxides could be painted on top of white glazes to give fused lines or crisp strokes during the firing, a technique called *majolica*.

Bernard Palissy in the 1560s in France experimented, and J. F. Böttger in Meissen, Germany, succeeded in making porcelain about 1710. In 1760 Josiah Wedgwood discovered how to make a porcelain clay body from English china clay and bone ash, and to fire it to high density.

After the furious pace of mass-production resulting from the industrial revolution that was completed by the 1850s, history witnessed a period of revolt against everything looking alike. William Morris, in England, was one of the first to call for a return of the individual craftsperson and craft techniques. In the 1860s he reestablished the "workshops" and "guilds" we had seen in Renaissance times, and craftspeople began to collabo-

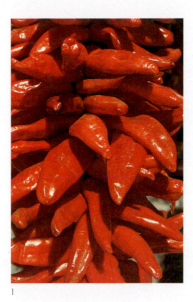

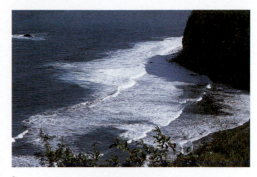

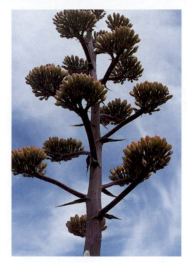

Nature is a design influence:

1. Design in nature: chillis from New Mexico, USA
2. The sea from the Big Island of Hawaii
3. Yucca, California, USA

rate. In 1925 a large German work-shop, the Bauhaus, inspired a revolutionary new trend in design that is still influential today; the schools at Weimar and Dessau laid emphasis on ceramic art among other art forms.

Before and after World War II, various countries began to investigate new ideas and to become known for their own design criteria. Scandinavian design, especially that of Sweden, promoted bright colors and simplicity of form; the ritual of the tea-ceremony emphasized the role of clay in Japanese culture; folk art, particularly ceramics, in such countries as Mexico and other parts of Central and South America, Morocco, Turkey and the like, exerted great influence on their other arts. Europe in general responded to the Bauhaus influence, while the trend in the United States was toward the freedom of Abstract Expressionism in painting and in craft. All these trends continue today.

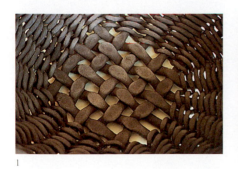

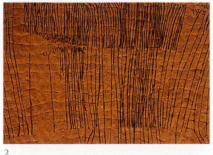

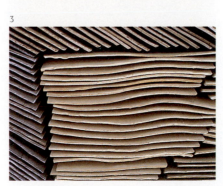

Surfaces reflecting the design ideas of nature:

1. Detail of weave from a clay basket by Rina Peleg

2. Detail of stain drawing with hypodermic needle over a coiled, glazed surface by Bruno Lavadiere

3. Unglazed colored paperthin porcelain layers, detail of a sculpture by Marylyn Dintenfass

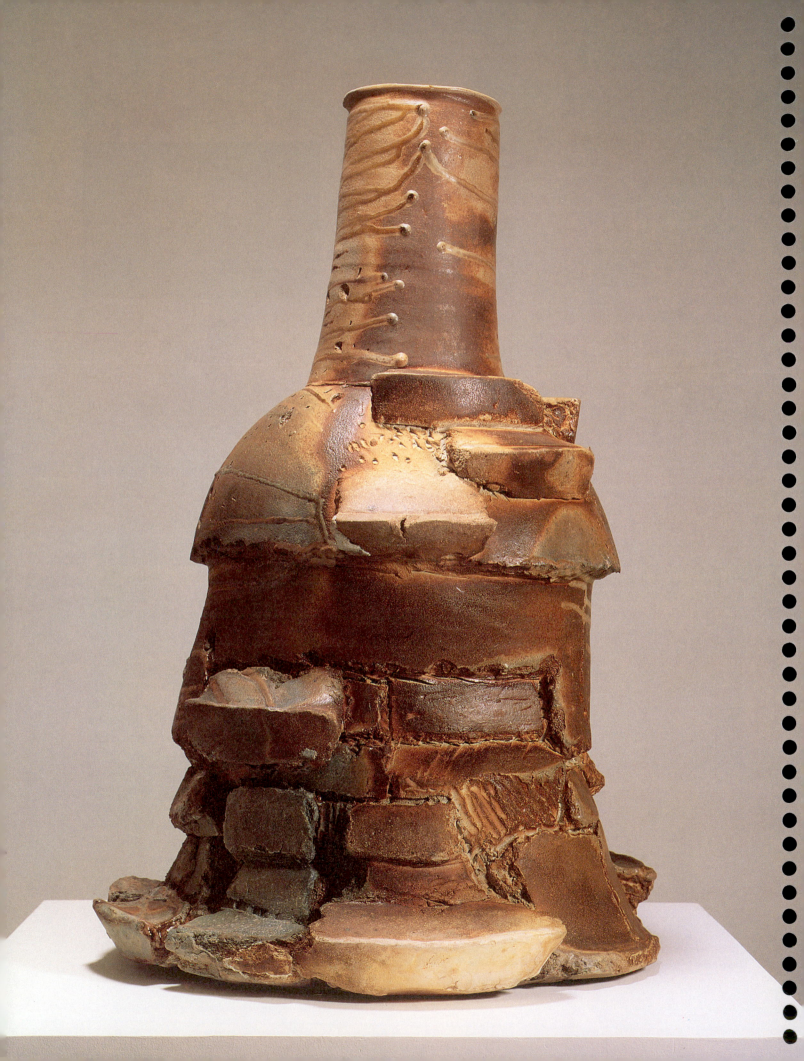

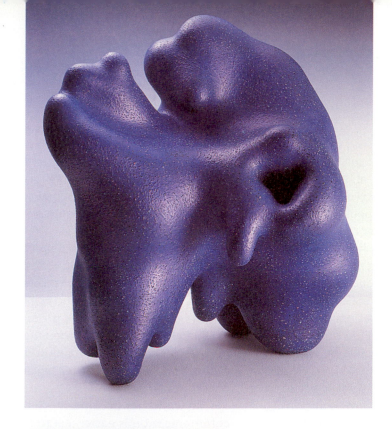

LEFT Ken Price's recent ceramic sculpture bears the illusion of glaze, about which this artist knows a great deal, but the surface is in fact a meticulous rendering of various acrylic paints on fired clay

RIGHT John Mason's vertical sculpture, "Figure Ember," 62 x 23 x 23 ins. (157 x 58 x 58 cm), is a brilliant example of slab-building technique astonishingly engineered to stand upright at cone 10 reduction firing

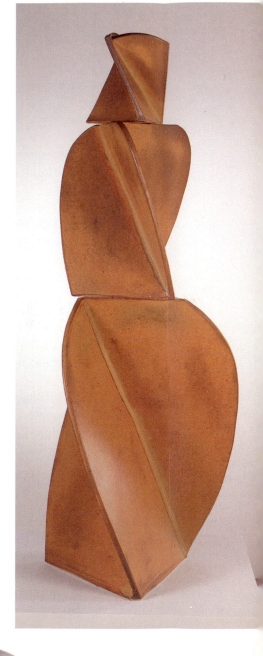

LEFT Shoji Hamada, the famous potter and ceramic National Treasure of Japan (1894–1978), at his Chinese chestnut hand-powered wheel, throwing a tea ceremony bowl in his studio at Mashiko, c. 1970

FACING PAGE Peter Voulkos' (1923–2002) thrown and altered wood-fired stoneware "stack," 45 ins. (114 cm) high; a magnificent piece that illustrates how influential this artist has been in the ceramic world

LEFT Bernard Leach (1887–1979), the so-called father of "studio pottery," worked in stoneware and porcelain at his well-known pottery in St Ives, Cornwall, UK, from 1920 to his death; this stoneware pot with engobe and sgraffito design dates from 1950. He wrote an early handbook for potters, which remains hugely influential

REMEMBER

- Creative expression is an individual need; it is not a specialty reserved for the "fine artist."
- Clayworkers direct their materials, their processes, and their techniques into an expression of their personalities.
- There is no definite line between craft and art, they are both of a piece.
- A "pot" is not necessarily a container, nor any longer needs to be thought only functional.
- Today ceramic art is a characterization of our time, continuing to be an energizing and captivating challenge to clayworkers as one of our most important methods of self-expression.

Early American ceramics came with the European settlers after 1620. From that point up to the 1800s ceramics began to be made in small potteries on the eastern seaboard: slipware, salt glaze, Delft, peasant redwares, luster, some with an aristocratic aesthetic. Ceramic chemistry in the New World embraced the three types of wares already current across the Atlantic ocean – earthenware, stoneware, and porcelain.

The western coast of the United States was influenced by Spanish and Mexican earthenwares, and by the porcelains brought by early Chinese settlers. The USA became a melting pot of world clay styles and cultures, until in the early 1950s a change occurred, causing a revolution in ceramic art that still goes on.

In California, about 1954, a young Pied Piper named Peter Voulkos began to handle enormous chunks of clay in a radical manner on a potter's wheel and to alter the shapes created on the wheel by cutting them, slashing them, beating them, and combining them into large sculptural forms. Jack Peterson and I had designed the first variable-speed electric potter's wheels west of the Mississippi. Voulkos and Paul Soldner used this wheel design but added more horsepower, so more pounds of clay could be thrown at one time. With Mike Kalan, a ceramic engineer, I designed the first high-temperature fast-firing open-fire up-draft gas kilns in the country. These developments made possible the huge thrown and handbuilt forms that other ceramists began tackling in the fifties and that are part and parcel of the ceramic objects being made today. We should not forget that the contemporary ceramics movement is only about fifty years old, but ceramic art is as old as time. A group formed around Peter, each experimenting individually, that included myself, Paul Soldner, Jerry Rothman, Henry Takemoto, Mac Maclain, Michael Frimkess – Pete's students – and John Mason and Ken Price, my students, among others. (I had come to Southern California in 1950 and was already teaching at Chouinard Art Institute when Voulkos came to teach at the nearby Los Angeles County Art Institute.)

About the same time I brought Bernard Leach, who had written the formative *A Potter's Book* in 1943, his old friends Shoji Hamada, the foremost potter of Japan, and Soetsu Yanagi, the scholar of Zen Buddhist aesthetics, to Chouinard for several weeks of lectures and demonstrations before an invited audience of clay-workers. The work, writings, and philosophies of these three mentors spread across the world and, even after their deaths, are a powerful inspiration for potters today.

Of course there were other important clay artists in the world at the same time, but the force of the Voulkos personality, and the awesome work that was flowing out of the group in Southern California, provided the major factor in the rapid evolution of ceramics from a functional, utilitarian concept to an art form.

The world has become smaller, communication is easier, ceramic schools, workshops, suppliers, and museums proliferate across the globe. The transformation is spectacular. Ceramic art can vie for prices and clientele similar to those for painting or sculpture. Furthermore, working in clay is a fascinating experience for nearly everyone who comes in contact with it.

FUNCTIONAL VS SCULPTURAL

Recent generations have debated the old argument of functional versus sculptural, of art versus craft, and still not solved it. Historically the controversy has been considered from the monetary standpoint as well as from the point of view of aesthetic values. Ceramic sculpture today sells for higher prices than functional vessels. So-called "fine art" has usually sold to collectors for more than so-called "decorative art."

In past ages there were countless potters throughout the world making functional pots for daily use. Many of these were indigenous potters, fitting the folk art category, as the one million potters of India still do, or those in Morocco, Mexico, Africa, Japan, Indonesia and elsewhere. Many others were individual potters who worked alone in their studios making objects for everyday use. Today functional potters are still very active, but more clay-workers make sculpture.

Some of the functional potters became famous and were called artists by the critics. Among them were the late Shoji Hamada, Bernard Leach, Michael Cardew, Marguerite Wildenhain, and in our day Warren MacKenzie, Sandy Simon, Jeff Oesterich and their ilk – but they might not call themselves artists.

There is a fine line between, on the one hand, functional pots for daily use or functional shapes that might or might not be used, which could be called sculpture, and on the other, forms that are traditional but into which one would not think to put food or drink but instead would use for decoration or contemplation – as in sculpture.

A sculpture is more particularly defined as a non-functioning object that exists in space, is meant to be looked at, and generally carries intrinsic meaning to the observer. Ceramic sculpture can – but does not have to – expand into a mixture of media using clay and other materials, or into installations that assemble groups of clay objects, with the possibility of other added materials.

Claywork goes on the floor, on walls, on the table, in the garden, on façades of buildings, and into space technology. The beginner in clay must learn the basics, then proceed toward determining the final goal, and ultimately execute his or her own ideas of ceramic art. Fine functional vessels produced by hand or wheel methods are still valued, though little publicized. The feel of a beautifully crafted cup, mug, or plate is unquestionably serene.

TYPES OF CERAMICS

The differences between the red brick and the white translucent porcelain cup are different clay and a different firing temperature. All clay products, ranging from bricks to porcelain cups, are the result of the same two variations. Clay is clay (and a clay body composition acts as its principal component clay type acts) and heat is heat – more or less – but it is the variations between the two factors that cause the differences in the end products.

Earthenware

A fired claywork that is porous, relatively light in weight, easily chipped, and makes a clunking sound if tapped with your fingernail is called "earthenware." Most tribal societies such as Native American, African, Aboriginal,

Burnished earthenware, raku-fired bowl with stain decoration by Carol Rossman (Canada)

Collage earthenware plaque with commercial glazes by Annabeth Rosen

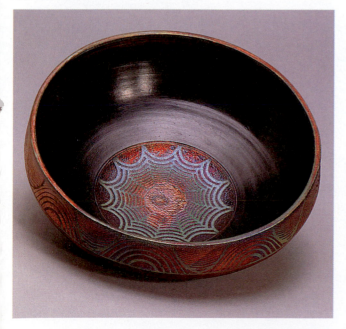

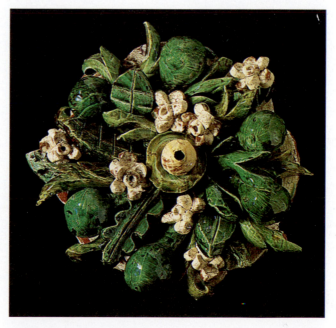

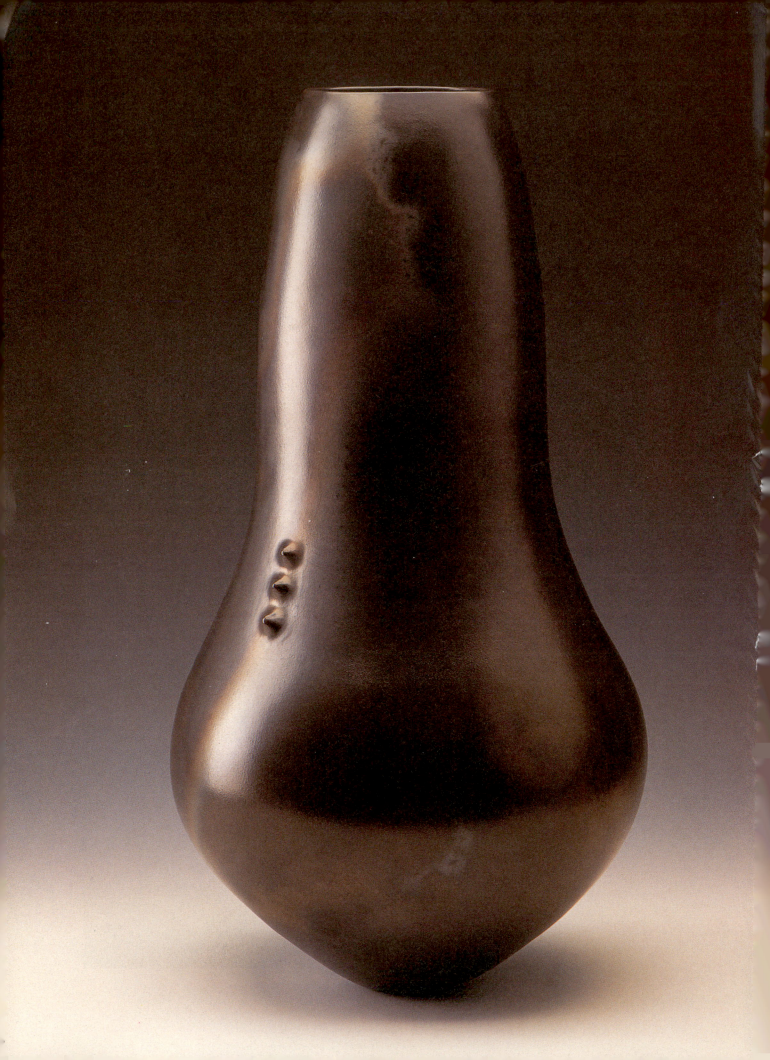

and other outback peoples use common surface clays because they are at hand, and fire them in low-temperature open fires to produce earthenware. So-called sophisticated societies make earthenware plant pots, tableware, bricks, and similar items, plus sculpture and installations, because they want to.

The technical definition of earthenware is that it will have an absorption of 10 to 15% of its unglazed weight when boiled one hour in water. China/ball clay bodies fired low will be very porous; most earthenwares are made from common surface and fire clays.

Stoneware

A fired claywork that is quite hard, holds liquids, is not easily broken, and rings when tapped is called "stoneware." Stoneware developed in China over 2,000 years ago, and in Europe during the Middle Ages; the technique was brought to North America by the early settlers who arrived from Europe. For a clay body to become stoneware a higher firing temperature is needed than for earthenware, or more flux can be added to high-temperature clays to make them dense at low heat.

The technical definition of a stoneware piece is that it absorbs 2 to 5% of its unglazed weight when boiled in water for one hour.

A huge coiled and thrown stoneware sculpture by Toshiko Takaezu shows the throwing marks of centrifugal motion in contrast to the vertical splashes of glaze

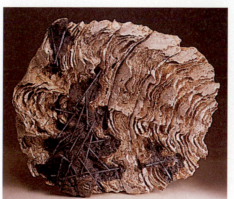

This unglazed plaque shows a heavy, utilitarian, coarse stoneware body; the piece is textured by ripping and attaching layers, and accented by the crispness of density achieved in a high-temperature fire. Sculpture by Claudi Casanovas (Spain), 36 ins. (91 cm) diameter

FACING PAGE Magdalene Odundo (UK), burnished earthenware sculpture, 16 x 8 ins. (40.5 x 20 cm)

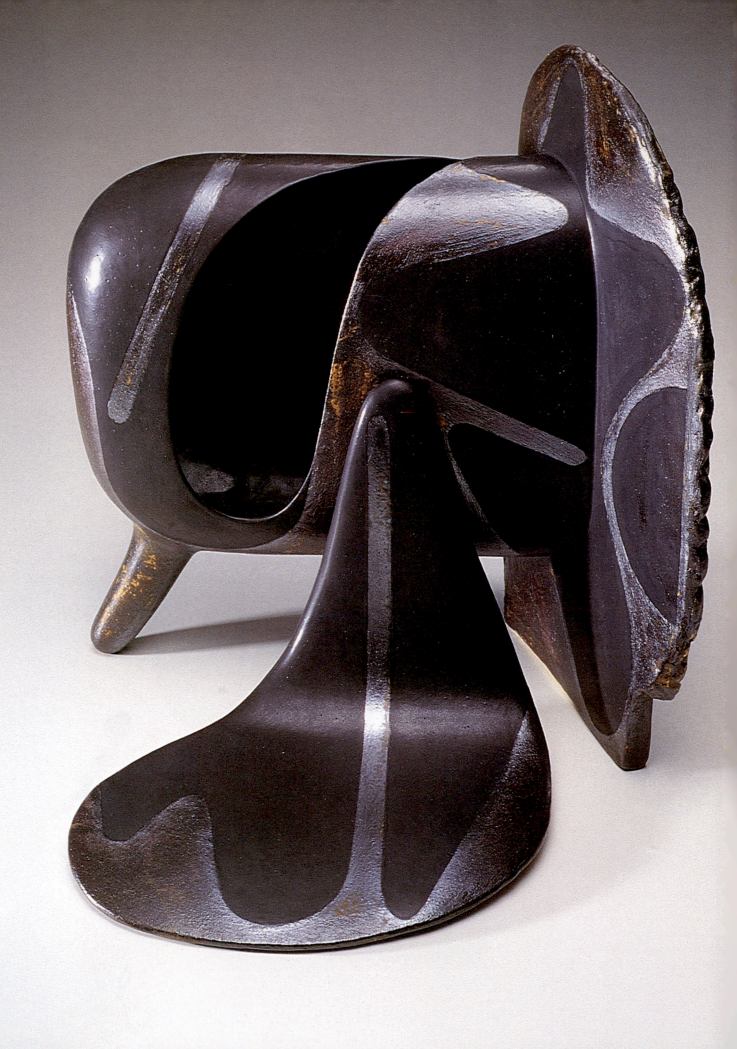

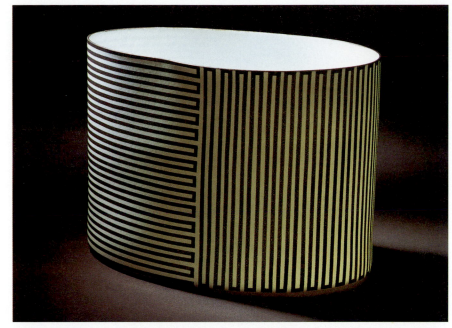

Bodil Manz (Germany), extraordinarily thin, translucent porcelain, oval form decorated with her own hand-made black decal, 8½ x 5 x 8½ ins. (22 x 13 x 22 cm)

FACING PAGE Hand-built; the sharply shaped and smoothed stoneware sculpture with black matt and lustrous glaze requires a silky clay body. Sculpture by Mutsuo Yanagihara (Japan)

Porcelain

A fired claywork that is hard, dense, and vitreous, usually translucent if thin, and generally white or off-white, is called porcelain. As previously stated, we think that the Chinese were the first to make it, several thousand years ago; they were the first people to understand the effects of, and how to get, high temperatures in an enclosed chamber such as a cave or a kiln.

The technical definition of porcelain is 0 to 1% absorption of the weight of an unglazed piece after it is boiled in water for one hour.

Because fired porcelain is so nearly glass-like, porcelain clay body ware must be evenly dried to prevent warping and will deform in the fire if the shape is not properly engineered.

Earthenware, stoneware, and porcelain products can result from clay body components **at any ceramic temperature** as long as they fit the above definitions

Nobuhito Nishigawara (Japan), figure, hollow-built porcelain sculpture, burnished to a marble-like texture, cone 12, 22 ins. (56 cm) high

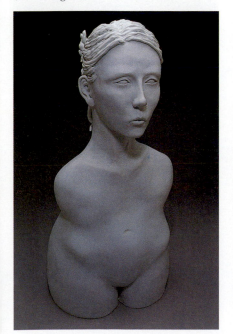

Enid Legros-Wise (Canada) has carved and textured her hand-built bisqued porcelain bowl so that it is translucent

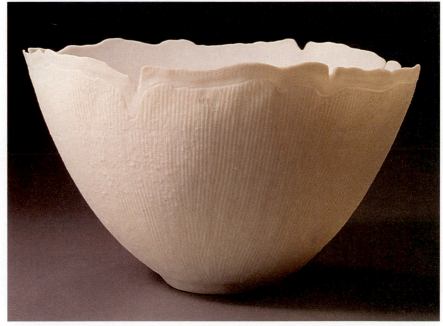

WHAT IS CLAY?

As long as we have a world, there will be clay. Clay is a mineral mined or dug from the earth, composed of alumina, silica, and chemically combined water. Its chemical formula is $Al_2O_3 - 2SiO_2 - 6H_2O$. Clay is continuously being formed from igneous rock – granite, which itself was formed through a process of fire. The great granite mountains of the world decompose, so to speak, through physical processes, such as rain, wind, earthquake, and glacial movement, and chemical processes, such as weathering from the acids and alkalis of the earth's atmosphere. **How clay has been weathered and where nature moves it determines its ultimate color and workability; the more impurities it has, the more plastic it is, while the fewer impurities, the less plasticity** (see glossary).

Geologically speaking, all native clays fall into five general categories.
1. China clays. The first clay that forms at the base of the mountain is virgin, with few impurities. It is the whitest-burning, most heat-resistant, least plastic, and rarest on the face of the globe, and we call it *kaolin* or china clay. Clay that has not moved from the spot where it was formed is termed "primary" or "residual"; hence *primary kaolin*. When primary kaolin is carried away by whatever natural means, contamination occurs, the clay becomes more plastic from the movement, and the color on firing is somewhat off-white. Clays that have been moved are called "secondary" or "sedimentary." *Secondary kaolins* are not as rare, and are more workable than

primary china clays. Both types of kaolin become hard, dense, and vitreous (glassy) by themselves when fired at temperatures of 3100°–3300° F (1740°–1785° C). Most china clays are found in Asia, Britain, Germany, and several in south-eastern USA.
2. Ball clays, the next in purity and the most plastic of all clays, are always secondary clays and have always been moved by water. Because of their fine particle size, brought about by water movement and rock-grinding, these nearly white-burning clays have high shrinkage in drying and firing, and become dense at 2300°–2500° F (1260°–1370° C). **Kaolins and ball clays are the usual components of porcelain.**
3. Fire clays, readily found in mountain and desert areas of the world, are the work-horses of ceramics. These clays have particle sizes of varying coarseness and flat or round platelets depending on their formation. In addition to the clay molecule, fire clays include extra uncombined silica. Beige, tan, gold, red, brown, are the colors that these clays fire; most become dense and vitreous around 2200°–2400° F (1205°–1260° C). **Potters like these clays for their resilience, their strength, and their ability to stand tall.** Industry uses fire clays for firebricks, flue linings, blast furnaces, and other heavy clay products.
4. Stoneware clays. This category is debated by geologists: is it really a separate kind of natural clay? So-called stoneware clays are very rare – in the USA we have Jordon (not mined now), Perrine, and Monmouth. A few other stoneware clays have been found in Europe,

China, Japan, and India. Because stoneware clays have the properties of both ball and fire clays, they are remarkably workable, firing dense, in off-white to brown colors, around 2200°–2300° F (1205°–1260° C).
5. Surface clays. The most prevalent clays on the earth, under your feet

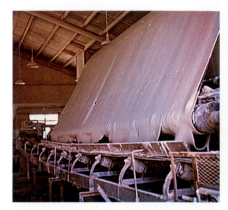

The commercial process of washing china clay (kaolin) removes all impurities

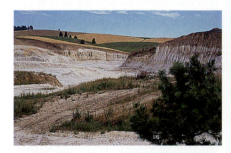

Yellow and beige fire-clay deposit being commercially mined

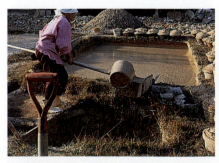

Slaking and screening natural clay in Kitagoya, Japan; after about three weeks in water the clay slurry is ladled into plaster tubs to dry to the plastic state

everywhere, are rightfully termed *common surface* clays. Because they are rich with impurities, and have enjoyed millions of years of movement, they are very workable, and are generally the only clays that can constitute a "clay body" and be used entirely by themselves with no additions of flux or filler (see below). **All indigenous societies use common surface clays, with little or no addition, to make functional vessels, effigy figures, bricks, and water pipes.** The usual fired color is rusty red, but common surface clays can fire to any color – except white – depending on the metallic oxides that have combined with them in the earth.

Clay, as opposed to dirt, when mixed with water will form a plastic mass that can be molded into any shape and will hold that shape. When left to dry, most clays will shrink in size as much as 10%. Further shrinkage takes place in the firing. When fired in a bonfire, approximately 1300° F (700° C), all natural clays become somewhat hard and durable, but probably will not hold liquid for longer than it takes to have a drink from a vessel.

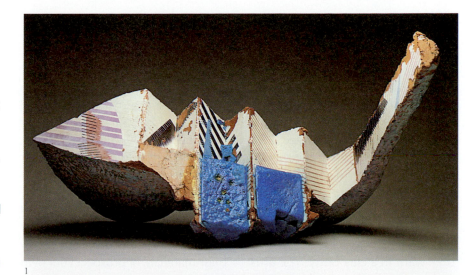

1

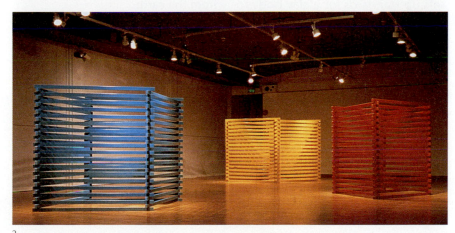

2

Many types of clay and combinations of clay with other materials are used to make ceramic art:

1. Ron Fondaw's earthenware sculpture has additions of turquoise "Egyptian paste," which was developed over 3,000 years ago by the Egyptians (see Chapter 7)

2. Jun Kaneko's museum installation of 8-ft by 2-ins. (244 x 5 cm) slabs was constructed in a low-shrink clay body at the Otsuka factory, Shigaraki, Japan

WHAT IS A CLAY BODY?

Inert or active materials can be added to natural clays to alter the basic properties of the original clay. This combination of clay and other ingredients is called a "clay body," and is built according to the visual and structural needs of industry or artists.

To the basic clay component (one or more natural clays) we add:

1. Filler, to subdue the sticky quality of plastic natural clays: sand, dirt, ground-up particles of already fired clay called "grog" or "temper," silica sand (fused silica) or pure silica. Some of these additions also add texture to the fired clay body.

2. Flux, to change the normal firing temperature of a given clay or group of clays. This can be feldspar, found all over the world, or bone ash – found mostly in England, hence "bone china" – or ground glass, or combinations of other low-melting minerals such as soda ash.

Thus a clay body consists of three components, clay, filler, and flux.

The clay body should contain at least 50% clay, plus the added materials, to keep plasticity; a better ratio for excellent workability is 70% to 80% clay plus added material. The clay content can consist of several clays for different reasons, such as color, degree of fine or coarse particle size, temperature required for a particular density, and fabricating specifications. Experience will help you figure this out. Without a good clay body you cannot hope to make good claywork.

Most clay artists know exactly what they want in a clay body. The artist sets up standards for a clay body to suit a particular kind of claywork: how pliable does it need to be? Must it stand up and hold weight? Is color impor- tant? What density or porosity is required for the finished product? The artist then makes up his or her own mix.

Clays of most geological types are mined in various parts of the world and can be purchased in bulk, or dry, ground to 200-mesh, easy to mix. Feldspars, ground glass, and other fluxes exist everywhere; everyone like- wise has access to various fillers. **Make up a clay composition, test it, and revise it until you like it**. Anywhere in the world you can probably buy these materials, or prospect your own from the earth.

Alternatively, a ready-mixed clay body can be purchased from a ceramic supplier, ready to use in the plastic state in 25 lb (11 kg) bags, or dry in larger quantity. You should specify your requirements for workability, fired color, and the temperature you will fire. You hope the ceramic material supplier can give you a ready-mixed clay body to fit your needs, although the company will keep the ingredients secret.

A famous natural clay body is found in YiXing village, China, well known for traditional and avant garde teapots in this special clay. Zhou Ding Fang's (China) teapot with mouse, 7 x 5 ins. (18 x 12.5 cm), is an example. She is one of the few female potters to have made a name in China

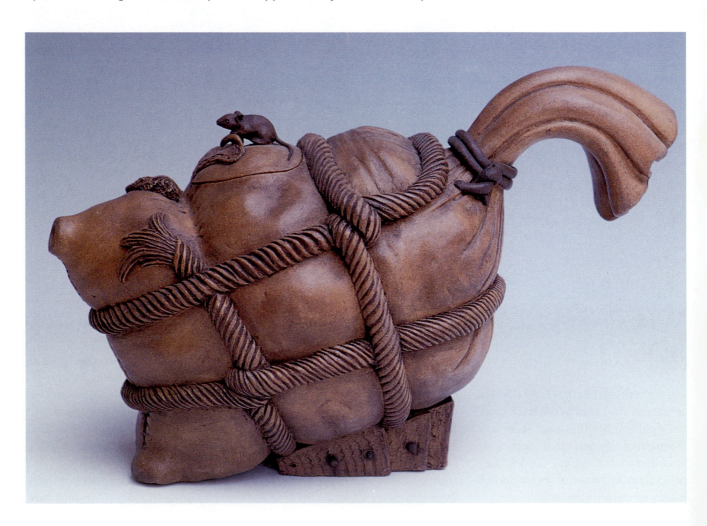

PAPERCLAY

In past ages papyrus, paper, cloth, adobe earth, and other materials were added to clay to make it more easily fashioned into varieties of complex shapes, or very thin shapes, or to enable functional and decorative use without firing. Today we see an experimental revival of those practices.

Paperclay body. Begin by trying all kinds of paper and all types of clays or clay bodies, mixed about 50–50 by hand or with an electric blunger.

Graham Hay, of Australia, one of the most inventive artists working with this material, mixes it in various consistencies – slurry, like whipped cream, plastic, for hand-building and for use in plaster molds, and drier for rolling thin flat slabs. Parts can be made individually, dried, and attached together with paperclay slip before firing, or dried parts of other sculptures can be put together into new forms. Hay says he throws paperclay on the ground to create large slabs with earthy texture.

Dust and bacteria are important issues with paperclay. "I tell people to think about paperclay pottery like gardening: both have organic material for bacteria to grow in, especially if your environment is warm and damp. My advice is to wash with soapy water before coming into the house or eating food."

All clayworkers can make a paperclay slip to repair cracks, patch chips, reattach pieces, or build new parts, in the raw or bisque state of your own claywork. Mix your own regular clay body with soft tissue paper in a blending apparatus when you are ready to use it; you won't notice the patches after glazing and firing.

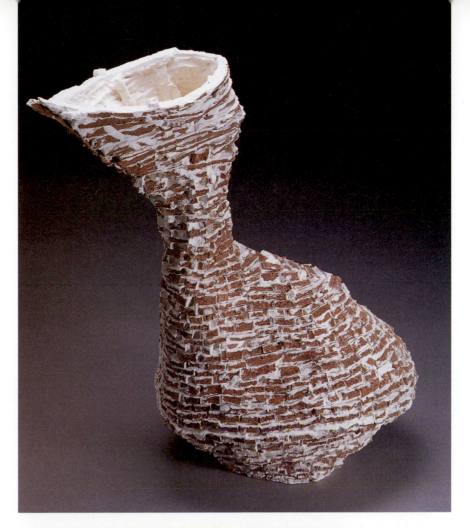

ABOVE Graham Hay (Australia), paperclay form, earthenware, 22 x 11 x 8 ins. (57 x 28 x 21 cm)

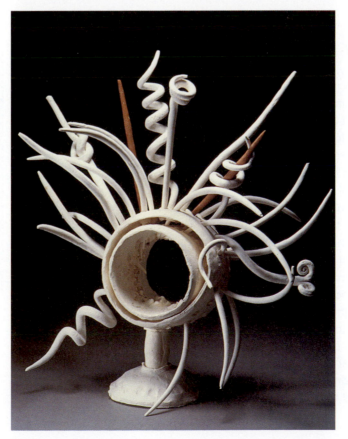

Graham Hay's (Australia) wildly invigorating sculpture illustrates the amazing versatility of a paperclay body. 43 x 47 x 24 ins. (110 x 120 x 60 cm)

Alternative clays and additions: paperclay for kilns

The idea of adding inert material to clay to lessen its propensity for thermal-shock destruction is probably as old as time, but has been recently resurrected. Using papier-mâché-like strips or particles of water-soaked paper added in varying proportions to a clay body is popular now for very thin large slabs, from which sculptures can be built, or for the actual construction of kiln chambers for any kind of fuel except electricity. This clay body will create a paper-like look when fired, and is particularly favorable to print or painting techniques.

Adobe, natural mud-earth that has some clay chemistry, is another age-old material that can serve well for certain sculptural and installation uses. Adobe will set in air, or can be fired. Concrete, another member of the ceramic family, is a possible addition to the sculpture vocabulary. Try adding concrete in varying percentages to your clay body for airset or fired sculpture, or the concrete/clay mixture can become a kiln construction material for very low-fire work only.

Actually mixing various materials into a natural clay or a clay body composition is one way to think about additions. Another way is to physically add stones, fired clay or glazed shards, nails and other hardware, wire and the like, pressed into or wrapped round the exterior of a clay piece before firing. Firecrackers or popcorn embedded in clay will cause interesting explosions that you can actually plan ahead in the concept of your piece.

FACING PAGE Hollow forms can be quickly molded and attached wet or dry as shown in this Graham Hay (Australia) sculpture, paperclay body, earthenware, 15 x 15 x 11 ins (37 x 37 x 27 cm)

The resurrection of the ancient concept of paper and clay mixed together has been a boon to contemporary artists and to students. The easy manipulation with paperclay allows for extraordinary squiggles, cantilevers, degrees of thinness, and easily fabricated large scale. Paperclay is best for decorative objects because it doesn't have as much strength as regular clay bodies. It makes excellent wall hangings that are lightweight and can be huge. rints from stencils, rollers, free brush, and lithography techniques are appropriate.

PAPERCLAY KILN

Patty Wouters in Belgium has developed a simple method of constructing a kiln made of paperclay, which is usable at least for temperatures up to cone 1, depending on the maturing temperature of the type of clay combined with paper. Such a kiln could fire clay bodies of any kind, but not higher than the temperature of the paperclay used in the furnace. The clay used in the body for the furnace must be a higher-maturing clay than the clay in the pots it will fire. Paperclay bodies have the advantage that they do not burst or blow up from thermal shock during a rapid firing.

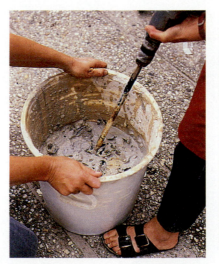

Blunging paper and clay with an electric mixer to make a paste. Lay the mixed paperclay for the kiln over an armature of chicken wire and cardboard for any size, whether sculpture or pots

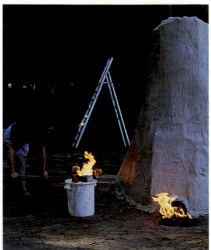

The paperclay kiln, loaded with wares, begins firing at the base stoke-holes, with charcoal first, then wood; or propane or gas burners can be inserted

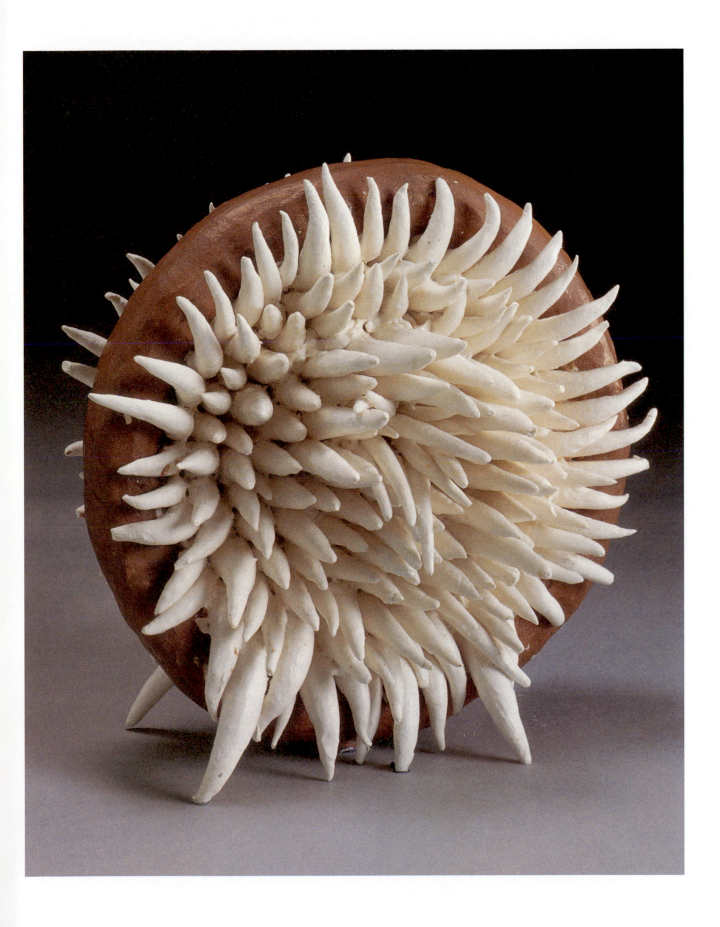

CLAYS/FELDSPARS/SILICA=CLAY BODY

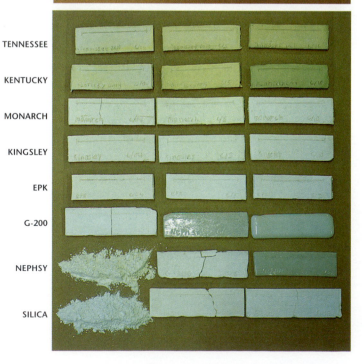

	C/04	C/5	C/10 (OXIDATION)
RED ART			
C-RED			
LATTERITE			
NEWMAN			
IMCO 800			
LINCOLN 60			
IMCO 400			
SUTTER 200			
LINCOLN			
GOLD ART			
MISSOURI FIRE			
TENNESSEE			
KENTUCKY			
MONARCH			
KINGSLEY			
EPK			
G-200			
NEPHSY			
SILICA			

A good clay body is paramount in doing good claywork. A bad clay body will present problems from start to finish. If you can understand this, you will be miles ahead. However, some artists – especially traditional ones – have enjoyed the challenge of working with poor clay bodies. Shoji Hamada, one of this century's best-known and finest potters, said of the coarse, unreliable clay that was dug for him on a hillside near his studio in Mashiko, Japan: "It is better to make good pots out of a bad clay than to make bad pots out of a good clay."

Concoct your own 100% clay body batch by choosing according to color, texture and temperature, from available clays that you dig or buy, common surface clays, fire clays, ball clays and/or china clays – plus a flux (feldspar) and a filler (silica).

Generic clays mined in the USA are illustrated in barmolds of exactly the same size, marked with a 2-in. (5 cm) line which can then be measured for shrinkage, fired at c/04 low fire, c/5 median fire, and c/10 high fire. Absorption is recorded for each fired tile. G200 is a potassium feldspar, and nepheline syenite is a soda spar. Silica and nepheline syenite remain powder at c/04.

The first 11 bars are fire clays, representative of all fire clays. All but Red Art and Gold Art, from Ohio, and Missouri, are from California, USA.

Tennessee and Kentucky are ball clays from USA. Monarch and Kingsley are primary china clays, EPK is a secondary china clay, from USA.

Note the variety of differences among the clays and spars.

Use the figures on the chart opposite for these clays or similar clays, for similar feldspars, and for silica, to develop a blended clay body to suit your needs for throwing or hand-building, for low shrinkage, and for desired density. Remember, earthenware has 10–15% absorption, stoneware 2–5%, porcelain 0–1%. More density means higher shrinkage. Test your own local materials by making bars like these and firing them at these mean temperatures, or just the temperature at which you want to fire.

Shrinkage: Measure the line on the bar wet (say 10 cm), then dry, then fired. Formula: Shrinkage wet minus shrinkage dry divided by X x 100; shrinkage dry minus shrinkage fired divided by X x 100
Absorption: fired weight wet minus fired weight dry divided by fired weight dry x 100 = % of absorption of water by bar

		SHRINKAGE									ABSORPTION		
		c/04			c/5			c/10			c/04	c/5	c/10
		WET TO DRY	DRY TO FIRE	TOTAL	WET TO DRY	DRY TO FIRE	TOTAL	WET TO DRY	DRY TO FIRE	TOTAL			
FIRE CLAYS	Red Art	6%	2%	8%	6%	4%	10%	6%	9%	15%	14.5%	1.5%	1.0%
	C-Red	10%	0%	10%	10%	3%	13%	10%	5%	15%	19.9%	14.9%	10.5%
	Latterite	5%	3%	8%	5%	10%	15%	5%	12%	17%	25.5%	14.0%	10.9%
	Newman	9%	1%	10%	9%	5%	14%	9%	6%	15%	24.5%	18.7%	11.1%
	Imco 800	9%	2%	11%	9%	6%	15%	9%	12%	21%	21.8%	7.1%	1.6%
	Lincoln 60	8%	1%	9%	8%	10%	18%	8%	11%	19%	21.5%	6.8%	1.4%
	Imco 400	10%	1%	11%	10%	7%	17%	10%	8%	18%	20.4%	3.7%	1.6%
	Sutter 200	7%	4%	11%	7%	16%	23%	7%	18%	25%	27.2%	1.9%	1.3%
	Lincoln	6%	3%	9%	6%	12%	18%	6%	13%	19%	28.0%	9.5%	0.7%
	Gold Art	6%	2%	8%	6%	6%	12%	6%	9%	15%	12.7%	4.8%	1.7%
	Missouri Fire	5%	3%	8%	5%	7%	12%	5%	9%	14%	13.5%	5.0%	2.9%
BALL CLAYS	Tennessee	8%	3%	11%	8%	6%	14%	8%	7%	15%	22.5%	11.8%	4.5%
	Kentucky	10%	3%	13%	10%	5%	15%	10%	7%	17%	19.9%	7.5%	1.2%
CHINA CLAYS (Kaolins)	Monarch	5%	1%	6%	5%	4%	9%	5%	5%	10%	30.2%	26.4%	25.0%
	Kingsley	3%	4%	7%	3%	5%	8%	3%	8%	11%	29.0%	26.0%	19.0%
	EPK	6%	7%	13%	6%	7%	13%	6%	12%	18%	19.3%	17.9%	17.4%
FELDSPAR	G-200	0%	0%	0%	0%	5%	5%	0%	12%	12%	dissolve	16.4%	0%
	NephSy	powder	powder	powder	0%	11%	11%	0%	melt	melt	24.0%	0%	0%
	Silica	powder	powder	powder	0%	0%	0%	0%	0%	0%	powder dissolve	21.9%	25.5%

WHY MIX YOUR OWN CLAY BODY?

The best reason for developing the proportions of various materials on a 100% clay body batch and then mixing your own clay is that you will know exactly what is in it. You will understand the properties of the individual components, which will help you to do exactly what your ideas demand.

If you are determining your own clay body – and clay is the basic first thing in making any ceramic object – you will be thinking of the whole project, of the whole piece and of the final result. You will be starting at the beginning and can set your own boundaries. Furthermore, if you mix your own clay body you will do so in a rather large quantity, perhaps as much as 100 lb (45 kg). When we buy plastic-bagged clay made commercially it usually comes in relatively small amounts, rectangularly shaped. Mentally we are restricted by the size and shape of that bung of clay, which limits the mind and the work.

> **REMEMBER**
> A clay body consists of:
> ● **the plastic material** – any clay or clays;
>
> ● **the flux** – feldspar, glass or bone ash;
>
> ● **the filler** – silica, sand, ground shards, or grog (also called chamotte).
>
> ● Check the charts on pages 28–29.

If you have a big mound of wet clay on the table or floor in front of you, ready to work with, there are no limits to your conceptual thoughts.

METHODS OF MIXING CLAY BODIES

Besides combining your clay body from refined materials such as those on our chart (pages 28–29), you might dig from the ground a natural clay, which must be treated and tested as follows. It should be dried out and pounded into small bits, then screened to remove sand, leaves, and debris. Next, add water and test the clay for workability by making a small pinch-pot. If the clay is sticky, add filler. Fire the pot if you can, and if it is too porous or fragile at the temperature to which you fired it, add flux to the clay, make corrections, work it, and fire a new sample. Repeat until you have a good, usable clay body mixture.

Mix without a machine:
1. Mix the batch dry – thoroughly – by stirring, sifting, or rolling in a closed container.
2. Next, hand-mix wet:
a) put clay and water in a bucket,

> Whether you use materials from nature or buy 200-mesh refined materials, your clay body needs several ingredients. You must mix them thoroughly, with or without a machine

> An example of a generic clay body that will fire at any temperature is:
>
> 70% clay (any kind or combination)
> 20% feldspar (any kind)
> 10% silica or sand
>
> At low fire this body will be porous, at high fire it will be dense, depending on the materials chosen

stir to smooth slurry, remove excess moisture on porous surface to plastic stage;
or b) make a 4-inch (10 cm) high mound of the dry body mix, make a center depression, add water, mix, and knead to plastic stage – a large quantity of clay can be mixed this way on the floor with a rake.

An example of a clay mixer. This one was designed by Paul Soldner, but there are innumerable types available all over the world. Most clay mixers blend the dry materials and water with a revolving paddle into your desired plasticity

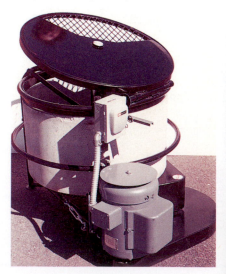

Mix with a machine:

1. Blunger. Put your dry batch in a barrel with water and mix liquid with an electric drill modified with a metal stirring blade on the end of a rod.

2. Clay mixer. For 100 lb (45 kg) of plastic clay, put about 4 inches (10 cm) of water in the bottom of a commercial clay mixer, add the dry ingredients, and mix for about 20 minutes. Note: for mixing deflocculated clay body slip clay for casting in molds, see page 61.

STORING THE CLAY

Clay dries when exposed to air, but will keep moist if it is stored airtight. Metal garbage cans used for clay storage should be galvanized and lined with several sheets of plastic. Plastic containers are satisfactory if lined with sheets of plastic and kept moist with damp towels. Other possible storage containers are wooden tubs, bath tubs, old sinks, or the like. If the clay does dry out, pound it into bits, remoisten, and keep it airtight a few days until it becomes plastic again.

How important is fired shrinkage and absorption?

As shown in the illustrations of fire-clays, ball clays, china clays, feldspars and silica (pages 28–29) – the components of a clay body – you will note the variety of shrinkage and absorption percentages at three mean temperatures: cone 04 = 1922° F (1035° C),

cone 5 = 2150° F (1162° C) and cone 10 = 2350° F (1273° C).

Clay shrinks as it dries in air, shrinks more as it fires, depending on how dense it becomes on firing. **Percentage of absorption – i.e. porosity – is the degree to which a fired clay will absorb water. Shrinkage and final density are particularly important when building and firing large claywork.**

Many ceramic sculptors use high-firing clays at low temperatures so that the shrink factor will be small, but porosity and fragility may be great. When clay becomes very dense, it will have maximum shrinkage; high shrinkage can cause deformations but dense work will be strong!

Thus a fired porcelain piece may turn out to be 20% smaller than it was when it was made; the density it attains could necessitate making several to get one correct form. Density in porcelain contributes to the visual effect. Functional pottery often has a higher percentage of absorption: cups, bowls, and the like should be dense enough to hold liquid or food without leaking. Low density – high porosity – makes for fragile, easily broken ware, hence earthenware dinnerware is in general cheaper to buy than stoneware or porcelain.

Density or conversely porosity is controlled by the firing qualities of the clay itself and by the amount of *flux* that is added to lower maturing temperature and increase density. Silica, almost always added to a clay body to alleviate stickiness, will lessen shrinkage. Concocting your clay body focuses your attention on the kind of workability your ideas require, on the shrinkage your forms can stand, and on the density or porosity demanded by the function.

How to reclaim scrap clay

Clay is only workable in the so-called plastic, malleable stage. The more you work it, the more it dries and loses its plasticity. To make it usable again:

1. if it is leather-hard (semi-dry, like cheese), poke finger-holes in the chunk, add water, wrap in a plastic sheet and store in a lidded container for a week or so until the clay softens;

2. if the scrap is bone-dry, collect it in a wooden box or some low flat receptacle, pound it into powder, and – in a metal, wood, or stoneware container – add that dry powder in layers alternating with sprays of water. Cover with damp cloths and plastic, leave for several days and the clay will be workable again;

3. or, add the ground dry powdered clay to an excess of water; in a few weeks it should be a slurry that can be dried to a workable stage on a plaster or wooden table.

4. If you add leather-hard, partially dry, and bone-dry scrap in various lumps to water, you will never get an un-lumpy mass of clay. Don't do this!

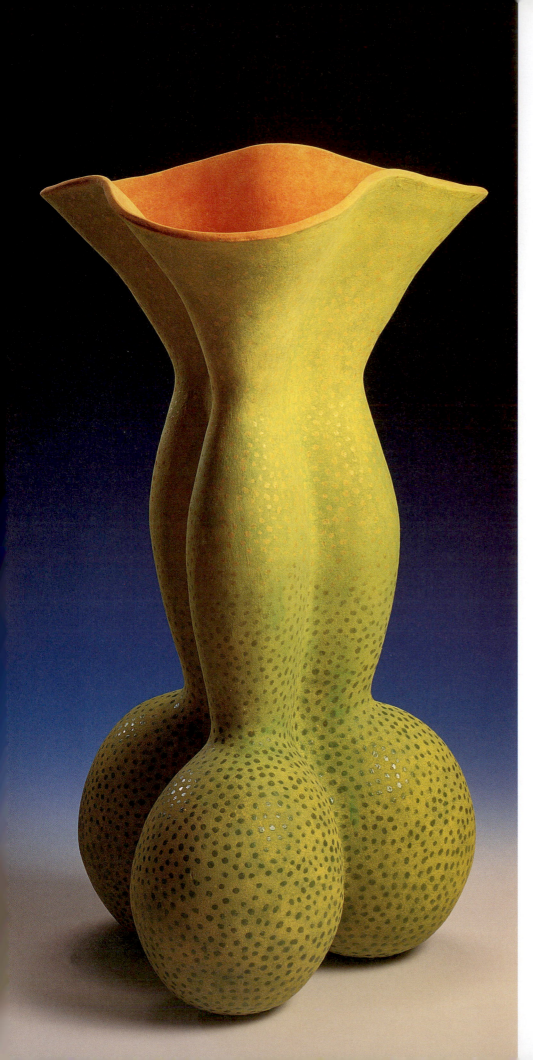

WHAT IS GLAZE?

Glaze is a type of glass, which melts in a fire at a given temperature, but does not melt enough to run off the object it coats.

Unlike glass, which stands alone, glaze needs to be bonded to something like clay or metal.

Glaze is made of silica (the glass-forming oxide), plus other oxides that will cause the refractory silica to melt at lower temperatures. In glass the fluxes are generally soda or lead. In glaze the fluxes vary according to the temperature required to fire the clay.

Glaze contains one more component than does glass. It needs the addition of an oxide that will hold the molten glass on a surface. That oxide is alumina, which acts as a binder and a viscosity controller. Remember, clay contains alumina. It turns out that clay is one of the important constituents of a glaze, in addition to silica, which is the same oxide that is a filler in a clay body. Both clay and glaze therefore contain these two ingredients in different proportions.

Glaze can be matt (dull) or glossy; transparent (see-through) or opaque in varying degrees; rough or smooth; colored with metallic earth oxides or left uncolored. Glazes can be mixed by you or commercially purchased ready-mixed, but of secret composition.

Glaze provides:
• an easily cleaned, sanitary coating;

White earthenware clay body vase with low-temperature matt and glossy glazes by Elisabeth van Krogh (Norway)

• a vehicle for decoration and color;
• acid and chemical resistance;
• durability.

Glazes can be "made up" from:
• an original molecular oxide formula;
• experimental tests of various raw materials in different percentage combinations;
• batch "recipes" found in ceramic books or magazines;
• original batches, altered according to experience or caprice.

Glazes are colored with:
• small percentages of oxides of a few metals that resist high temperatures, such as cobalt for blue, iron for brown, chrome for green, copper for turquoise, vanadium for yellow, and others;
• salts of various metals such as carbonates, sulphates, nitrates (e.g. copper carbonate, copper sulphate) – sulphates and nitrates are less strong, carbonates are stronger but oxides are strongest, used with appropriate percentages;
• "stains" that are commercially prepared from metallic oxides and other chemicals that are stable at certain temperatures and that provide a much wider palette of color than the basic oxides.

More about glazes and glazing in Chapter 4.

FIRING CERAMICS

Humans made and used pottery for many thousands of years, knowing that sun-drying did not make the pieces durable, but not aware of what else to do. They added papyrus, dirt, and other organic materials to the clay to increase the vessel's sun-dried strength. But in rain the clay reverted to mud, and disintegrated with use.

No one knows how humans discovered that the heat of a real fire was necessary to produce the chemistry in clay body ingredients for a modicum of hardness and stability. 1300° F (700° C) is the measurable temperature of flame in an open fire. This "red heat" is the lowest temperature at which minerals in a clay vessel can achieve minimum durability, but it will still be fragile and liquids will seep out. When potters learned to enclose the heat, they realized greater density and permanence. Pots stacked for bonfiring could be covered with brush and a thick coating of clay all over to enclose the fire. American Indians used cow chips around their wood-fired pots. The first "kilns" were probably caves cut deep into hills, blocked up with stones after the pots and wood were placed inside. The cave idea progressed

Peter Hayes (UK) pulling a red-hot piece out of a raku kiln. Usually artists use metal tongs or a shovel mechanism to extract large pieces hot from the kiln, but properly refractory gloves, as shown here, also suffice

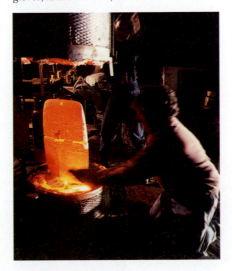

to kilns built like a dragon, upward on sloping ground with fire at the bottom and a flue at the top.

Potters found that different temperatures and lengths of time in the heat created different colors in the same clays. White-burning clays didn't change, but colored clays stayed lighter at low fire and darkened if temperature and time were extended. Ceramic chemistry has been called the earliest science. Museums are full of the evolution of pottery from earliest times, showing a variety of clay colors, shapes, and forms. We don't know why the Chinese were the first people in the world to determine, thousands of years ago, how to build kilns that would stand up under the high temperatures they were learning to attain – nor do we understand why they were the first and only culture to want to try.

Clay does not like thermal shock – it breaks. Ancient potters put "temper," ground shards of broken fired pots, pulverized nutshells or bones, grains, sand, or volcanic ash into clay to make it more resistant to an instant flame. When clayworkers used enclosed chambers, which we call kilns, they also worked out how to control heat with flues and dampers in extraordinarily complicated ways.

In a kiln, clay can be fired slowly, especially in the initial stages, to expel the moisture that made it workable and the water that is combined chemically with the alumina and silica in the clay molecule. Generally a six- to eight-hour firing curve, consistently rising to top temperature, is sufficient for normal claywork; cooling must be slow also. Exceptionally large works require much slower firings, which can take several days or even weeks.

Look for more about firing in Chapter 5.

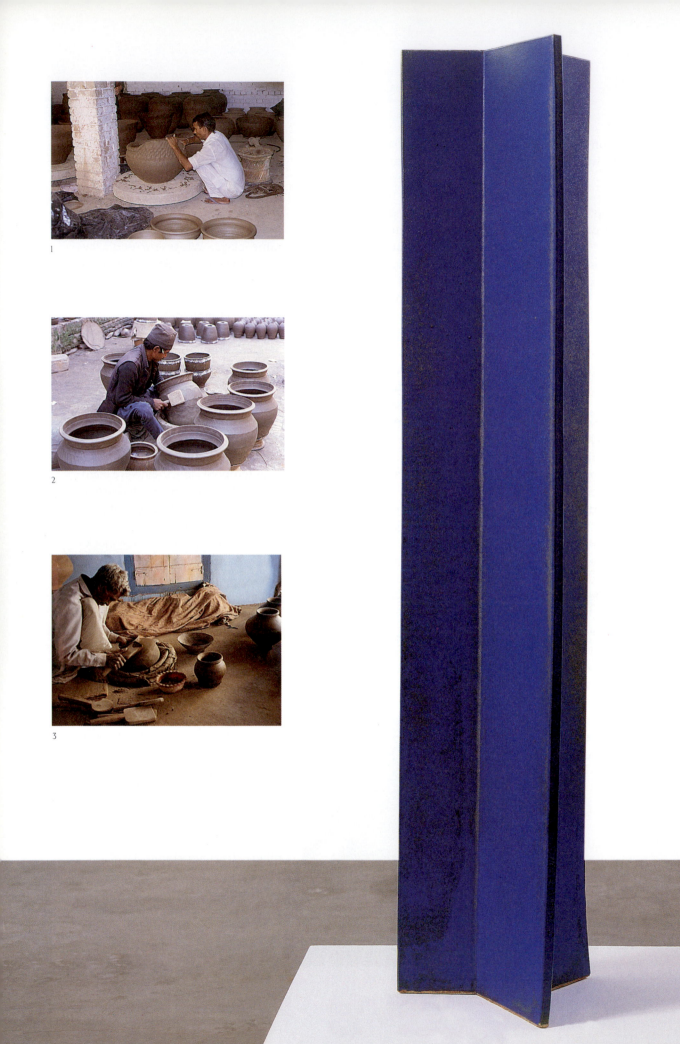

1

2

3

2

THE CRAFT OF
WORKING WITH
CLAY BY HAND

GETTING STARTED

Hand-building is the oldest method of clayworking, probably beginning at least 30,000 years ago.

Throwing developed in Egypt, China, and Mesopotamia about 5,000 or more years ago. Throwing on the potter's wheel (see Chapter 3) is the most direct way of shaping a clay piece. Thrown work made round on the wheel can be altered to make other shapes. Working on the potter's wheel is a skill that requires many years of practice, but it is only a skill and anyone can learn it.

FACING PAGE Another extraordinary vertical slab-built sculpture by John Mason, 62½ x 13½ x 13½ ins. (159 x 34 x 34 cm)

INSETS The techniques shown here for making large pots are necessary because the wheels, or the potter's skill, are too imperfect to throw the shapes. Beginners can take advantage of these methods, too:

1. A potter at Tulsi Farms, Delhi, India, throws and coils a large container

2. In Nepal a potter paddles a shape both inside and outside from the thickly thrown cones visible at the rear, stretching the clay by hand in an almost unbelievable fashion

3. A potter in Maheshwar, India, paddles from the thrown shape you see in front of him to the shape you see at the far right

Pressing over or into another shape is another way to design clay. The earliest humans probably pressed clay against rocks, or turned round shapes in a basket or another clay form, using a part-hand, part-wheel technique.

Reproducing the same shapes in a fired-clay or plaster mold is ancient too. The Egyptians and Greeks mastered mold-making by 2000 B.C. Today commercial ceramics are made mechanically, by mold reproduction processes called slip-casting, jiggering, and ram pressing. Some processes done by machines turn out hundreds of wares automatically every day. Potters can use hand variations of these methods.

Space ceramics involve other ways of forming, which may one day be part of the potter's vocabulary.

The clayworker decides which method to use according to the special requirements of the piece that is to be fabricated. His or her emotional response to a particular method may also affect the decision.

If the skills are not known, then they should all be learned and practiced in order that an intelligent choice of method can be made. The clay body, as I have said, must be the best, or the best pieces will not be made. It behoves you to take time to develop or find a good clay body. If you are a student you may be limited to what is in your school. If you are working on your own, you can afford the time to experiment and test until the right mixture proves itself.

On the following pages I will show you beginning steps in the wonderful vocabulary of clay work. Some of the photographs of finished pieces may seem too complicated for beginners, but it's OK to try. It's also OK to feed your brain with lots of ideas and images, to keep your mind flying high.

TOOLS FOR WORKING

Potters can use many tools, or just a few, or none. Most clay artists make collections all their lives of various tools – or objects that will function as tools – from the hardware store, from their attics and garages, and from nature.

Water is essential in the hand-building process, but should be used very sparingly. A plastic squirt bottle of some sort is required to spray water, as work must be kept uniformly damp throughout construction.

A basic set of tools for hand-building could be:

• metal knife and wood knife
• small sponge or chamois
• cutting wire
• half-moon-shaped wood or rubber rib
• texture tools such as rocks, sticks, buttons, shells, etc.
• metal scraping tool, wire-end tool, hacksaw blade, or metal rib
• silver or steel fork, knife, spoon
• wooden paddles

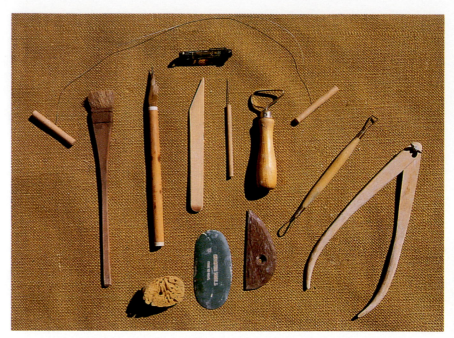

Potters can use hundreds of tools, or a few, or none, but a basic set is probably a good idea. Shown here are a flat and a round *brush* for decorating, a twisted *cutting wire*, a small finishing *sponge*, a *wood knife* for texturing and trimming, a rubber and a wooden *rib* for shaping, a *needle on the end of a stick* for cutting, a small *level*, a small and a large *wire-end trimming tool*, and a *calliper* for measuring lids or attachments

WEDGING CLAY

Clay must be in the best possible plastic condition for working, without hard lumps, without air bubbles, and absolutely even in consistency throughout. *Wedging* is the hand process by which we get clay into working condition. Industry, as well as some schools and potters, use a pug mill to "wedge" clay, but even then, more hand wedging is essential. Wedging puts the clay into an even condition while the potter is "feeling" the clay. Clay will tell you what it wants to do, what it CAN do. See also page 69 for more on the wedging process.

Of course you must start each project with an idea of how the finished object will look. Some balls of clay just do not feel as if they want to become wide bowls or tall bottles, in which case change your perception of what you wanted to make, or try another ball of clay. Ideas always should come first. Flawless wedging is the initial step.

BUILDING BY HAND: INTRODUCTION

Because ancient peoples first made pots and clay figures by hand processes, and only later on the wheel, we sometimes think that the making of pottery by coil and slab techniques is easy.

Actually, learning to control shapes made from coils, slabs, and pinches by hand, or learning to support the line of the profile and the weight of

HOW TO WEDGE

1. Start with a relatively soft ball of clay slapped into a rectangular shape, on end, pointing up to the right.

2. Left hand grasps the left side of the lump, fingers towards the back; right hand rests gently on top of the mound. Left hand presses down into the clay,

3. right hand pivots the lump to the left, counterclockwise. After the pivot, left hand presses downward again, right hand pivots.

4. Repeat until the clay feels even. Wedging dries clay out – expect it to get stiffer as you work. Although all forming methods with clay require the potter to be ambidextrous, to use both hands equally well, left-handers may want to reverse the above directions.

5. This wedging routine results in "petal" shapes, and is called chrysanthemum wedging.

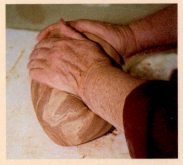

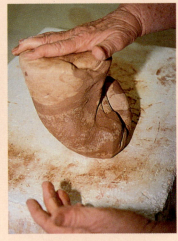

Beginners can check their wedging capability by using two different colors of clay and wedging until they are completely amalgamated into a single color:

Turn the ball of clay on its end, push the left hand down into the clay, and…

… pivot with the right hand. Repeat the process, left hand down, right hand pivot, until consistency is even. The air is forced out through the petal layers you can see developing above

the form, are techniques probably more difficult to master than wheel-throwing.

Solid clay shapes are used for making plaster molds, into which clay, plaster, or even molten metal may be cast. **Hollow clay shapes.** Clay shapes to be fired, whether vessel forms or sculpture, must be built hollow; solid shapes produce firing difficulties.

Some clayworkers build forms solid but carve them out while the clay is still moist; this does not allow for an even cross-section, and disaster is likely in the firing. Thick, solid clay shapes can be finished in a very elongated kiln firing and cooling period. Bricks, one of the thickest clay shapes, may take weeks to fire. The larger and thicker the clay form the more slowly it must be fired.

Shrinkage. Furthermore, clay shrinks as it dries. Thin walls dry and fire most easily. Understanding the movement of clay from wet to dry to fired is the first and most necessary step in thinking of clay shapes. Clay is a living, moving thing until after

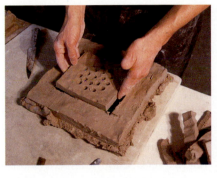

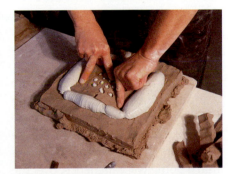

HAND-BUILDING TILES

Ron Kovatch devised this simple, quick method. Extrapolate for any size module:
• for instance, hollow out a 12 x 2 ins. (30 x 5 cm) thick slab of clay like a picture frame
• decorate a 7 ins. (18 cm) square stoneware tile with a punctured design, to fit into the frame
• make a white porcelain thick slurry and fill the stoneware frame
• squeeze the tile into the slurry
• sagger fire with charcoal, dried food, pine needles, sawdust, salt and the like. Tumble-stack tiles together.
Temperatures from c/5 to c/11 work best, with a long firing

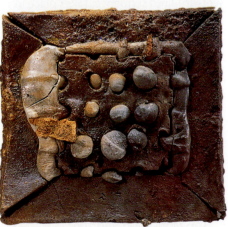

Stoneware: fire clays 80%, china clay 10%, feldspar 10% plus coarse grog
Porcelain: china clay 50%, soda feldspar 25%, silica 25%

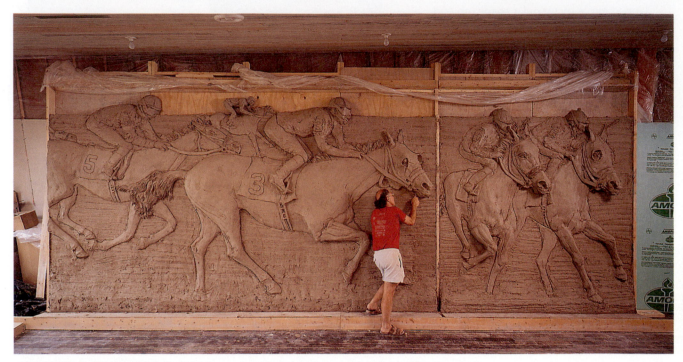

Bruce Howdle builds a wall 23 ft (7 m) long against a wooden easel, carves directly into the moist clay, keeps it damp with plastic covers for the weeks of work, and will cut it into sections for firing

it is out of the kiln. Clay moves because it shrinks physically from the wet to the bone-dry stage; more shrinkage takes place chemically in the course of the firing. The maximum shrinkage that a potter will experience, over the wet-dry-fired sequence, takes place in a vitreous porcelain piece.

Cantilevered shapes, that is, wide bowls on tiny feet, or pot-bellied bottles on small bases, are likely to slump or warp in any direction, or to crack. It simply is not feasible to create the same shapes in clay that can be achieved in wood or metal.

> Allowing for the movement during shrinkage is crucial to the fabrication and the design in all claywork. Build on 2-inch (5 cm) thick newspaper or thick cloth

Weight and thickness – that is, the cross-section of the clay wall – are important. Like a tree, clay shapes need to be somewhat heavier at the bottom and lighter toward the top, not vice versa. Clay movement (shrinkage) should take place evenly, which implies that the clay wall should be even. Thickness of the wall should be ideally not more than ½ inch (1.25 cm).

If cross-sections vary too much from thick to thin over the entire piece, then drying and shrinking will also be uneven. **This is almost always the reason for cracked pots**. Cracks resulting from uneven drying may not be seen until the first firing, the so-called "bisque" firing. Sometimes the clay waits to crack until there is further shrinkage, at the stage when the glaze is fired to higher temperatures. But the strain will almost always have been the potter's mistake, set up during the fabrication and the drying.

The clayworker is in total control when using the basic hand methods such as pinch, coil, and slab. In throwing, the wheel determines a great deal of the weight and wall of a piece.

It is possible to use combustible cores for construction of hand-built pottery. Again, you have to know what you are doing. If clay is fastened against paper, cardboard, or fabric without room to move, then it cannot shrink properly and it will crack at the pre-fire drying stage. Combustible cores are supports that burn out in the fire, but they must be soft enough to allow movement of the wet to dry clay before firing, or must be covered with layers of soft paper or cloth that will give as the clay moves.

Wooden or metal armatures should not be used unless they can be removed before firing, unless the cracking that ensues is part of the design, or unless the armature is stainless steel or nylon wire (page 50). Sculptors who work in stone or bronze often make solid clay models on metal armatures as "sketches," or they work clay on metal armatures from which a mold will be made for further casting in metal. Potters are limited to hollow, relatively thin and even-walled work. **Ceramic sculpture is best made by building hollow, bottom to top, controlling wall thickness and weight all the while**.

Children enjoy making small clay figures or objects solid, and they can be successful, especially if they are shown how to poke needle or pin holes through the thick clay for even drying and firing. Something children particularly like is to put the little groups of figures or objects together on a flat clay pancake, making a whole story on a stand of clay.

Some of the most beautiful objects ever made in clay have been made by hand techniques, without the use of a wheel or template. Today some of the best ceramic sculpture on an architectural scale is made this way. If you respect the technique and learn to use it properly, if you understand the principles of hand-building, there is no limit to size or design.

Coil-built basket sculpture by Rina Peleg

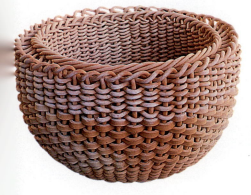

HAND-BUILDING TECHNIQUES

Pinching clay

Pinching a ball of solid clay into a hollow form, with the fingers and without tools, is one of the oldest methods of building with clay. Pinching can be combined with coiling or with paddling, so that larger shapes can be obtained. Much satisfaction – akin to meditating – can be gained from holding a ball of clay in the palm of one hand, making a hole in it with the thumb of the other hand, and then rotating the form and pinching the wall up and out with the thumb and fingers.

Pinching is the first technique to use with any new clay, or with clay you have just prospected in nature. It is the ideal method for developing that absolutely vital sense of the clay wall thickness. The best way to measure clay thickness is by feel, although you can push a needle through the clay wall to measure it. Feeling the wall is also the proper method of teaching yourself to sense whether the clay is in good condition, that is, without lumps or air bubbles that will cause trouble in firing. Gaining these perceptions takes practice; pinching a clay form is a good way to practice (see page 40).

Coil method, smooth or textured

As old as time, this is one of the most difficult ways of making clay forms. We give kindergarten children the assignment of making a coil pot, and then expect them to do it!

Coils placed one on top of the other will cause the vessel to grow tall and straight; a coil edge placed outside the previous one will expand the vessel outwardly; a coil edge placed inside the previous one will move the shape inward. Thus a shape is easily controlled, whether straight up or out and in

Ropes of clay are rolled out, one at a time, and attached to each other by a process called **luting**. Each coil is scored with a knife, the tines of a fork, a comb, or a similar tool. The scored edges are moistened with water or with a clay slurry (a thickish mixture of clay and water) and attached sturdily. **Scoring must be deep so that each coil mates solidly with the other** (see page 41).

Stoneware clay body coils from a hand-pushed extruder mound together in a large sculpture by a Hunter college student

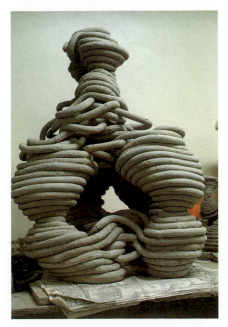

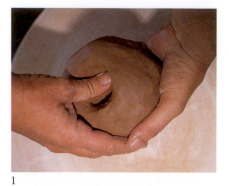

PINCHING A CLAY POT

1. Begin a small pinch-pot from a ball of clay you can hold in your hands. Press a hole downward with your thumb, turning the ball in your hand

2. Thumb inside, fingers outside, or vice versa as here, squeeze and pinch upward while rotating the ball; repeat to perfect the form

3. Turn pot upside down, fingers squeeze up a foot pedestal, thumb indents

4. Finished form can be pinched thinner, wider, taller, right side up; a paddle can refine the form or add texture
Large pinched forms are possible in similar fashion to almost any scale

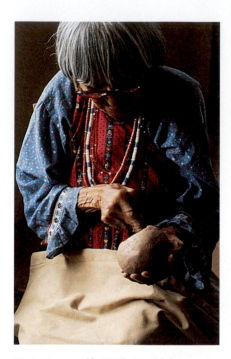

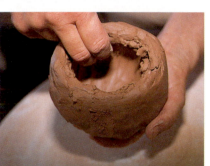

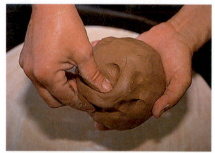

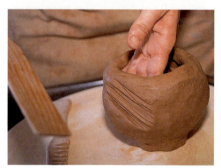

Maria Martinez (d. 1980), San Ildefonso Pueblo, New Mexico, pinching out a form which she has started from a solid ball. The 50–50 clay–volcanic ash composition causes the body to become moist and sluggish quickly, making it difficult to control. Maria used to build jars as tall as 3 ft (90 cm) and bowls equally wide, but by her 90s, above, her arthritis prevented large-scale pieces and she preferred only shapes she could hold in her hand

BELOW A large pillow form by Marea Gazzard (Australia) illustrates the pinching technique and is a good example of the concept of enclosed space. It is quite difficult to give the feeling of volume in clay sculpture

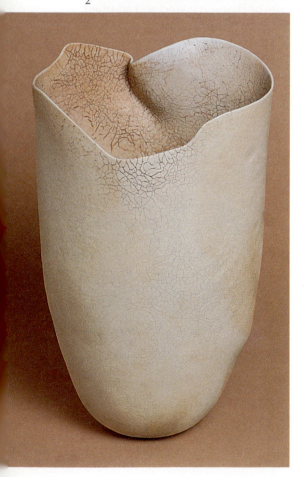

Richard DeVore's thinly pinched, articulated vessel is coated with a crackle glaze enhanced with black pigment after firing

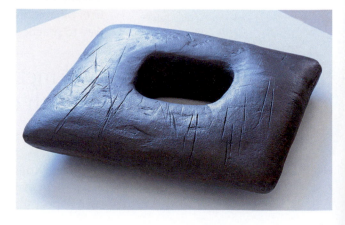

Coils must be added while the clay is moist, or "leather-hard," not dry. Because clay shrinks and must dry uniformly, the piece must be constructed all at once in the same state of wetness, even if this means keeping it damp for weeks until the fabrication is finished.

Weight, thickness of the wall, and the profile line of the form are the determining factors in whether or not a coiled piece will stand up without cracking or warping in the fire. The texture and pattern of the coils can be kept as part of the design of the work, or the coils can be smoothed inside and out with a tool. Evenly rolled coils make evenly controlled lines, but unevenly rolled coils can be interesting too. Coils rolled into rosette shapes, or snakes, or U's and W's, laid sideways or vertically, will achieve pattern and structure at the same time.

If a smooth surface is desired on very large works, build with fat coils that can be flattened before they are attached. Usually one coil is wound round to form one circle and the two ends are luted together. More complicated forms are possible if the coils are kept narrow in diameter, but the building process is slower. It is also possible to wind the pieces round and round in a continuous coil, which will create a different kind of texture and form.

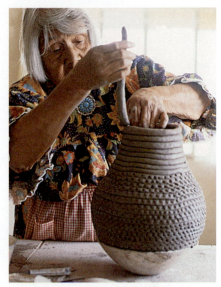

Lucy Lewis (d. 1992), Acoma Pueblo, New Mexico, coils and textures a storage vessel. In order to achieve the traditionally rounded bottom, she is working in an old clay shard

COIL BUILDING

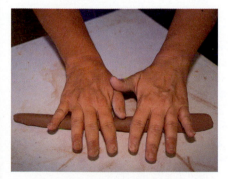

Two hands may be easier than one hand for rolling a coil of even thickness and soundness; roll from center out, on canvas, plaster, wood, or towel

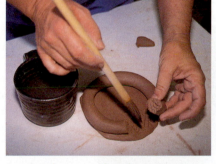

Attach coil to a patted-out base: score base and coil deeply with a sharp tool, moisten, press together strongly. Score (lute) both ends, moisten and join

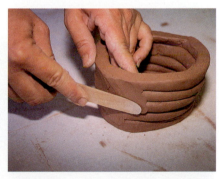

Exposed coils can form arbitrary patterns during building of the shape, or coils can be obliterated with a tool for a smooth surface

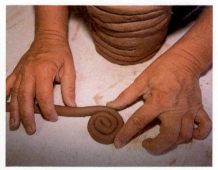

Rolled coil forms …

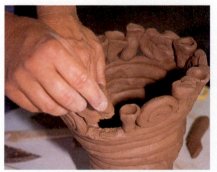

… can add decorative elements to finish the work; be sure to score and wet both sides for the attachments

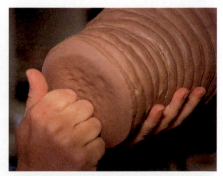

The base of the form can be indented with your fist or palm, for ease of drying and firing

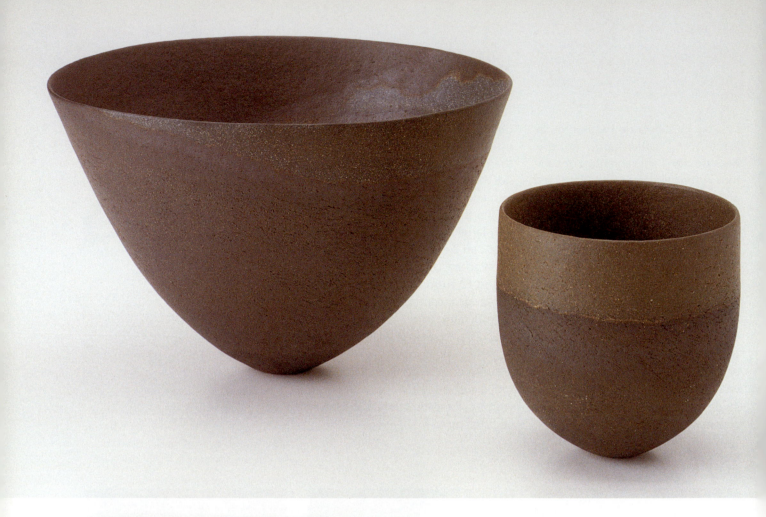

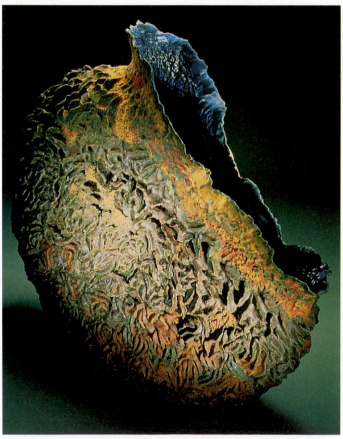

Jennifer Lee (UK) is a master at pinch and coil technique using stains and metallic oxides added to a variety of clay bodies for a range of colors and textures. She works one pot at a time over several weeks; pinch and coil marks are smoothed with bamboo and wood tools; some surfaces are scraped, some are burnished. Pots are once-fired, oxidation, to cone 9; no glaze is used. 6 x 9½ ins. (15 x 24 cm); 3¾ x 3½ ins (9.5 x 9 cm)

Joanne Emelock's large coiled floor pot, 42 ins. (106 cm) high, meticulously carved and textured, has been coated with low-fire earthenware glazes

Slab building

Coil building is for round shapes, slab building is for squares or angles and sharp edges. However, slabs can also construct round forms where there is not much profile change, and coiled shapes can be pounded into off-round objects.

Depending on the size of the work to be constructed, one slab can become one whole vertical wall, or a number of slabs may be laid vertically one on top of another in a manner similar to building with the coil process. A natural line-change takes place where slabs join, making an artful conjunction. Fabricate slabs against a canvas board, or other porous surface from which the clay will be easily released.

Different ways to make a slab:
1. Roll a lump of clay flat between two horizontal sticks; the width of the sticks will determine the thickness of the slab, usually ½ to 1 inch.
2. Shape a lump of clay into a rectangle; hold two sticks upright either side of it, with a string or wire stretched between them; pull the string or wire through at different levels to obtain a number of slabs.
3. Pound a lump of clay into a flat slab with your fist; turn it over and pound the opposite side; repeat several times for structural strength (page 48).
4. Several slabs can be luted together to make one large clay blanket.
5. "Throw" out a slab: hold a flattened lump of clay from its top with both your hands and fling the clay down toward the table, repeating several times until it has

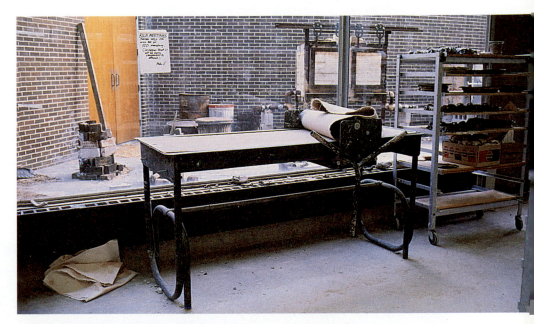

Slab roller, a mechanical means of producing slabs of varying thicknesses

SLABS ARE BEST FOR ANGULAR FORMS

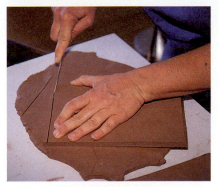

Cut shapes from preformed slabs (see Different ways to make a slab)

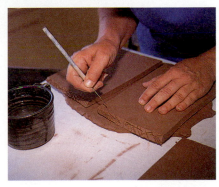

With a sharp tool, deeply score mating edges, and moisten with water; repeat several times

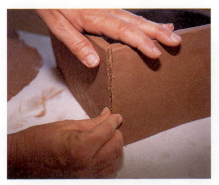

Squeeze scored, moistened surfaces together tightly; paddle to strengthen the bond

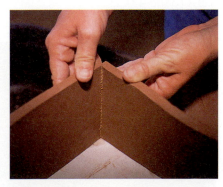

A thin coil can be pinched into the interior seam for strength; reinforce with a tool

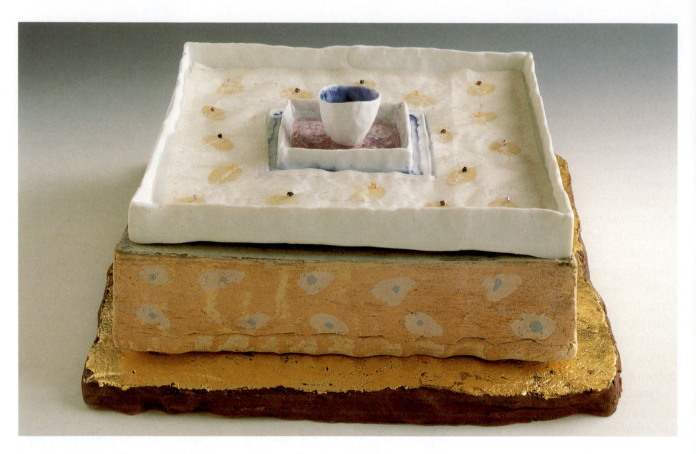

expanded to the desired size. This method works for small or huge slabs, once you get the hang of it, and yields a relatively even cross-section (page 46).

6. Use a rolling pin and roll a lump of clay as if it were biscuit dough (page 48).

7. A "slab rolling" machine helps, especially in making extra-large slabs (page 43).

8. Cast a liquid clay slab against plaster (page 52).

9. Cast a thicker slab into a sand mold (page 60).

10. Press a slab from plastic clay in a mold.

Màrta Nagy's (Hungary) charming slab-built sculpture is constructed of stoneware and porcelain, decorated with engobes and gold leaf, multi-fired from c/12 down, with added accessories and silk

Some of these slab methods will give a more even, some a relatively uneven result. Select the method most suited to your design concept

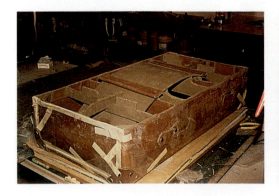

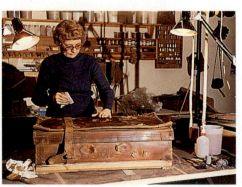

1. Marilyn Levine's slab-built suitcase with slab buttresses is encased in plastic and taped to keep it damp and ready for the top to be added

2. The artist applies an oxide patina after the whole piece is finished, before firing. After firing, wax is added for leather-look

Slab construction is ideal for large scale; it is a faster method of building than pinch or coil. Slabs for large work can be laid over combustible cores made of cardboard wrapped in fabric, or scrunched-up paper, or sand-stuffed pillows – the sand must be let out as the piece reaches leather-hardness. Clay can be rolled against nylon screens, which burn out, or against stainless steel screens, which will stay in the structure up to 2150° F (1175° C).

Potters through the centuries have added inert materials to the clay body to enable the handling of large, weighty constructions in the moist plastic state. Today short nylon fibers can be wedged or mixed in clay bodies to serve this purpose. Clayworkers need to become magicians with inventive ideas.

A SLAB-BUILT FIREPLACE

Paula Winokur is well known for slab-building large sculptures of porcelain clay body. For this commissioned and installed fireplace she began with a clay maquette presentation to the client. To do the work she:

• cut large-scale cardboard templates for the sections for the entire piece, allowing for 14% fired clay shrinkage;

• rolled the clay slabs according to design; allowed them to stiffen; scored edges, and moistened several times before attaching sections of surface slabs with torn edges.

• Fired porcelain shapes were grouted together, installed on site, with Paula's hearth of flat tiles

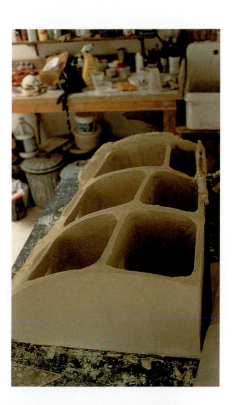

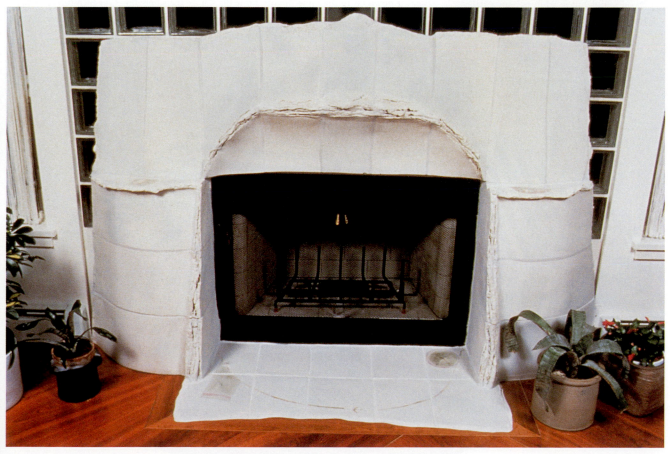

ONE METHOD OF MAKING A SLAB BY HAND

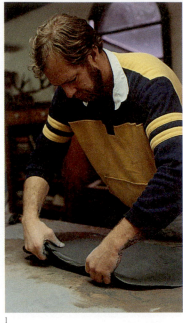

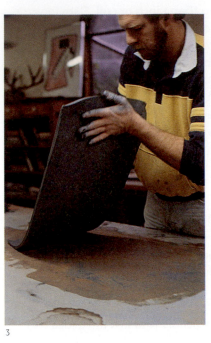

1

2

3

David Middlebrook "throws" out a slab: **He picks up the flattened slab and . . .**

. . . flings it down on to the table. If you throw the slab in the same direction each time it will become longer; if you throw it in opposite directions it will become round or square. Several slabs can be luted together to make one huge slab

John Mason's large pentagonal form is a virtuoso piece of slab-building, as well as of graphic surface decoration

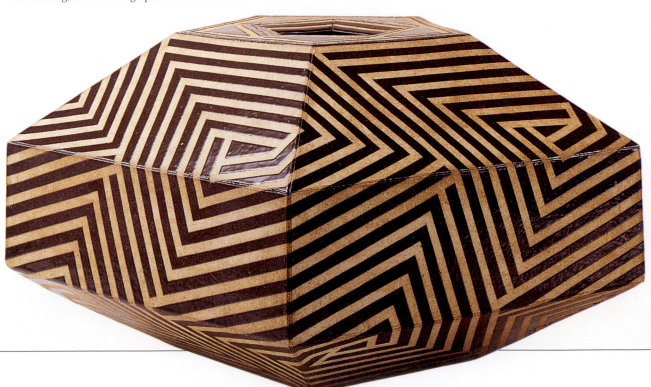

YIXING TEAPOT

Shao Junya (China) uses the famous YiXing natural clay, prospected near her home, to fabricate teapots of traditional and avant-garde forms

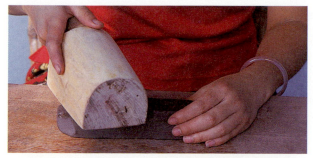

She pounds clay slabs hard many times, with a heavy wood hammer to achieve a very thin, even thickness of ³⁄₁₆ in. (5 mm)

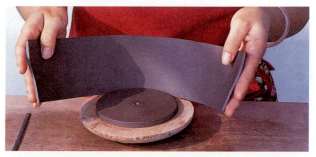

Scored and moistened slab is attached to base

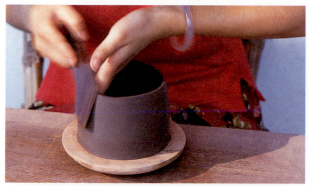

Cylindrical form is paddled round (no wheel is used)

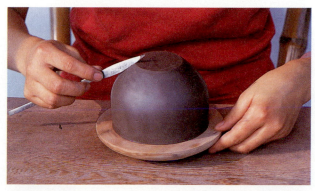

Upside down, the foot is shaped

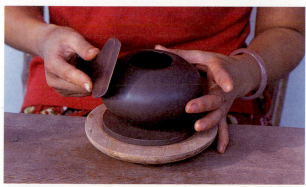

Right side up, she turns and gently paddles the final shape, which rests on a pad of clay to turn pot without scratching foot

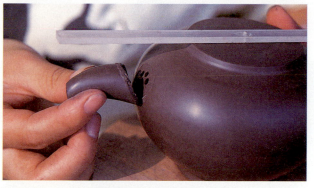

Hand-formed spout attaches at tea-straining holes; top slab will be cut open to accommodate the lid

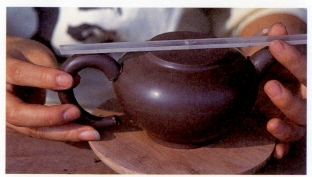

Hollow formed handle is placed directly opposite spout

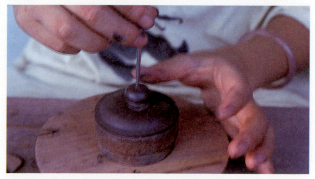

Lid with flange and knob is similarly fabricated

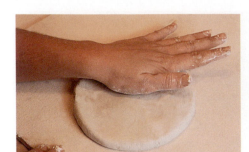

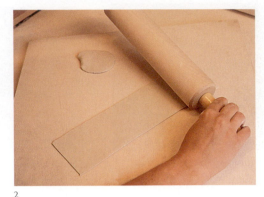

HAND-BUILD WITH THIN FRAGILE PORCELAIN

1. Using a very clean canvas board, Jan Peterson pats out a porcelain clay pancake

2. She rolls very thin slabs and cuts them to size for a tumbler

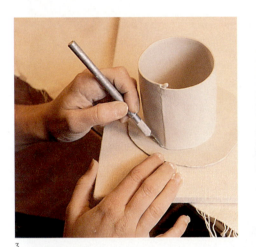

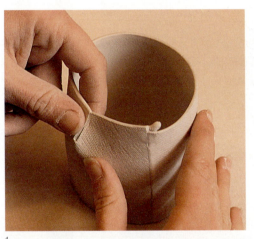

3. The cylindrical shape, thin enough to be translucent, is placed on an equally thin slab base, and the two are scored and luted together

4. She cuts and folds the edge to alter the shape

5. Finished tumblers, glazed inside, unglazed outside, with airbrush and tape resist stain decoration, c/10 oxidation

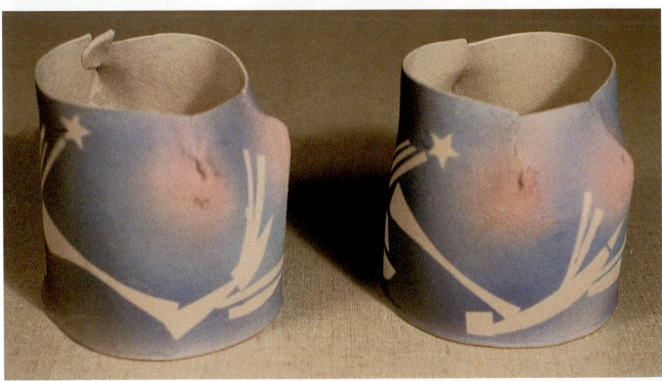

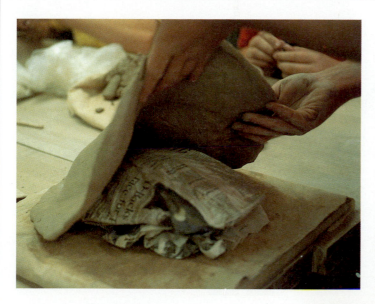

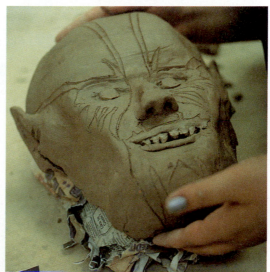

MASK MAKING

Students at Highland High School, Gilbert, Arizona, enjoy making monster masks as a ceramic project. Piles of newspaper, of almost any size and height, form the basic shape; stoneware clay slabs are laid over to form the mask. With the paper core support, facial features, pinched, coiled, or slabbed, can be added. When leather-hard the mask will be lifted off the paper, decorated with colored clay engobes and fired to cone 10. Finished mask at right is 36 x 18 x 6 ins. (91 x 45 x 15 cm)

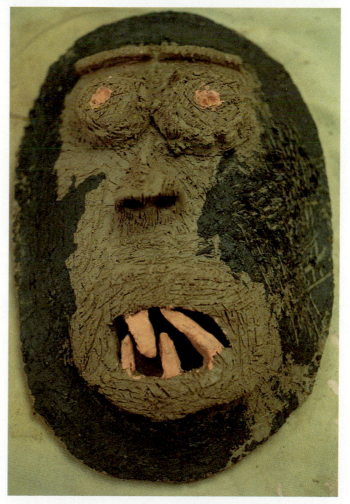

Using an armature

Stainless steel will withstand 2150° F (1175° C), cone 5, and such an armature will remain in the piece to give strength to large work, but must be wrapped with enough paper to allow for the clay to shrink against it. A clay body should be developed for minimum shrinkage.

Nylon mesh or nylon wire armatures may burn out depending on the firing temperature, but will add structure during fabrication. Supports of wood, glass bottles, or pipes must be wrapped and extracted before the plastic clay begins to dry.

If the clay piece is a model for a plaster mold or for metal casting, the armature buttress will remain in until the clay is removed from the mold.

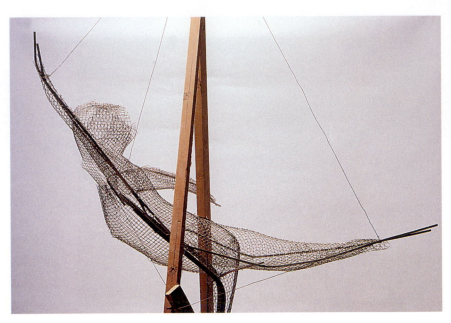

Jerry Rothman's low-shrink clay body will be laid over this stainless steel armature that will remain in the piece while the sculpture below is fired at a median stoneware temperature

Clay on the steel armature is supported by wood while it dries

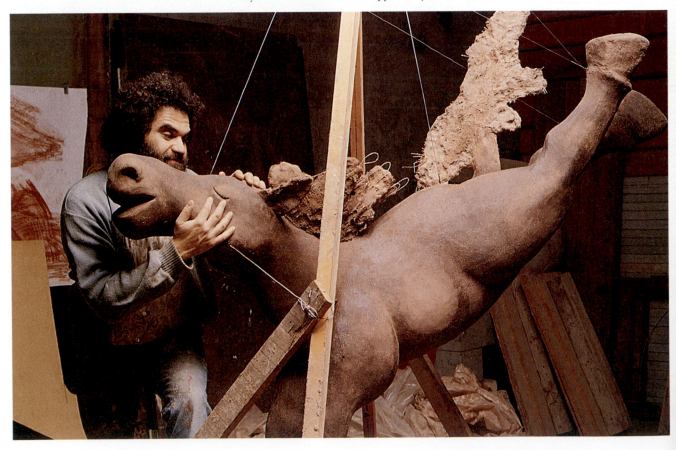

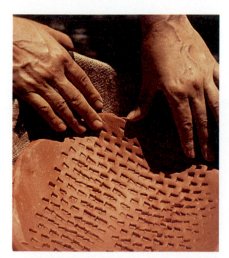

Susan Peterson lays a textured clay slab into a burlap hammock draped in a cardboard box

it. The form must be such that the clay will be released from the hump without getting stuck. It must therefore have no "undercuts" (see page 60), or the clay cannot be removed. You can create your own form from clay or plaster instead of a found object; fire the clay to keep it, or use it moist for one time only.

Place a sheet of plastic or paper or fabric over the hump before laying the clay slab on top, so that it will be released easily when it is lifted off. The hump method, the opposite of the sling method, provides the opportunity of working on the back of the shape, for instance if you want to add a foot or any other appendage to the vessel.

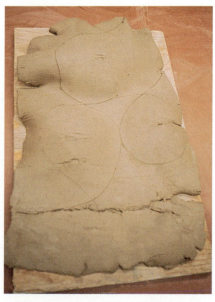

She uses newspapers under layered moist clay slabs as a "hump" to give form, then draws on the surface

Drape in a hammock

Drape a cloth to form a sling of desired depth and width by pinning or nailing the fabric to the inside of a cardboard or wooden box, or suspend material from the legs of an upturned stool, or in any way you can, as a receptacle for a slab of clay. Platter and plate shapes are easily made in this manner. Alternatively, the slung clay can become the base for a sculpture, with pinch, coil, or slab additions. The hammock supports the clay until it is dry enough to be moved.

Several slings can be utilized at once, so that the clay forms may be joined together into hollow vessels or sculptures.

Over-the-hump slab building

Choose a contour – a rock, a pot, a balloon, or the like – that will create the interior shape of the vessel when a slab of clay is placed over

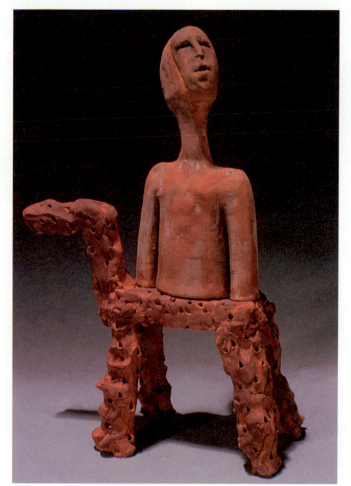

BUILDING ON A CORE

Christine Federighi's unglazed figure is built over a cardboard core which burns out in the firing

POURING A SLAB

Jan Peterson hand-builds a porcelain plate from slip-cast slabs laid over a plaster hump-mold

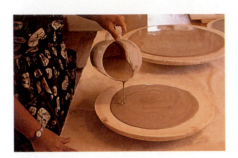

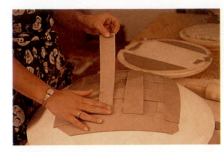

Leather-hard slab cut into patterns, laid over a plaster hump form; moist slabs are rolled together for strength and design

Pouring liquid clay on to plaster to create flat, thin slabs

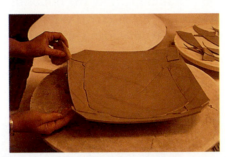

Plate turned right side up shows pressed pattern created by the slabs; edges are smoothed with a damp sponge

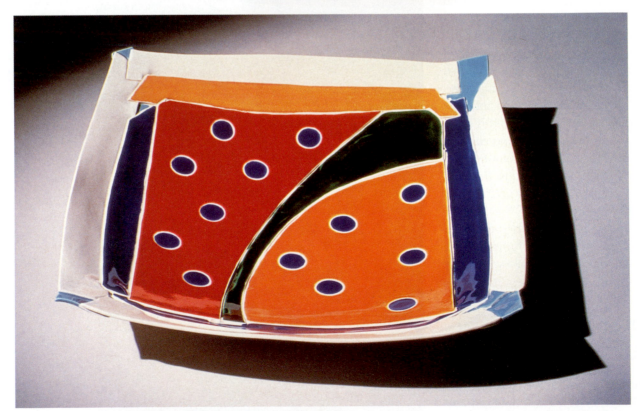

Jan Peterson's finished porcelain platter, bisque fired c/10, glaze fired c/04

Ceramic sculpture

Any method of clay construction may be used for the purpose of sculpture, but hand-building techniques are probably the most versatile. A misconception is that sculpture must be large. If the piece is small and narrow, or if long-time firing is possible, the work could be solid. However, as we have said, it is best to think of ceramic sculpture as hollow, like a pot, and to build it bottom to top as a pot is built.

Making a small solid clay model prior to constructing the large sculpture will help in the complicated thought process of building hollow from the bottom up. Parts of a sculpture can be made separately and attached when the clay is leather-hard. Any size of work is possible, the only limitation being the kiln size. In fact, this can be overcome by making your piece in units that will fit the kiln and can be fired separately. These can be combined after firing by non-clay methods, such as glue, plumber's cement, nuts and bolts, wire, or similar methods. The only real limitation is the clay-worker's imagination, and even that can be strengthened and enriched with knowledge and time.

In one of the largest ceramic projects ever undertaken, Jun Kaneko created monolithic shapes of extraordinary technical difficulty with conspicuous success:

1. His slab and pinch-built "dango" shapes, 11 ft 6 ins. (3.5 m) high, were constructed within a sewer-pipe kiln in Fremont, California

2. The beehive sewer-pipe kiln in which the dangos were built and fired was 30 ft (9 m) in diameter

3. Jun Kaneko glazing an 11 ft (3.4 m) tall dango, following his doodles and codes for color notes

4. Dangos packed and ready to be trucked for storage in Kaneko's Omaha studio

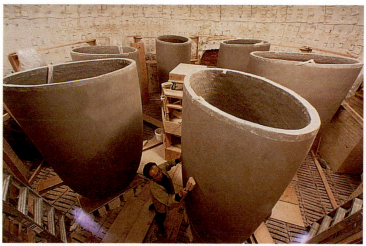

1

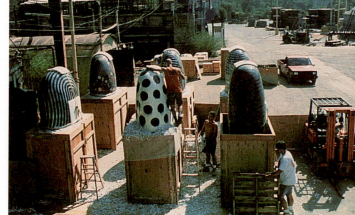

2

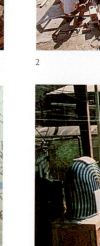

3

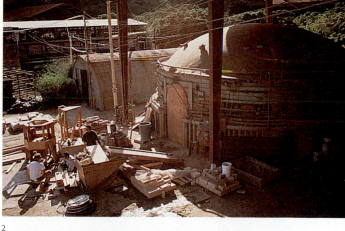

4

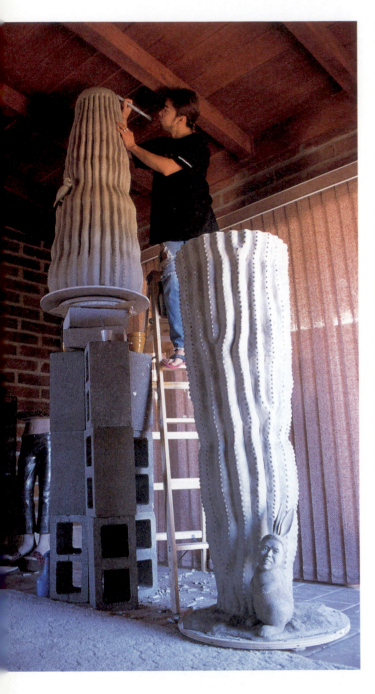

Hirotsune Tashima (Japan) is known for building larger than lifesize figures and installations, usually in sections to be assembled later

LEFT Hiro is constructing a colossal stoneware cactus. Engobe decoration and glazing are done next; firing in a gas kiln takes place at c/5 to c/10

BELOW Here the clay figure, modeled after himself, is about to receive a head similar to his own. The base of the figure is kept damp by being wrapped in plastic; the cement blocks allow him to climb up to continue the piece

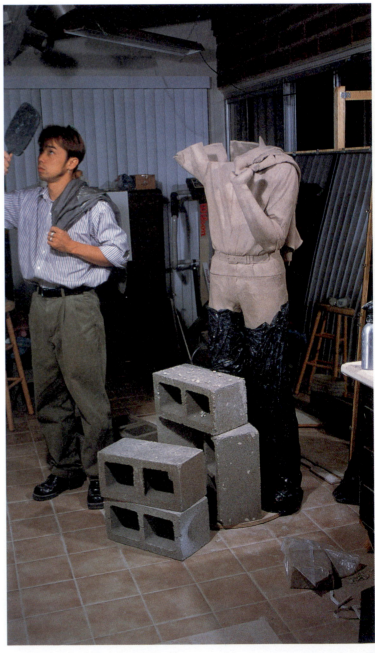

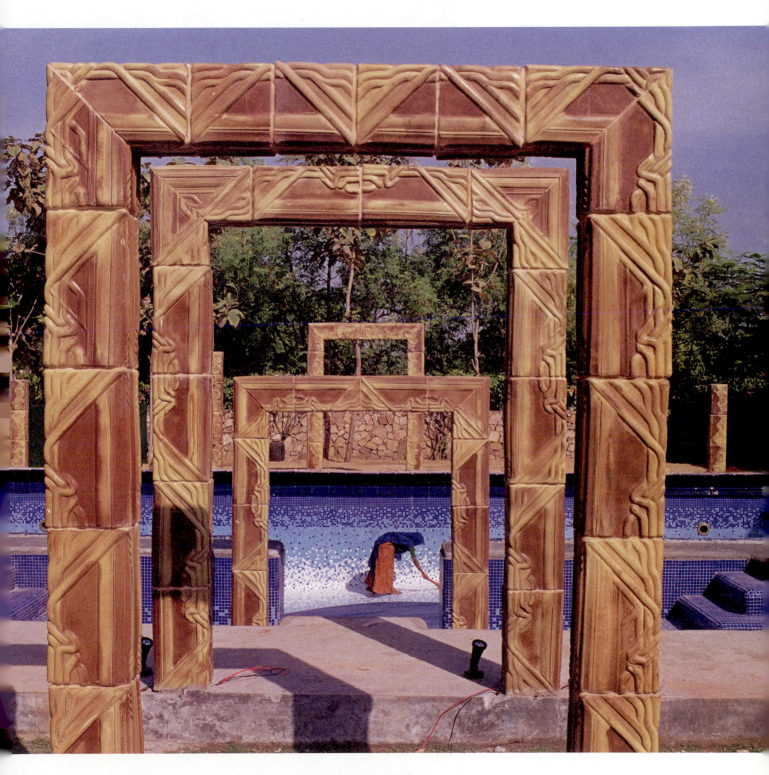

P.R. Daroz (India) is one of the very few artists creating large-scale ceramics in India. His monumental gateway, a private commission in Gujerat, India, consists of four arches and six pillars, slip-cast or extruded in 2-ft (60 cm) stoneware blocks built to a height of 9 ft (2.7 m) and width of 5 ft (1.52 m). Iron oxide accents on a dolomite glaze, fired in a tunnel kiln fueled with oil, are the finishing touch to the three months' work prior to the installation

LEARNING FROM TECHNIQUES USED BY INDIGENOUS PEOPLES

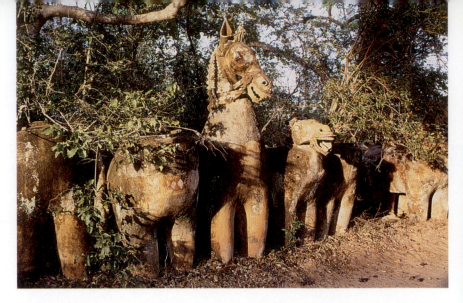

One-hundred-year-old oversized coil-built Ayyanar horses in a hidden shrine in Tamil-Nadu, South India; wood-fired, some are as tall as 13 ft (4 m)

These techniques are still widely applicable, and are well worth practicing whether you are a beginner or not.

Methods of forming

1. Using a natural form as the interior shape:
• coil over a convexly curved rock;
• lay clay over or into a reed basket;
• shape clay over a ball of wax, melt wax out;
• form clay over a ball of bark, twigs, or string, pull the fiber out of finished piece;
• lay slabs or coils of clay over fruits or vegetables such as melon or squash.

2. Pushing natural forms into solid lumps of soft clay to create a pot:
• use sticks, starting with thinner ones, working up to sticks of successively larger diameter up to log-size;
• ram solid clay with smooth, elongated rocks;
• dig down into a soft lump of clay with clam shells or pot shards, turning the clay and widening it with the shape of the shell;
• shape a hollow piece by paddling the outside with a stone against a paddle inside.
• use a wheel made of bamboo or an old tire.

ALTERING WHILE BUILDING

Texture a fresh clay surface with:
• paddles: carved of wood in various shapes, or wrapped with string, weeds, or fabric, or made of bark from different trees or brush;
• roulettes: natural forms that can be rolled against soft clay, such as bones, pine cones, seed pods, animal teeth, wads of leaves, rocks, carved wood rollers;
• combing: pull a toothed or serrated edge across a clay surface;
• stamping: use carved clay stamps, dried or fired, or vegetables, shells, bone ends, twigs, or broken pots.

Changing clay surface

• burnishing: polish the leather-hard clay with a smooth water-washed stone or a gourd to produce a sheen;
• resin: drip tree resin or pitch against a hot pot as it is pulled from the fire.

An Indian pot at Tulsi Farm Pottery, Delhi, is supported on a grain bag while it is burnished with a smooth stone

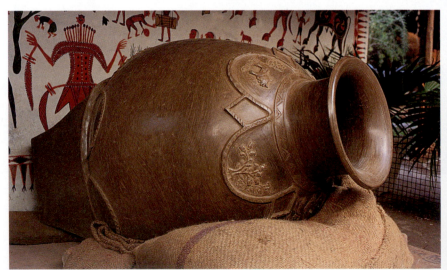

TEXTURE

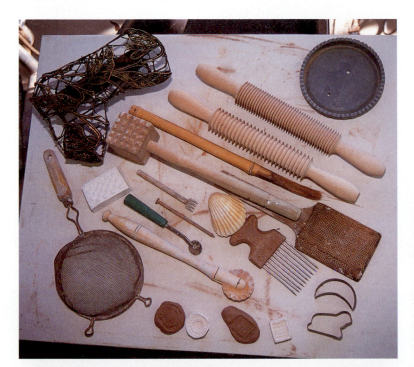

These modern tools imitate natural ones that might have been used by indigenous peoples

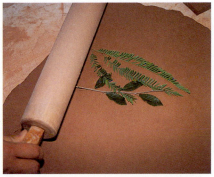

Rolling or pressing plant material into clay for pattern-making is an ancient technique

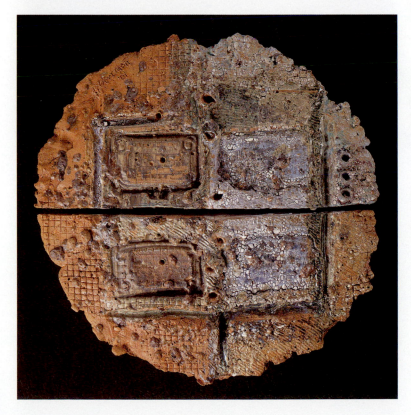

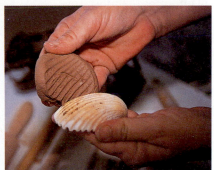

Today we often use 'found objects' such as shells to obtain textures in clay

Barbara Sorensen's contemporary shield sculpture, inspired by prehistoric images, is encrusted with textural impressions and earth oxide colorings; stoneware, stones and mixed media, 27 x 15 x 4 ins. (68 x 38 x 10 cm)

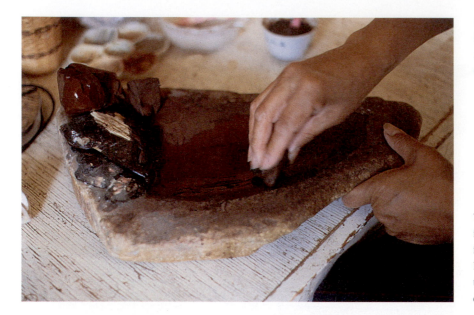

Rocks containing mineral oxides are ground for paint pigment on a stone *metate* at Acoma Pueblo by Emma Lewis Mitchell, one of Lucy's daughters

The late Lucy Lewis uses the ground pigment for painting, with her yucca-frond brush, her famous fine-line design (see Contents pages). Painting this size of jar would take her three to four weeks of daily work, sun-up to sun-down, on the electricity-free Acoma mesa

Coloring with mineral/vegetable matter

• Add the powder from grinding metallic oxide rocks such as hematite or copper to the clay surface;
• use plant juices – almost any plant will do, but yucca is a favorite – painted against a burnished surface to produce a dull matt design; some plant juices cause color on the clay in the fire;

• change all the clay colors by smothering the fire or making smoke.

It is stimulating to increase your awareness of all the ceramic processes that have been in use for centuries by primitive and studio potters. If you have a chance to travel in rural areas or in countries where clay is still the prime material for functional objects, take note of the various techniques and adapt them for yourself. Books and photographs of these areas are also a wonderful help.

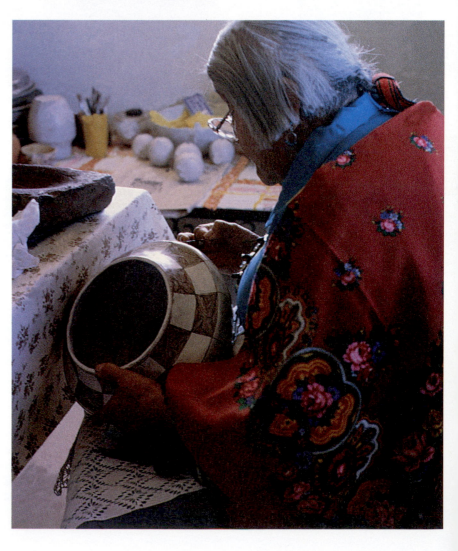

WORKING WITH PLASTER

Potters use plaster as a means of reproducing ceramic forms, or as a form against which to work. Plaster can also be used as a mold for casting metal, but then so can bisqued clay. As potters we usually use plaster for making molds, into which liquid clay slip is cast, or into or over which plastic clay is pressed.

Plaster is a gypsum (calcium) product, available from lumber yards, hobby shops, hardware stores, and the like. Good pottery plaster is not the same as dental plaster. Most pottery plasters are labeled as such in all parts of the world, yet there can be many types. For instance, in the United States, U.S. Gypsum and Blue Diamond, the most noted companies, have different trade-names for types with various setting times, and different plasters for degrees of hardness. Potters usually prefer a setting time of 20 minutes from when the plaster enters the water to when it is the proper consistency for pouring; stirring the plaster shortens the time, as does hot instead of cold water.

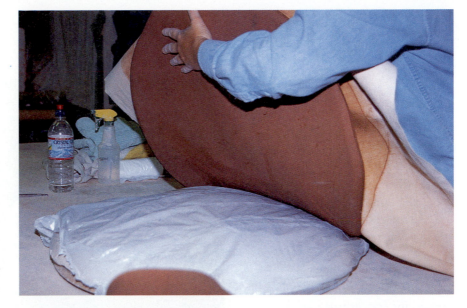

Linda Speranza creates outrageously large platters from previously made plaster one-of-a-kind hump molds. She layers paddled chunks of clay on the canvas bed of a slab roller, sometimes using fiberglass strands between layers, to give strength for the large proportions of her slabs

The carved plaster face of the mold imprints the clay slab laid over it; a coiled foot attached to the back several inches high supports the piece or, when pierced with holes, forms a rack for hanging

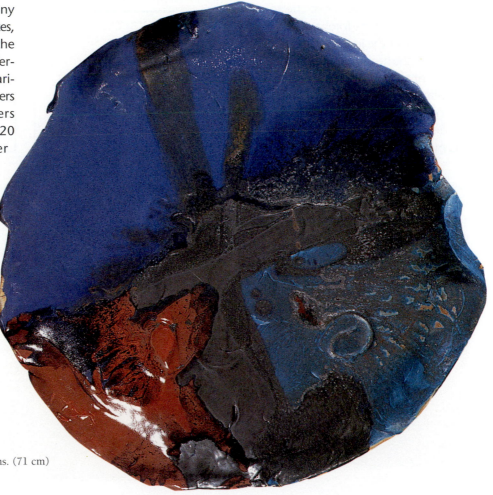

Finished platter, reduction fired c/10, 28 ins. (71 cm) diameter

How to make a mold

To make a mold requires making or acquiring a model first. The plastic clay you use for hand-building is the usual substance for a **model** you create yourself, but Styrofoam, cardboard, sand, wood, newspaper, or fabric can be used, as well as "found objects" such as rocks, fruit and vegetables, tools, and so on, which can provide images for conceptual pieces.

"**Undercuts**" determine the number of pieces a mold will have. An undercut is a line that goes under from another line or curve. Your face would need at least a two-piece mold, divided either around the head or down the middle from the center of the top of the head, over the forehead, down the nose, over the lips, over the chin, and down the neck. If you make a solid model of a head you will make all the planes and curves recede from that center line. Think about how you will detach the mold from the model. You must be able to lift it off, so if there

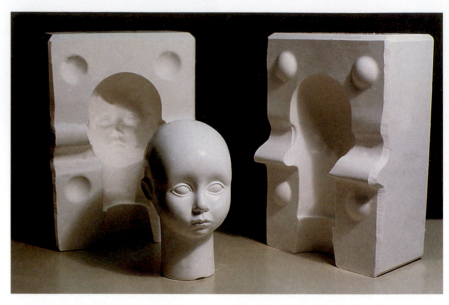

A Lennox china doll head model with its two-piece mold for hollow-casting

One-piece mold (left). A two-piece mold is necessary if there are "undercuts" (right)

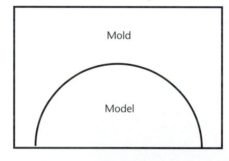

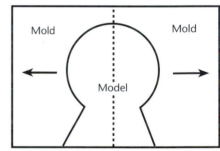

Virginia Scotchie constructed two-piece molds from street lamps, kick balls, beach balls, baseballs, for a large multi-balled site sculpture. Clay was pressed 1 in. (2.54 cm) thick into both halves of the plaster molds, which were joined at the edges; balls were removed leather-hard

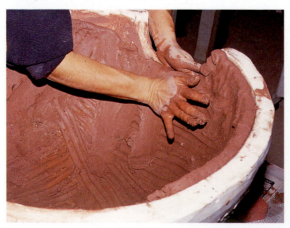

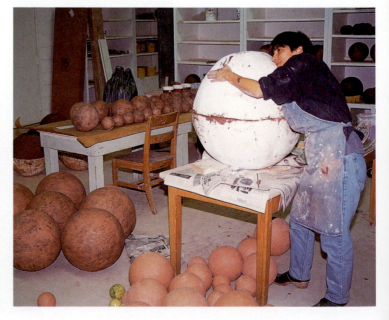

> **Hollow-cast molds** – either one-piece or multi-piece – are open voids that form only the outside shape; clay slip is poured into the top of the shape and poured out as soon as a cross-section of ³⁄₁₆ in. (5 mm) or so sets against the plaster

> **Solid-cast molds** shape the inside and the outside form of the piece; the hollow between the two or more pieces of the mold fills with slip and nothing is poured out. Plaster is porous and absorbs moisture from the clay slip, so that the skin of the piece hardens in minutes. Molds cannot be used more than a few times a day or they become too wet

are undercuts, necessary to form such features as nostrils or ears, they will necessitate further pieces of the mold.

If the model is made of clay, metal can be inserted to be used as a separation line, against which to cast the first piece of the mold. If the model is any other material, the separation line could be a slab of clay. After you have cast the first piece, use Vaseline or potter's soap between each section of the plaster mold to separate the pieces as you cast the plaster over your original model. You now have a mold. When the clay that is cast into the mold is set, the various parts of the mold come apart and are removed; the piece then stands alone.

MAKE YOUR OWN CASTING SLIP OR BUY IT READY-MADE

Clay casting slip that is poured into hollow or solid-cast molds is a specially **deflocculated** clay body. If we make clay liquid enough to pour into a mold just by adding water – three to four times the weight of the clay would be needed – the proportion of clay becomes so tiny that when the water evaporates there is not enough clay left to hold the form together.

Deflocculating a clay slip means adding a catalyst, called an electrolyte.

A percentage of 0.2 to 0.5% of this will make a batch of 100 parts of clay body plus a maximum of 40% water into a liquid that weighs 1.7 specific gravity, just a little heavier than water. The most satisfactory deflocculant is usually sodium silicate (also called waterglass) or soda ash, or a combination of both, although tea, dishwashing soap, or manufactured chemicals such as "Darvan" also work.

Any clay body will deflocculate, but tests should be made with small quantities before mixing a large batch. Store the casting slip as airtight as possible. If it seems less liquid when you come to use it, add a small quantity of water to the slip, or adjust it by weighing for specific gravity.

Readymade deflocculated casting slip can be bought in jugs ready to use. Alternatively, you can buy the dry casting body; make it liquid with 40% water by weight (as described above) and add the deflocculant. Clay bodies for earthenware, stoneware, and porcelain are available commercially all over the world. Potters in England and France are particularly lucky in being able to buy casting bodies from famous factories. Mixing your own casting slip gives you the advantage of knowing exactly what the ingredients are and how they will function.

Tiles for wall installations are slipcast in previously carved or textured plaster molds by Karin Bjorquist (Gustavsberg, Sweden)

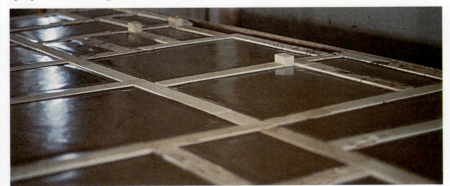

Karin Bjorquist's tile façade in Stockholm

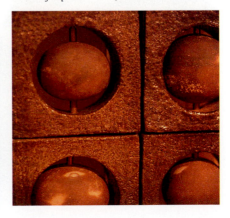

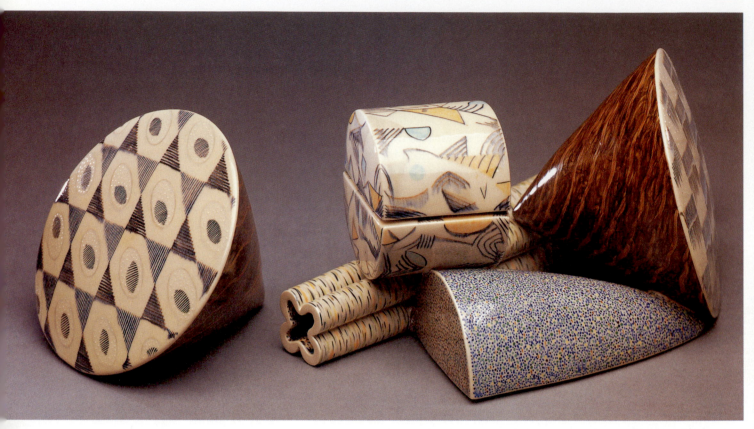

ASSEMBLING MULTIPLE MOLDED FORMS

Karen Massaro's porcelain slip-cast conical elements, to be freely arranged in varying "installations," are finished in underglaze stains and glaze, fired c/10; china-painted overglaze decoration c/013

Victor Spinski's installation, assembled from ceramic objects which have been pressed or slipcast from plaster molds taken from real life

Mold forms of various units can be cast individually and assembled in different ways, as shown in this porcelain sculpture, one of a series of outdoor installations by Patriciu Mateiescu, 6 ft x 6 ft x 6 ft (182 x 182 x 182 cm)

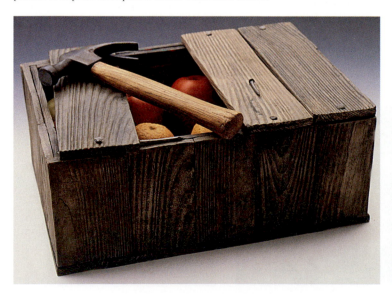

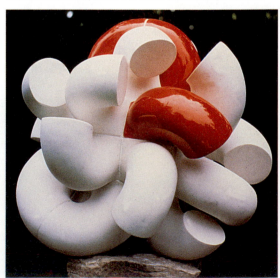

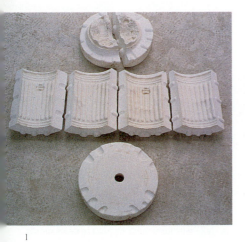

1

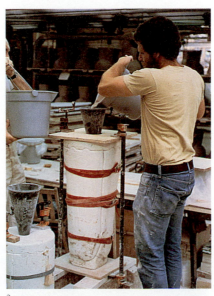

2

CASTING MULTIPLE MOLDS

Richard Notkin casting the pieces to be assembled into a finished sculpture:

1. **Exploded view** of seven-piece hollow-cast mold of garbage can image

2. **Pouring slip into mold**

3. **Draining slip** from the huge mold

4. **Mold pieces** being removed from the cast garbage can

5. **Finished object** in porcelain, celadon glaze, electric hardware and wood. Many more molds of the fantasy images were employed and slip cast to form the final composite

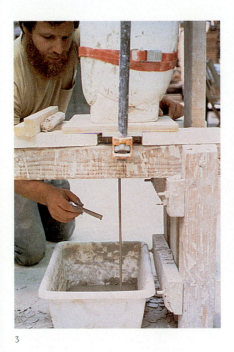

3

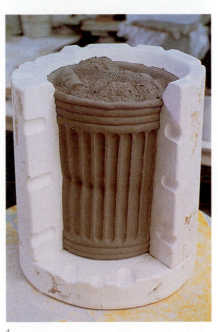

4

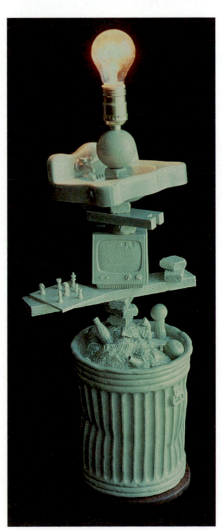

5

Casting a 6 ft (2 m) tall piece from multiple molds is challenging but fun:

• clay must be removed from the molds as soon as possible;
• all shapes must be kept moist until final attachment;
• or shapes can be glued together after firing;
• deflocculated slip must be kept at 1.7 specific gravity (s.g.) in an airtight container as long as the individual units are being cast

HOW TO MIX PLASTER AND POUR A FORM

Some clay artists mix plaster and water willy-nilly, as bronze sculptors do, but sculptors use plaster as a throw-away material. Potters want their plaster models and molds to last a long time and to be used over and over. Therefore it is important to use the proper plaster/water ratio your particular brand of plaster requires and to mix in a regulated manner that will produce the most durable mixture.

This is a regular mix for bats, models, and molds, for use with Blue Diamond or Gypsum Pottery Number One plaster in the United States. Plasters in other countries are similar. Do not use so-called Plaster of Paris.

1. Calculate how much plaster is needed in cubic inches for the area to be poured. That is, measure the three dimensions of height times width times depth. If the area is round rather than cubic, multiply the cubic inch total by 0.8. Then divide the cubic inch total by 81, as 81 cubic inches of space require one quart of water plus 2¾ lb plaster (generic ratio for most plasters). (Metric equivalents: 1325 c. cm, 1.18 litres, 1.25 kg.)
2. Measure the correct amount of cold or lukewarm water into a plastic, rubber, or metal container; weigh the correct amount of plaster.
3. Shake plaster into water slowly – not too slowly – so it mounds up in the bucket; allow plaster to slake a few minutes in the water until it all seems moist.

4. Begin to stir with your hand around the bucket in a wide motion, then a figure-of-eight motion on the bottom, palm up, moving upward to the top of the mix and around again. As bubbles come to the surface, scoop the foam off with a paper towel.
5. As soon as you can make a mark that holds its line slightly on top of the mix, the plaster is ready to pour. **Pour down the side** of the wood or linoleum coddle surrounding the model, or down the side of the mold area, so that the plaster fills up the space and air comes to the top; shake the bench or table under your mold, to break the bubbles. **Remove the cast mold** when the plaster becomes hot to the touch, at which point it pulls away most easily; otherwise

Peter Hayes' (UK) raku-fired sculpture (6 ft, 180 cm, tall) was fabricated in plaster press molds

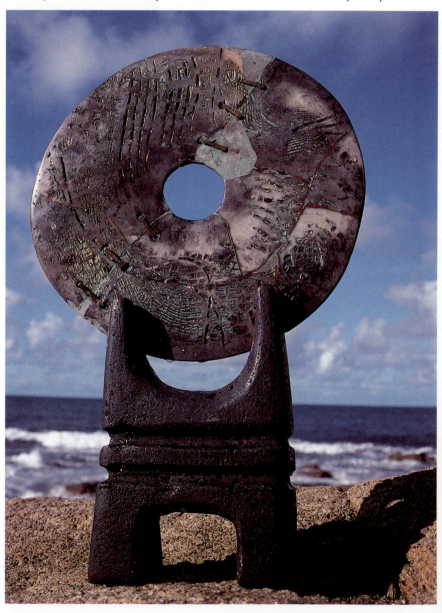

you may need an air hose to part the plaster from its core.

6. If there is excess plaster, pour it onto newspaper to set, and discard it. Do not pour plaster down a household or schoolroom drain. Rinse the container in lots of cold water.

Making molds is a complicated process. Frequently, artists use casting or pressing mold techniques to create multiple images or exact replicas of objects for use in sculptures. Molds are also used as a means of reproducing forms when many similar items are needed, such as for dinnerware or accessory sets. Some artists use plaster as a sketch mechanism to see form quickly.

Carved plaster makes innovative stamps for decorative pressing into clay. To explore the capabilities and experiment with plaster requires explicit instruction. Don Frith has written the definitive book on making and using plaster molds.

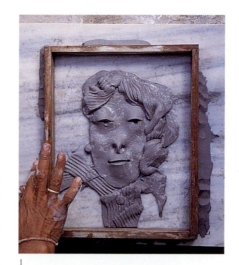

1

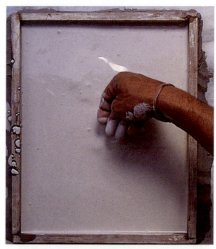

2

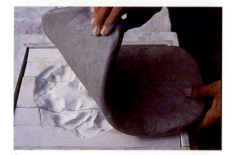

3

P. R. Daroz, a sculptor in Delhi, India, illustrates his technique of making molds for pressing images to construct a wall:

1. Clay model encased in wooden frame

2. Plaster is poured over the model within the frame; the image will be indented in the plaster

3. Pressing the clay slab into the plaster image

4. Assembling variations of the molded clay tile into a wall piece

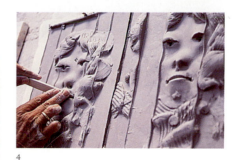

4

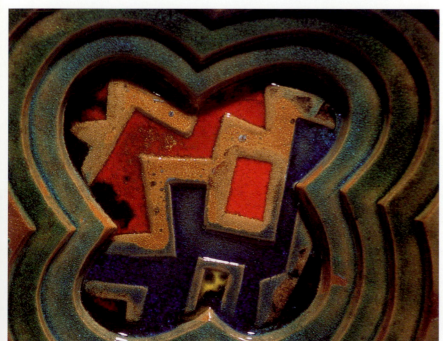

Charles Nalle makes his living designing press-molded plaster shapes for clay and slumped glass. Shown is a detail of one of his many stoneware oxidation-fired tiles, 22 x 22 x 3 ins. (56 x 56 x 7.5 cm), fabricated from a carved plaster form

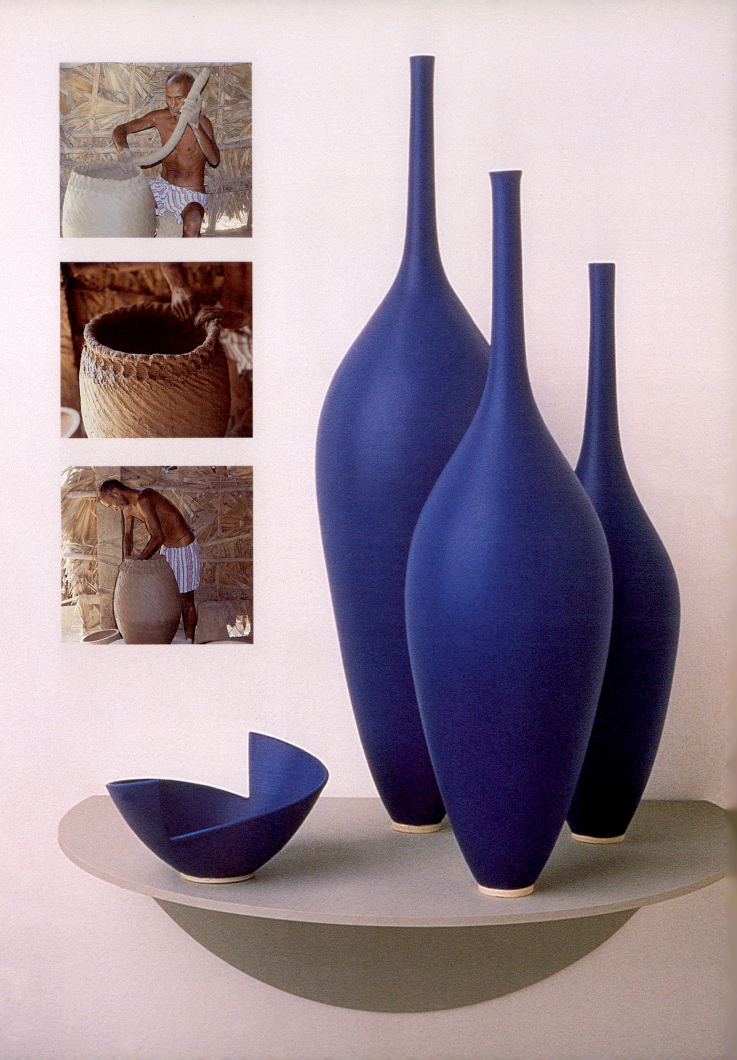

3

THROWING ON THE POTTER'S WHEEL

ANYONE CAN LEARN TO THROW . . .

The potter's wheel has not changed much in 5,000 years. We think that in ancient times a large wooden or stone disk was placed on a rock or stick fixed in the ground, and it bounced as it rotated unevenly. More sophisticated means of achieving balance and stability were gradually incorporated, until thousands of years later, in the twentieth century, an electric motor was added. The purpose of the potter's wheel – to revolve evenly and smoothly under the pressure of the potter's hands – has always been the same.

FACING PAGE Elsa Rady's wall piece is assembled of cobalt-glazed porcelain bottles on a painted aluminum shelf

INSETS A village potter in South India using coil and throw technique: a long, fat coil is rolled from very plastic clay and attached to the previously thrown vessel. The clay is very soft and fingers pinch an even wall which the potter throws into symmetrical shape. Eventually the huge thrown vessel will be enlarged and refined by hand with a paddle

It is a good idea to hand-build before starting to work on the wheel. It is important to learn to feel the clay, and to gauge its reaction to your hand pressure. These sensitivities are important through all claywork, but really important in throwing. You should have made at least a pinch pot with the clay you will be throwing to test plasticity, before trying to use the wheel.

Throwing on the wheel is the fastest way to get a hollow clay shape, ready to be finished or to be combined or cut up and added to something else ("thrown and altered"). But it is the fastest method only when the potter is skillful and has total command of the wheel. This accomplishment can take ten years to acquire, although some people have a natural skill that allows them to develop control faster.

Throwing is a process of working clay by hand on a revolving wheel that is kicked, rotated by hand, or motor-driven at speeds up to 120 rotations per minute. It is the only process by which a form can be so spontaneously created, so quickly made, involving the most direct communication between the creator and the material. Potters work a mass of clay under their hands, in tune with the speed of the wheel and the rhythms of their bodies, into a shape determined by their own sensitivity and skill.

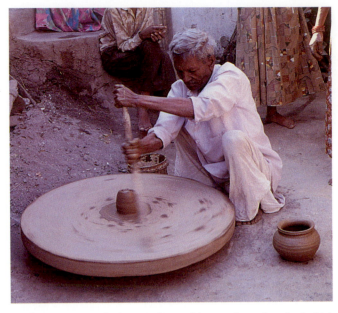

A village potter in Maheshwar, India, working on a large disc wheel which is turned by hand with a stick. The wheel has to be this size to keep up the momentum. The potter can stand or squat to the wheel, slowly working a shape during the few revolutions that occur between twirls

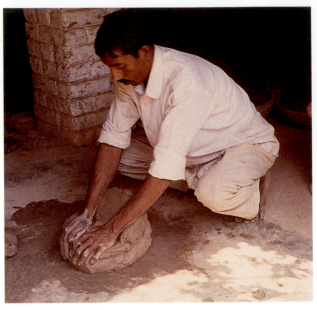

A potter at Tulsi Farm, India, wedging clay on the floor

During the process of learning, everyone will feel the sense of being one with the clay, of feeling the clay take shape – any shape – under the pressure of the hands. Not everyone will acquire enough skill to make thrown clay into an art, or be able to say the things an artist can communicate with this method, yet all who work on a potter's wheel will feel an expression of self. This degree of personal satisfaction can make throwing on the wheel an end in itself. M. C. Richards, a potter-poet, wrote a book called *Centering*, about the process of centering a ball of clay which she likened to centering oneself.

Consistency is very important. The clay must be soft enough to respond easily to any pressure. No hard lumps or foreign particles should be present in the clay body, except small impurities used for texture or color. Clay for throwing can be softer than clay used for hand-building.

TO THE BEGINNER

If you will read the following pages on throwing many, many times over, you will fix the words and steps in your subconscious memory. Your fingers will respond quickly because they are really being told what to do by my words in your mind.

Throwing takes years of practice before you will be in complete control of the clay and the wheel. But even in the beginning you can respond to the clay, react to the motion of the wheel, and make something, or make something that you can make into something else, by hand. The pleasure of throwing will be enhanced as control and skill improve.

Practice the whole process of throwing. "The whole is greater than the sum of the parts," as the Gestalt psychologist says. Practice center-

ing and opening the ball first. Then wedge five small balls of clay (approximately 5 lb/2 kg each).

After some days of practice at centering and opening the ball, then practicing the shapes, now begin to analyze where you are having problems and practice the trouble spots. When you have managed all the shapes pretty well, do the same thing again with balls of clay twice as large.

Remember the motion of the wheel. No change in the movement of your hands should be made until you feel that the clay has revolved under your hands one or more times, so that it has reacted to your pressure all the way round.

Remember that the smallest pressure point gives the most control. The smaller the area of clay that your hand or fingers touch, the less drag on the clay, and the better leverage you will have. Beginners tend to want to put their whole hand, or both hands, against the clay. This never works. Just a small point at the base of your thumb, or the tips of the fingers, should touch the clay.

Remember to pull from the bottom to the top every time you draw. This keeps the motion and rhythm of the lift. Finish the shape at the bottom first, then the top. Put your fingers on each side of the wall, feel the form from the bottom, as you move up, being careful not to exert pressure, except where you wish to further the shape.

Once you know intuitively where the pressure really is, and can feel the clay respond immediately, then you can make your own way.

STEPS IN THROWING ON THE POTTER'S WHEEL

Wedging

We have mentioned wedging in the hand-building chapter but must speak of it again here. The process of making a ball of clay into just the right consistency for working is more important for throwing than for hand-building. If the clay consistency is uneven, a really centered form is impossible. Any method of kneading clay works, but wedging is best: one hand rotates a lump of clay and the other hand presses the sides in, giving a chrysanthemum-petal look (see page 37).

Clay should be wedged free of air so that subsequent moisture pockets will not cause the piece to "blow up" during the bisque firing. If the clay

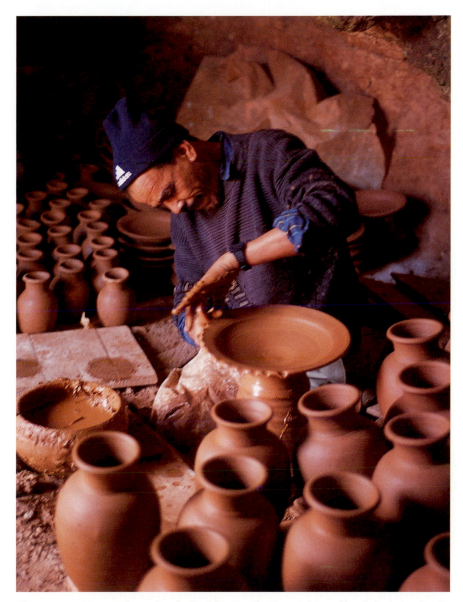

This potter in Morocco throws hundreds of functional tajines and jars of local clay every day. He will fire them stacked up in a tall updraft wood-burning kiln, unglazed, for his domestic market. Note the mound of clay behind the potter

is too wet, wedging against a porous surface will stiffen it; if it is too dry, water can gradually be wedged in to moisten it.

Many times in learning to throw, the clay will fall apart or be so off-center that it cannot be rescued. The potter should re-wedge the lump and begin again with the same clay,

until it is too worn out to be made into a satisfactory form. At that point, re-wedge the rebellious clay, wrap it in plastic, and put it into your storage bucket; get a new lump of clay and begin again, repeating until you too are worn out.

Wedging is so important that I am giving the instructions again here:

1. The basic ball
Take a lump of clay the size that your two hands will go round without quite touching.
2. Wedge clay
a. Left palm pushes into clay, right palm pivots the ball; continue and keep a steady rhythm.
b. Spiral shape develops which shows that the clay is moving and the whole chunk is being properly wedged.
c. Proper wedging removes air bubbles, puts clay in good condition for working; if dry, add water and wedge.
3. Put clay on wheel
Pat into a cone shape, and put the wide part down against the wheel head or bat. Turn the wheel on or begin to kick it; moisten the clay with water.

Position at the wheel

The position of the potter at the wheel is crucial. Some wheels are made for sitting, some for standing, some for squatting; kicking a wheel usually requires sitting and kicking a rotating flywheel. European wheels are often treadle-style, requiring a posture of standing on one foot and moving a treadle back and forth with the other foot.

Preferably, the potter should sit at the level of the wheel head, or above it, close enough and high enough to bend the back and shoulders over the clay. Arms should be relaxed but held against the body, and the whole body including the arms should move in toward the clay as hand pressure is applied; if the arms move alone, they become unsteady; clay goes off-center. Hands, wrists,

and arms must be steady and fairly rigid, although poised and relaxed enough to feel what the clay is doing. The body leans into the clay from the back and the shoulders, through the arms to the hands. **A steady, centered "self" is essential in learning to feel every tiny response of the clay.** It is important to stretch and relax the body now and then.

If the potter stands to a low wheel, it is usually to handle a huge amount of clay. The stance will be solid, with legs apart, arms braced from the shoulders. You work bent over the clay until the wall rises as high as you are and eventually you are standing tall, parallel with the clay. To make really large vessels or sculptures you may need to throw several shapes and attach them together, or to cut, patch, or paddle forms into other forms.

The left hand centers the clay.
The right hand lifts the wall.
The left hand shapes a bowl.
The right hand lifts a bottle.
**Two hands squeeze in to collar a
    neck.**

It is important to have only one pressure point on the clay at a time. If there are more pressures – more fingers or too much hand surface against the clay – the pot will absorb all those pressures and will be taken off-center.

In America the potter's wheel rotates counter-clockwise. In Britain, Japan, and some other countries it is rotated clockwise. It does not matter about the direction. The potter adapts to the motion and pulls up on the right side of the clay if the wheel goes counter-clockwise, or on the left side if it goes clockwise. The best spot for catching the clay with your pressure as it comes round is about 4 o'clock

on the right side, or 8 o'clock on the left side.

It does not matter what shape the wheel head is, or the bat on which the throwing is done. What matters most is that the potter learns to feel the centrifugal motion of the wheel and the clay as it responds to that motion and the potter's pressure. **Learning to feel is one of the big issues in clay-working.**

Centering

1. Begin centering
a. Squeeze the cone up with the base of the palms of both hands, squeezing into the clay and lifting up (see picture below).
b. Push the cone down with the base of the left palm lying on top of the clay; the base of the right palm, held vertically, perpendicular to the other hand, also pushes down (see picture opposite).

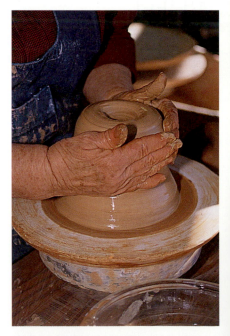

Begin centering:
1a. Squeeze the ball of clay up with the bases of the hands opposite each other

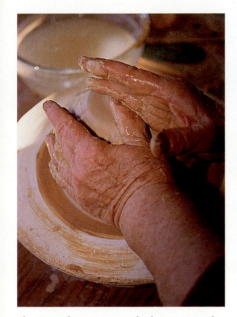

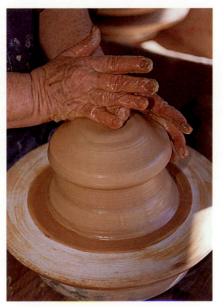

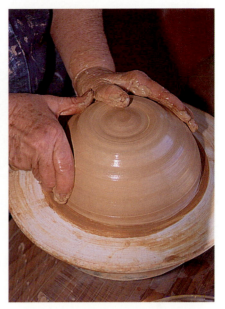

1b. Press down to center by leaning into the clay with the wrist flexed, using the base of the left palm; wheel revolves counterclockwise

2. Heel of left palm leans steadily against the clay at 8 o'clock position to center; base of right hand lies next to left thumb, pushing the clay straight down

3. First finger of right hand, buttressed by second finger at 4 o'clock position, pushes straight down from the top to true up the base

2. Lean in and center
Center by leaning in with the edge of the palm of the left hand, at the 8 o'clock position on the left side of the clay (if the wheel goes counter-clockwise), or 4 o'clock (if it goes clockwise). "On center" means running true with the centrifugal motion of the wheel – you must learn to feel that, but you can test it by holding a point against the clay; if it is centered the point will make a mark evenly all the way around.
3. Right fingers push down.

Opening the ball

1. Opening position 1
All directions are for counter-clockwise rotation. (Reverse for a clockwise wheel.) Left middle finger centered on top of the clay, with middle finger of right hand

over it; hold left finger rigid and push straight down, right finger guides.
2. *or* opening position 2
Left thumb finds center on top of clay, middle finger of right hand on top of thumb; thumb pushes straight down, guided by right finger.
3. Push to bottom
Push down to within about ¾ inch (2 cm) from the bottom.
4. Open
Position 1: pull the middle fingers, one on top of the other, toward you, *or* Position 2: push left thumb, with middle finger right hand supporting, from the bottom center out to the left.
    Pressure of either position will move to the wall of clay from the hollow now being opened; move far enough to make several inches of curved opening. Feel the thickness of the wall and try not to go all the way through.

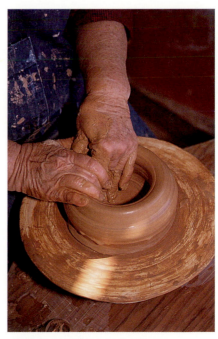

Position 1. Open the ball by pushing straight down, (a) with the middle finger left hand supported by the middle finger right hand, as above, or (b) by the tip of the left thumb supported by the right hand, and pull toward you to widen the hole

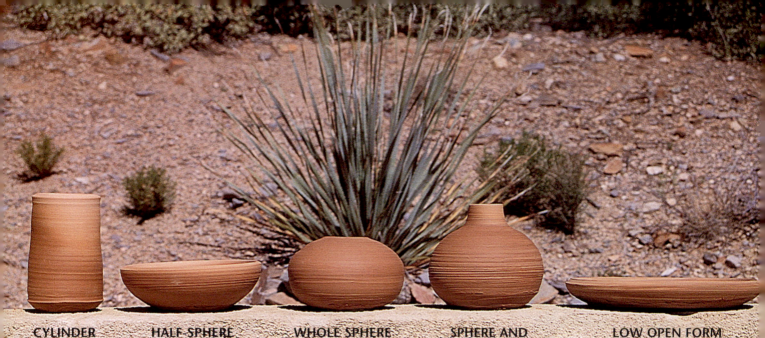

CYLINDER   HALF-SPHERE   WHOLE SPHERE   SPHERE AND CYLINDER   LOW OPEN FORM

ABOVE The five basic shapes a beginner should practice over and over have to do with form, not function; *cylinder, half-sphere, full sphere, full sphere and cylinder combined, low open form*

PRACTICE THESE FIVE SHAPES

Practice these five shapes, one after the other, in this order:

- cylinder;
- half-sphere;
- whole sphere;
- sphere and cylinder combined;
- low open form.

Repeat every day or as often as possible until you feel mastery over these five shapes

We could give functional names to the above shapes, such as bowl, round vase, bottle, plate, but we prefer not to do this.

We prefer you to think of the geometric form, not function, when you practice shaping on the potter's wheel

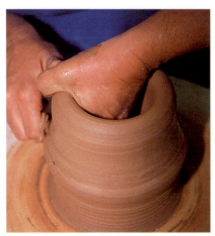

1. Pull up to shape cylinder

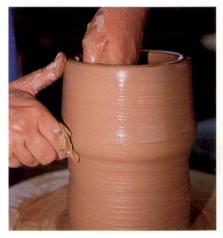

2. Draw up for height

a) Pull up and shape a cylinder

1. Hand position

Left middle finger-tip, buttressed by the left first finger, goes *inside* to the bottom and sweeps over to the right wall. *Outside*, the right first finger crooks toward you, the first finger-tip pushes into the clay on the outside for almost an inch (2.5 cm) and begins to lift upward. Fingernails must be short!

2. In repeated draws the outside first finger, buttressed by the second finger, does the lifting. Press in hard to really cause the clay to grow; the inside finger does not push, only follows straight up.
3. Squeeze with both hands to narrow the cylinder and thicken the wall for a further lift.
4. Outside finger continues pushing inward, lifting up to desired height. Both fingers or a sponge keep the lip smooth.
5. If the lip is uneven, cut it with a

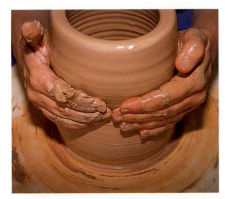

3. Squeeze to narrow cylinder

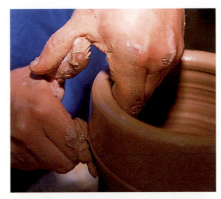

4. Continue pushing inward to lift

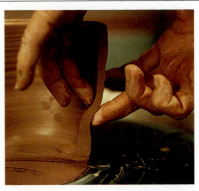

Cross-section of thrown piece; beginners should try to pull an even wall, slightly thicker at base, thinner at top, then cut with a wire to see what you have pulled

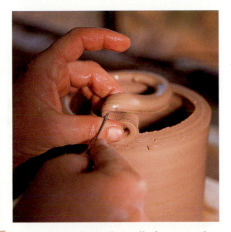

5. Cut uneven lip with needle from outside to inside finger, then lift

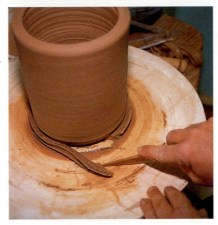

6. Trim excess clay from base

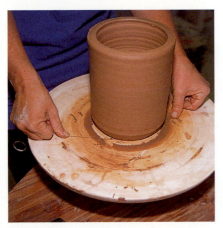

7. Wire cut to release

needle or a wire held on the right side of the clay even if you are left-handed. Push the point into the clay, wheel moving slowly for one revolution; quickly lift up the cut ring; smooth the lip.

6. With a wood knife cut excess clay from cylinder base several times while lifting the clay; at end, hold wood knife parallel to bat and cut into the clay base, then hold wooden point parallel to the cylinder and cut down to the bat; stop the wheel, remove excess trimming and clean the bat.

7. Holding the cutting wire with each hand, pull toward you from behind the cylinder as the wheel turns slowly. Lift the cylinder off the bat with both hands.

b) Half-spherical shape
(sometimes called bowl, see photo opposite)

1. Center a low wide mound
Push downward with the wrist-end of the left hand on the top center of the mound, the heel of the right hand against the left thumb; lower the mound. **Push down to make the base of the mound as wide as you want the base of the shape to be.**

2. Open the mound
Same method (1 or 2, 3, 4) as for the cylinder shape. The inside opening will be wider because this mound is lower and wider than that for a cylinder.

3. Pull up the wall
Lift a low thick wall, with three or four draws upward.

4. Shape the half-sphere
Inside, the left-hand middle finger, buttressed by the curled first finger, drops from the wrist; it moves from the center out toward the right side. When the fingers reach the

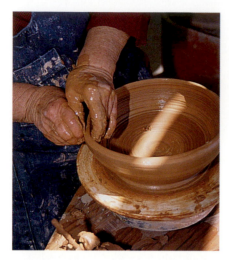

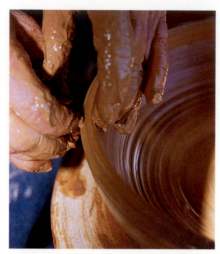

Half-sphere: after opening a low, wide cylinder, expand the clay into a half-spherical shape with the fingertips of the left hand exactly opposite the fingertips of the right hand. Pull up and out three or four times, slowly, so that the clay will not fall

wall, the right-hand first finger, on the outside, curled and with the fingertip pointed into the clay, squeezes inward to meet the "feel" of the inside finger. On the inside, the left middle finger, buttressed by the first finger, pulls over to the right and up to the top. Pressure from the inside fingers controls the round shape. Both left- and right-hand fingers together, with the clay in between, draw out and up in the desired profile line.

5. Finish the shape
Continue bottom to top, pulling outward with the inside left finger toward the outside right finger, and upward until the half-sphere is shaped and the wall is thin enough. True up the lip, cut if necessary, smooth it, and undercut the base with the wood knife, as in the cylinder. For beginners, the diameter of the initial mound of clay at the base should be 4 ins. (10 cm) less than you want the diameter of the half sphere. Carefully draw the curve on paper first as a guide.

c) Full spherical shape (see photo on p. 72)

1. Begin a half-sphere
Make a basic half-sphere, leaving a thick roll on the top lip. Shape the half-sphere curve from inside out, using the thick roll to lift up out and in toward the center in a diamond shape.

2. Expand the diamond
Push outward with the inside hand for the half-sphere, then the outside hand takes over to pull the diamond shape taller, rounder, and thinner. Keep the curve moving up at all times; don't push in horizontally, or the wall will fall in. Keep the top opening narrow; if you widen it to get your hand inside, narrow it again at the finish of each draw.

3. Make the full sphere
With one last draw, push out with the inside hand up to the middle, rounding the half-sphere, then "draw" the profile shape of a full circle with your two fingers opposite each other, one inside, one outside. The opening should be as narrow as you can make it.

4. Keep practicing
This is a difficult shape. Do it over and over.

Some potters use a sponge or rib for support while throwing large open forms, as Jane Dillon is doing at this wheel. Note her assembled thrown forms on the shelves in her studio

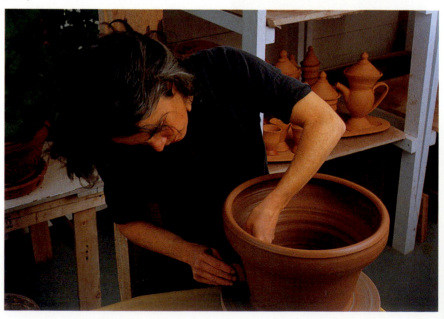

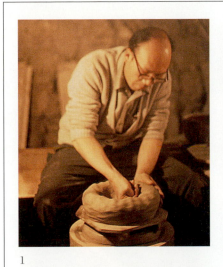

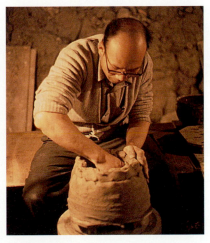

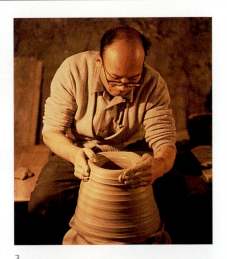

1

2

3

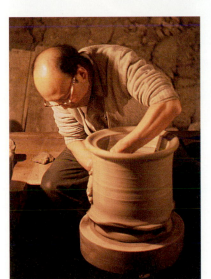

SHINSAKU HAMADA THROWS A BOWL

1. **He punches a hole** into a lump of clay, because his Korean kick-wheel moves too slowly for him to center a solid ball of clay

2. **He adds coils** to the first thrown base

3. **He throws the coils true**

4. **After straightening the cylinder** he sets a wide lip which will remain to reinforce the vessel

5, 6 **He expands the bowl**, being careful not to affect the lip

7. **He smooths the interior** with a thick wooden rib. Finished bowl is 42 ins. (107 cm) diameter

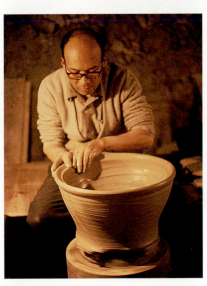

4

5

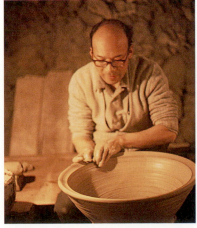

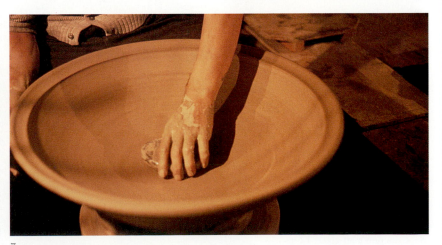

6

7

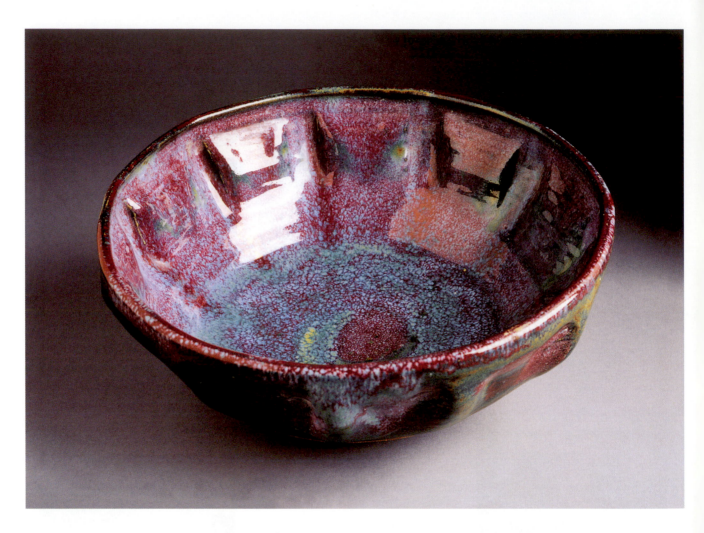

Susan Peterson's large thrown and altered bowl is stoneware, glazed with reduction fired copper red and blue glazes, c/10, 20 x 7 ins. (50 x 18 cm)

Bowls come in all sizes and shapes, age-old containers for everything imaginable, or wonderful bases for glaze and decoration

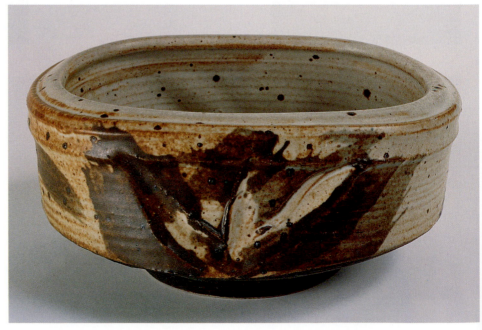

Stoneware bowl by Viveka and Otto Heino, reduction matt glaze, 12 ins. (30 cm) diameter

Bottles provide contrasts in form from wide to narrow, short to tall, round to angular, indeed any shape

George Bowes's stoneware bottle, brushed with engobes and glazes

Harrison McIntosh's stoneware bottle has engobe pattern under a translucent matt glaze

Andy Nasisse's thrown and hand-built jug, 15 x 9 x 7 ins. (38 x 23 x 18 cm), is made of a white earthenware body glazed at c/02, then overglaze decorated, refired c/09

Michael Frimkess's stoneware bottle is decorated with an Aztec design in brushed glaze

d) Sphere and cylinder combined
(sometimes called bottle, see photo p. 72)

1. Center, open, lift
Pull a cylinder about as tall as you want this form to be. Don't pull all the way to the top – leave a thick roll at the top.

2. Shape the sphere
Go to the bottom with left fingers inside, opposite the first finger of the right hand outside, and expand the spherical shape, out and in, like a grapefruit.

3. Lift the cylinder
When the circle form is made, take the thick roll you left at the top and lift it into a cylinder. It will look like a ball with a stove-pipe on top. It will not look like a normal bottle, but as we said we want you to learn geometric form, not function, now.

4. Cut lip, trim base
Cut the lip even, sponge smooth. With wood knife, after cutting parallel to the bat, carve a nice indented line at the base by pointing the tool downward and cutting against the profile of the clay shape down and into base.

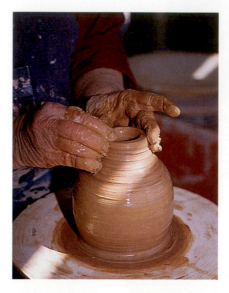
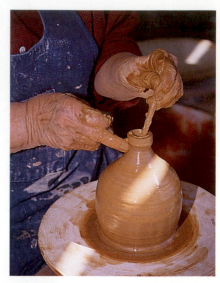

Bottle forms are made by keeping an extra roll at the top of the full spherical form from which to create the neck. Collar with the fingers of both hands squeezing in and lifting up. Use a tool such as a stick inside the bottleneck when your finger no longer fits in. Continue squeezing and lifting until the neck is the shape you want

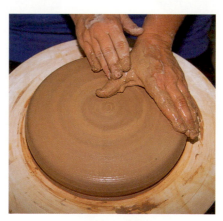
Low open form 1: center a mound of clay

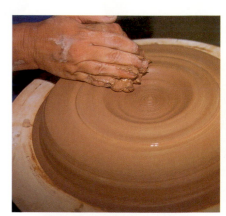
2. Begin opening the mound

e) Low open form
(sometimes called platter, see photo p. 72)

1. Center a mound of clay
Press down and out to expand and lower the mound of clay to the diameter you want the base to be. Right hand presses down, left palm leans in to center the mound.

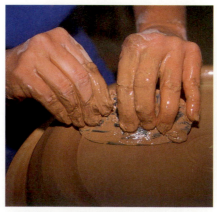
3. Use rib to flatten form

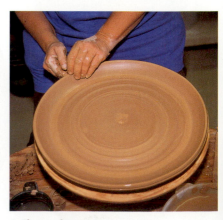
4. Shape edge

2. Begin opening the low form
Middle finger left hand supported by right fingers push downward in center and pull toward you to widen. You can continue lowering the entire mound while you open the center.

3. Use a rib
Move a rubber, wood, or metal rib from the center outward, pushing down to compress the clay and flatten the interior form.

4. Shape the edge
Left fingers inside, right fingers outside, pull the curve out and lift up to form a lip; press down to round and smooth the edge. Use wood knife to trim clay away from the base and clean the bat.

5. Cut under
With the sharp pointed wood tool, cut into the base down toward the bat to shape the outside profile.

> The five shapes you have just practiced are the basic shapes from which all pottery wheel forms come

OTHER SHAPES ARE VARIATIONS
Pitcher

A pitcher is a bellied cylinder with a flared top for the pointed **pouring lip**. Make this by holding the thumb and third finger of the left hand outside against the pitcher neck, and with the right-hand first finger down inside the neck, pull up and out into a lip-shape. This can also be done reversing the two hands, whichever you prefer. Sharpen and thin the lip to a sharp edge for pouring without dripping.

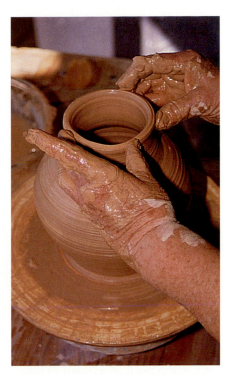

Most pitchers have a functional shape that is wider at the bottom and collars in to a flared neck which controls the liquid to be poured ABOVE **Lift a narrowed neck** from the full sphere shape

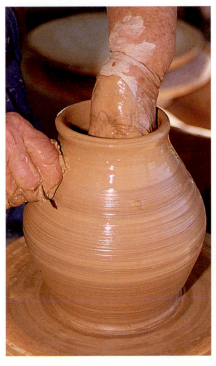

Form the pouring lip by pushing in with the outside thumb and first finger against the inside finger, lifting and pulling over to form a sharp point to cut the drip

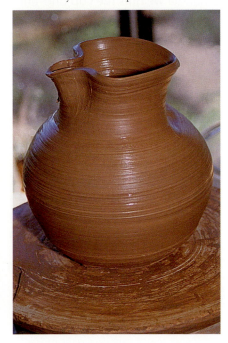

Collar in with fingertips of both hands and then flare the lip

Wire-cut to sever the bottom from the bat and carefully lift the wet pitcher off

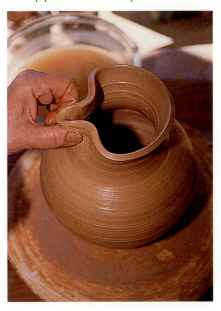

Handles

Handles for thrown pots can be hand-built by pinch, coil, or slab methods, or cut from thrown cylinders, or carved from bamboo or wood. More usually a clay handle for a thrown shape is pulled from a solid lump of clay, just as the pot was thrown from a solid lump.

Hold the well-wedged rectangular lump in one hand, moisten the clay and begin to pull downward, with thumb and finger of the other hand forming a circle around the clay; turn the pulling hand as you work to keep the handle shape even. When you have pulled a long enough, thick enough piece, pinch it off with your fingers, arch it and put it on a board to stiffen until you can attach it.

Cups with handles: think of how the hand will hold the cup, with one or more fingers or the whole fist. Think function: a handle sticking too far up or out will break off easily; too thick a handle weights the cup unevenly;

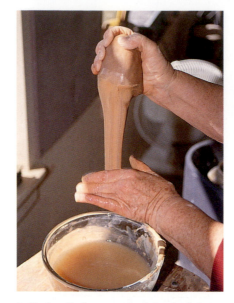

Pull a handle from a wedged chunk of clay by holding the clay between thumb and fingers, turning the other hand from left to right, pulling from the top downward until the desired shape is achieved

too thin a handle is not strong enough. Feel the handle as you make it, then it should feel right after firing.

Pitchers with handles: for functional success, attach a pitcher handle where

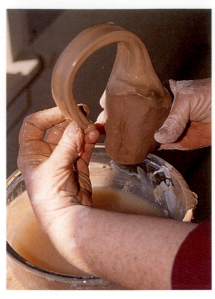

Curve the handle and set it aside to stiffen

the bulk of the liquid will be. Keep handles away from the lip of a pot, or else they break. Usually a handle is thicker at the top and narrower at the base, but this can be reversed.

Attach handles wet or leather-hard; score both edges, moisten, and push firmly together.

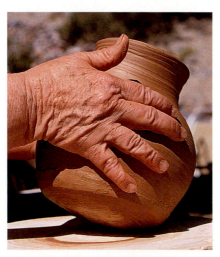

When the pitcher is dry enough to handle, **roll the bottom** against a flat surface to achieve a rounded foot. Cut the handle from its base, and fit it to the pitcher

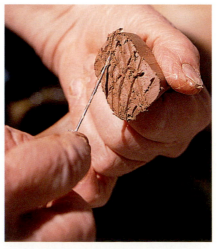

Score and moisten the ends that will be attached

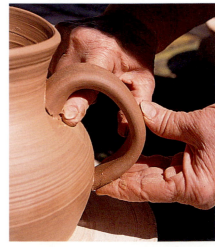

After scoring and moistening the attachment points on the pitcher, **fix the moistened handle on** and smooth it into the body

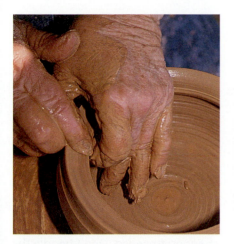

Make the flange for a lid by pushing straight down on a thickened cylindrical wall with the first finger of the right hand against the first finger of the left hand, which is underneath to support the flange

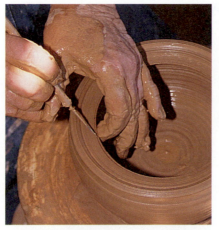

Cut the flange true with a needle at the 4 o'clock position

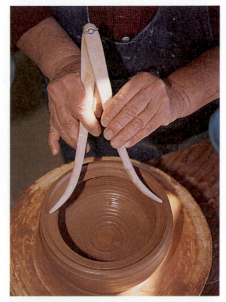

Measure with a wooden calliper the exact spot where the lid should sit, and throw the lid to fit. Lid is made as shown on page 82, but larger

Casserole

A casserole is a large half-sphere, with a horizontal flange where a lid will sit, or without a flange so that the lid must have a vertical flange that fits down inside the lip of the pot. Measure the opening the lid will fit into, or the casserole flange on which the lid will sit, very carefully because it is only a proper measurement that will make a lid fit. If it does not fit it is the potter's fault.

Lids

Lids for all pots are made in several ways, depending on whether they span very wide or very narrow diameters.

Lids made right side up, with no flange, can be thrown directly against a bat or off the hump, as shown here. Be sure to calliper the diameter of the lid and the diameter of the flange on the pot where it will sit.

THROW SMALL POTS FOR LIDS OFF THE HUMP

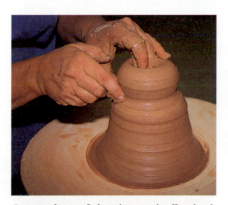

Center a lump of clay, then mark off a chunk for the pot size you want

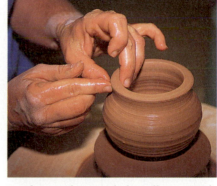

Pot shape with a straight lip will accommodate a lid with a flange to fit inside the lip

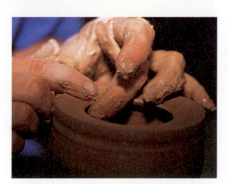

Left fingers hold the lip while right fingers flatten a flange for a flat lid

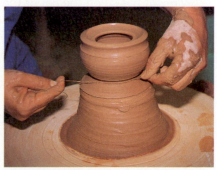

Wire cut flanged pot off hump, ready for a flat lid; pull wire from back, through clay, toward you

LIDS WITHOUT AND WITH FLANGE

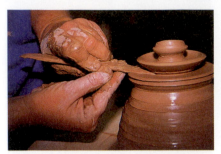

Right-side-up lid: center mound for width of lid

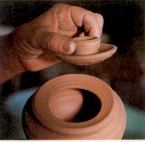

Check fit of lid on flanged pot

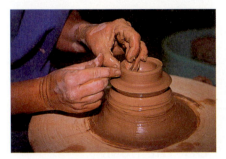

Upside-down lid: lift flange for lid

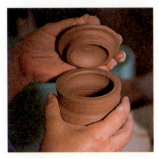

Check fit of flanged lid at leather-hard stage

Right-side-up lid: center a wide enough mound for the width of the lid; open the mound off center leaving clay in the middle from which to throw up a knob.

A lid made right side up can also have a flange: press into the clay at the base to achieve proper diameter and height to fit in the pot. This flange can stay solid or be trimmed out later.

Wire cut the lid off the bat or the hump; when leather-hard check the fit of lid to pot.

Flanged lids made upside-down: lids made upside down with a flange that fits into a pot can be dome-shaped or flat. Usually a separate thrown or hand-built knob is added later to the leather-hard lid.

Center a wide enough mound of clay – for the outside diameter the lid should be – directly on a bat or off a hump, as shown here.

Open the mound, pull up a thick wall, then press in with outside finger against the inside finger opposite, to create the flange diameter.

Lift the flange as tall as it needs to be. Measure again exactly; finish lip smooth.

For domed lids made upside-down, belly-out a round shape under the flange with the inside fingers. Keep measuring the flange diameter after each draw.

Wire cut the lid or let it dry on the plaster bat; add a separate knob, or attach a coil and throw on a knob.

Always check the fit of lid and pot in leather-hard state, and make changes if needed. Don't handle the pot or the lid more than necessary or you will cause warping or cracking later on. Almost all problems occurring in the firing are the result of too much touching with hands during wet to leather-hard stages.

Lids should dry on their pots. Lid and pot should bisque-fire together, but askew so that air and moisture can escape from the pot. For the glaze firing, scrupulously wipe the glaze from edge of lid and rim of pot so the two can be fired together. If you want the edge glazed, fire the lid separately.

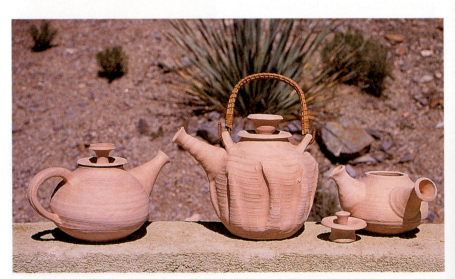

Three bisque teapot variations: left, a pulled clay handle, middle, a Japanese bamboo handle, to be fitted on after the glaze fire, and right, a thrown lug handle; the right-side-up thrown lid shows the correct depth of the flange

TEAPOT SPOUT

Throwing teapot spouts uses the same method as making a tall thin bottle neck, except that you can begin from a hump of clay and cut the spouts off, or throw each spout directly on its own bat.

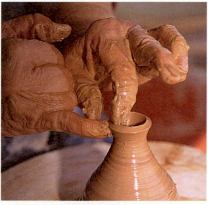

Throw the teapot spout by expanding it at the base and collaring in at the top, in much the same way as a narrow-necked bottle is formed

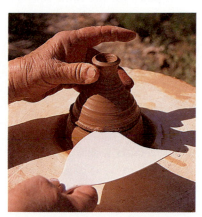

Wire-cut the spout base at the desired length, and lift it off when it is stiff

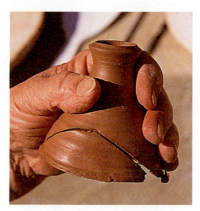

Arbitrarily cut away a triangular section to help fit the spout to the body

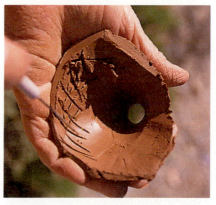

Thin the cross-section of the spout with a metal knife and score it in preparation for attaching

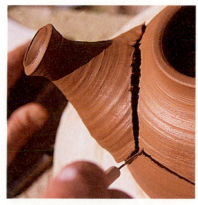

Hold the spout against the teapot body and trace around the base where it is to go. Use a drill bit or other rounded tool to punch holes to strain the tea-leaves. Score both the spout and the area to which it is to be attached, moisten, and meld the two

Teapot, coffee-pot

A tea- or coffee-pot shape is one of the most difficult composite shapes because of the complicated parts, the assemblage, and the reference of the parts to each other, but beverage pots are among the most exciting forms for the functional potter.

The body of the pot is made first; then throw the spout separately. Make the lid with a deep flange so it won't fall off the pot when it is tilted. The spout must be thrown so that, when it is attached at an angle, it is long enough for its narrow end to be as high up as the lid of the pot – otherwise the liquid will leak out.

Pull the handle when the body is trimmed, then trim the lid if necessary. Next, attach the spout, making a full hole in the body, or punch small holes at the point where the spout fits, to strain the liquid from the leaves when pouring. The pulled handle can be attached opposite the spout or it can fit in an arc over the top of the pot. If you prefer the Oriental-style bamboo or reed handle, make two small hand-built clay lugs on either side of the top opening, for the ready-made handle.

Sets

Making sets, all items alike or proportionally related, is difficult for beginners. Weighing balls of clay helps, as does taking proper measurements or making a template for the profile changes. Keep wall thickness, edges, and feet alike too.

Closed form

Throwing a closed form is similar to throwing a spherical shape, except that you will pull the clay wall all the way over and close the vessel completely; use a rib to press down at the closure to insure the seal (make a pinhole to allow expanding air to escape). Prior to closing you may want to blow into the shape to fill out the form.

Do-nut

Throwing a do-nut shape is difficult. Begin with a low wide mound of clay the diameter you wish the outside to have. Make a hole, not in the center of the mound, but off-center; raise and shape the outside wall. Next, open the mound in the center and go directly down to the bat, clean up that hole with a tool, and undercut it for shaping. Raise that wall also and pull the two walls up and over to each other, closing their edges together in the do-nut form; you now have a hollow do-nut shaped ring with a void in the center.

Do-nut forms can create such vessels as wine-pitchers and flower-holders.

Throwing off the hump

Start with a large solid lump of clay and center the whole thing, or just the top for the first pot. Take a bite of clay the size you think you need by making a line at the base of the top centered chunk, open that ball, pull up and shape the pot from that line, cut with a wire and lift off. Start another piece the same way and continue until all the clay is used up (see p. 81).

TRIMMING

Trimming thrown pots can be achieved in the classic fashion by turning the form upside down, re-centering it on the wheel, and trimming an indented, pedestal foot with a sharp tool; tool the profile on the right side of the pot if the wheel goes counter-clockwise and on the left side of the pot if the wheel goes clockwise.

Alternatively, paddle the foot shape, carve it, add legs or other standing supports, roll the bottom against a flat surface – or think of other ways.

Remember that it seems to take forever to learn to throw. No matter, a form of some sort will result each

Steps for easy progression in learning to throw will be found at the back of this book, as well as suggestions for individual projects that can be fabricated in any of the methods we have discussed, once you have gained some experience

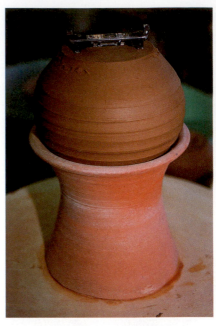

Trimming: a bottle form with a narrow neck must be trimmed in a chuck of some sort, whereas a bowl or plate can be turned upside down directly on a bat. **Level the pot in the chuck**, using a bubble level, and center chuck or pot. Beginners should paste the chuck to the bat with coils of clay

Hold middle finger in the center of the foot, push down gently to keep the pot in place. Hold a sharp tool steady on right side of clay, trim downward to "draw the line" you want, repeat until correct. Indent the foot by carving into the clay from the center out

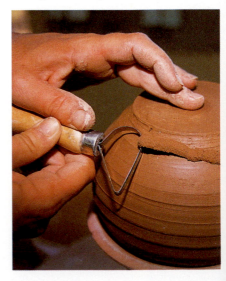

time you work at the potter's wheel. Use these uncertain shapes for glaze and decorative experimentation. Often beginner's luck creates really interesting works. Nothing is wasted; look carefully at everything you do, for inspiration, for self-tutoring.

Collectors and friendly observers who are reading this book, but are perhaps not involved in clay construction, will find that the information and perceptions outlined here are helpful in gaining a complete understanding of the ceramic medium.

LARGE FORMS

Making larger and larger shapes on the wheel comes after you learn the basic steps on so-called functional sizes. To increase your technique for larger forms, try adding 5 lb (2.5 kg) increments – start with a 5 lb ball, then a 10 lb (5 kg) ball, and so forth. If that is too much, reduce it to a 2½ lb (1.25 kg) increase at a time. Everyone can learn to throw, but some persons take longer than others – don't be discouraged, it *will* happen! Throwing larger shapes takes more time to learn. You can throw as tall as your arm is long, or you can throw what is comfortable, then add coils and throw each one up, or you can throw separate shapes and join them leather-hard.

Large thrown pots can be made several ways:

1. Throw and coil: throw as tall as you can, then begin to add large fat coils one at a time, each luted well into the last, and throw each coil up true until you have your desired height.

2. Make a number of thrown sections, measuring with a calliper

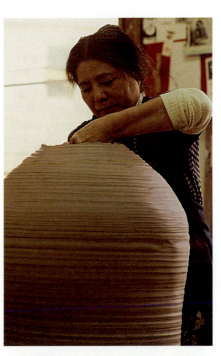
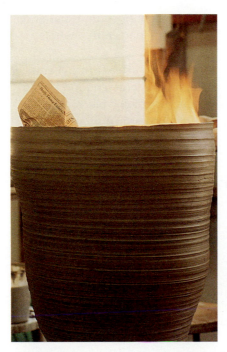

Toshiko Takaezu makes a 7-ft (213 cm) tall sculpture by adding coils and throwing them true. In the process of gaining height she stiffens the clay with a bonfire inside the vessel; eventually she encloses the form totally (see a finished piece by Toshiko on page 19)

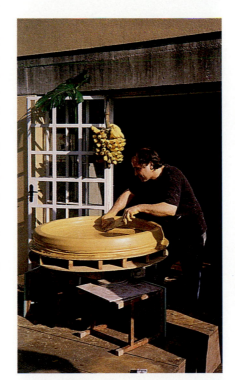

Neil Tetkowski throws a large bowl on a huge wooden bat for one of his mixed-media wall pieces

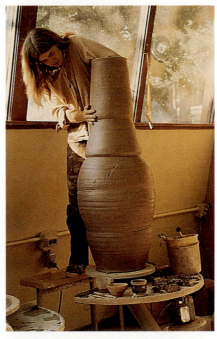

Taäg Peterson assembles previously thrown sections by luting and rethrowing. In order to be able to stand above the pot he has placed a rock on the wheel pedal to keep the motor moving

where they will fit together, and attach them in the leather-hard stage. Do not use a ruler: it is not accurate enough.

3. Combine sections creatively. Make a number of thrown sections without measuring anything and put them together in a frenzy of creative passion, cutting, slashing, pushing the parts into a whole sculpture.

4. Combine after firing. If you don't have a large enough kiln to fire the monolithic piece, fire the sections and attach them with a good glue or plumber's cement, or put them together by other means such as nuts and bolts, wire, wood or metal appendages, or even bandages.

COMBINING AND ALTERING THROWN FORMS

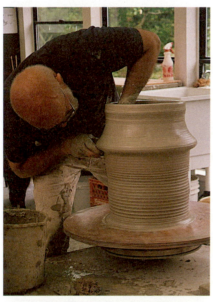

1

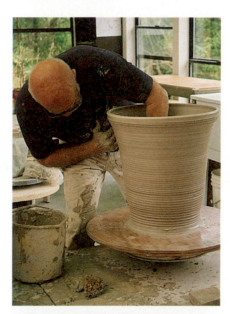

2

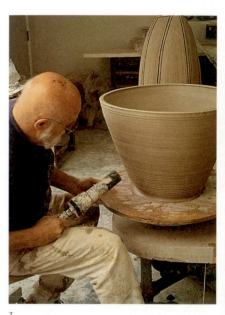

3

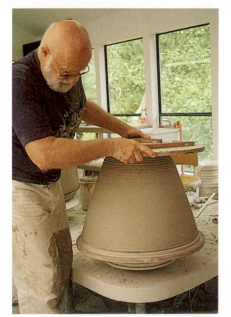

4

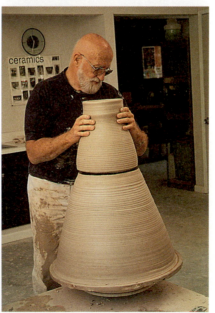

5

Bob Kinzie throws in sections, alters the shape, and carves a large sculpture:

1. **Throwing a huge piece on a low wheel**; note the position of the potter in relation to the wheel
2. **Raising and expanding the form**
3. **Stiffening the shape** with fire from a torch
4. **Turning the leather-hard shape upside down** on another bat on which the flat clay pancake base was thrown
5. **Adding another shape**, carefully measured to fit

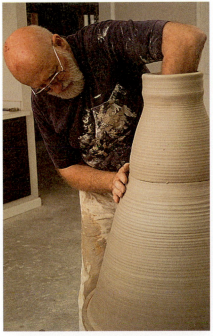

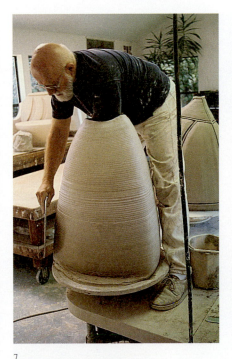

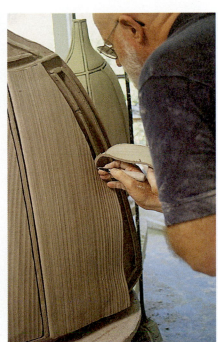

6

7

8

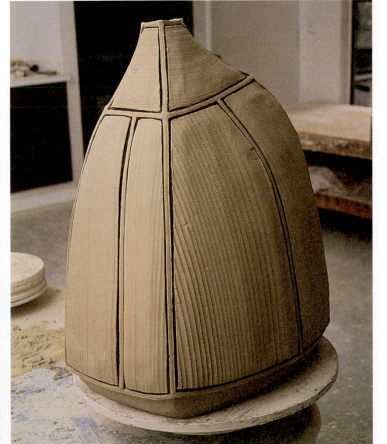

6. **Throwing the two shapes together**
7. **The top of the shape is cut off** and reserved, then the remaining form is paddled into a triangle
8. **The top is added off-center** and the form is textured and carved
9. **The finished stoneware piece**, 40 ins. (102 cm) high

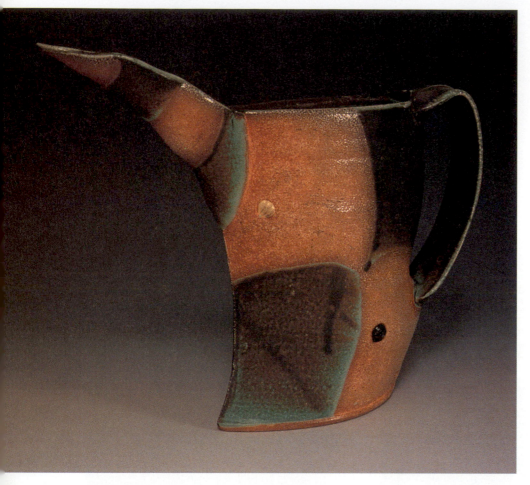

PITCHER

Pitcher shapes are almost as old as time, but still provide creative fun for clayworkers

Jeff Oestreich's beaked pitcher is thrown and altered porcelain, resist pattern, soda fired c/10; 10 x 10 x 4 ins. (25 x 25 x 10 cm)

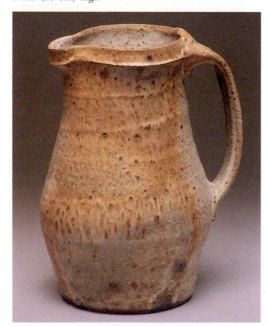

Classic matt glazed stoneware jug by Greg Miller, 8 ins. (20 cm) high

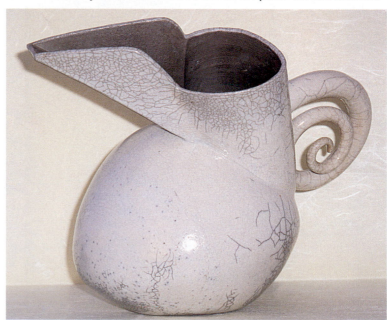

Goedele Vanhille's paddled and cut thrown earthenware pitcher has been raku-fired

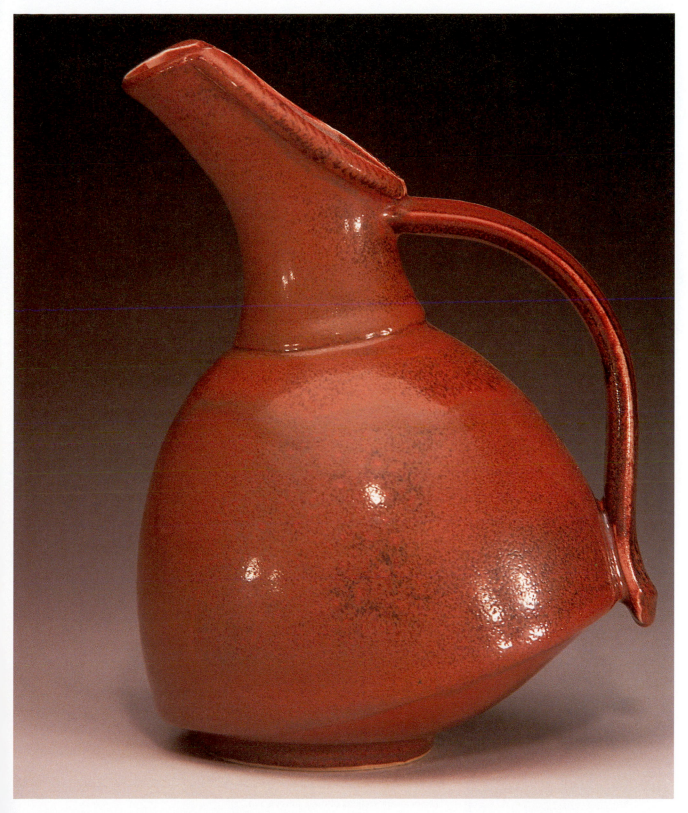

Rick Malmgren's thrown pitcher is reduction fired c/6 stoneware
with an iron persimmon glaze; 10 x 7 x 5½ ins. (25 x 18 x 12.5 cm)

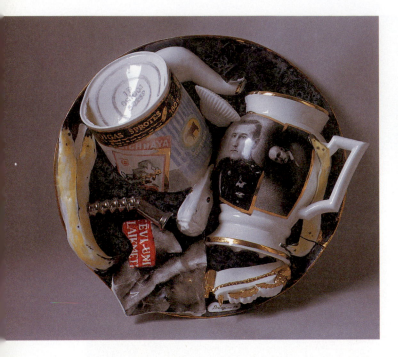

Juris Bergins' (Latvia) cup metaphor is a composite of porcelain forms, decals, china paints, transparent glaze, multi-firings, oxidation c/10 to c/013; 14 ins. (35.5 cm) diameter

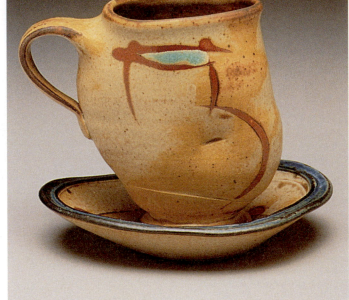

CUPS, SAUCERS, MUGS

Cups are functional forms that can be used every day or exist as sculptural objects

Nick Joerling's thrown and altered stoneware cup and saucer is stain-decorated

Linda Arbuckle's earthenware cup is majolica-decorated with stain washes over a white glaze

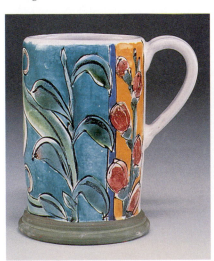

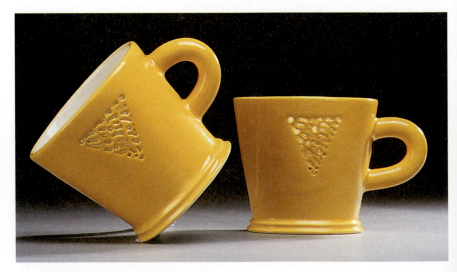

The openwork sections of these thrown and pierced porcelain cups by Sandra Black (Australia) are covered by translucent glaze

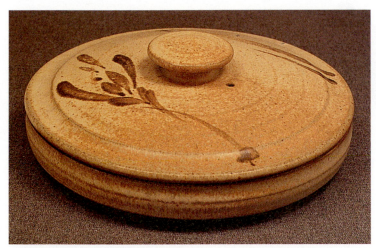

Deborah Smith's (India) lidded casserole has an easily grasped knob and is decorated with brushed oxides over the glaze

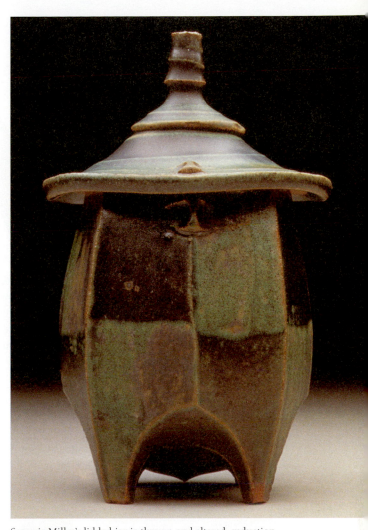

LIDDED POTS

Lidded pots are a challenge, especially large ones, first for fit, second for good proportion between lid and pot. Lid and pot should glaze-fire together, with no glaze between them. Bad fit is potter's bad measurement

Sequoia Miller's lidded jar is thrown and altered, reduction glazed c/10; 10 x 5 x 4 ins. (25 x 12.5 x 10 cm)

Linda Sikora's porcelain tureen is resist-patterned with glazes and fired in a wood- and oil-fueled salt kiln, 6 x 12 ins. (15 x 30 cm); plate is assembled from thrown sections

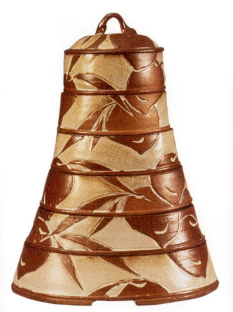

Ray Meeker's (India) tiered and lidded set of serving dishes is wax-resist and glaze decorated, 14 ins. (35.5 cm) high

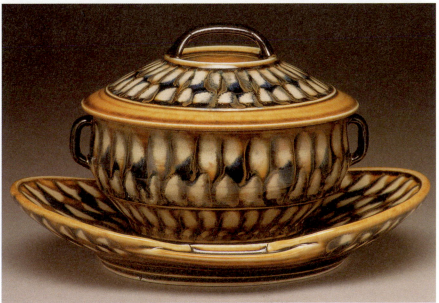

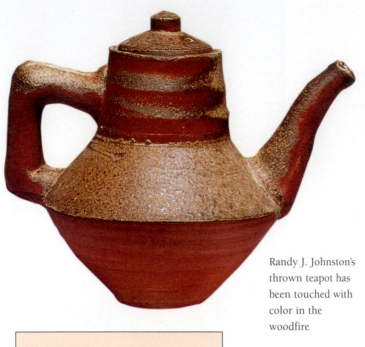

Randy J. Johnston's thrown teapot has been touched with color in the woodfire

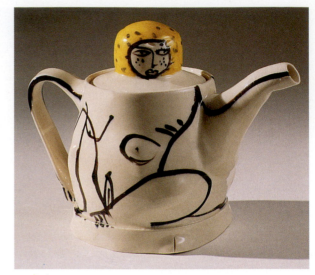

Sandy Simon's porcelain teapot is brushed with black and yellow glaze stains

TEAPOTS

Teapots or beverage pots are exciting to make but difficult to design and assemble. Think of the whole before you start

FACING PAGE Hwang Jeng-Daw's (Taiwan) thrown stoneware teapot of multicolored clay with coil-made appendages, 15 x 15½ x 8 ins. (38 x 40 x 20 cm) is c/8 oxidation fired; many supports hold the pot during firing

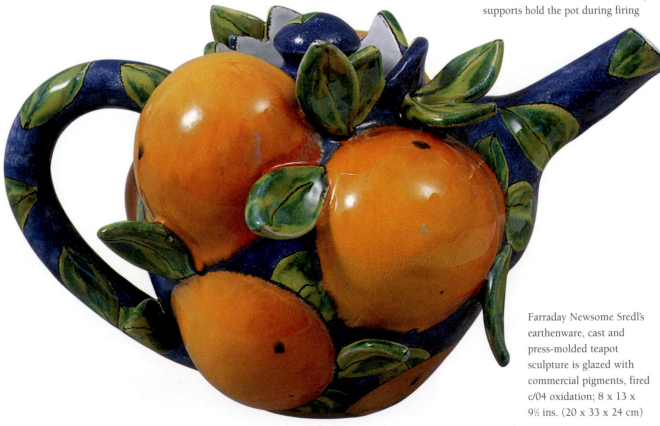

Farraday Newsome Sredl's earthenware, cast and press-molded teapot sculpture is glazed with commercial pigments, fired c/04 oxidation; 8 x 13 x 9½ ins. (20 x 33 x 24 cm)

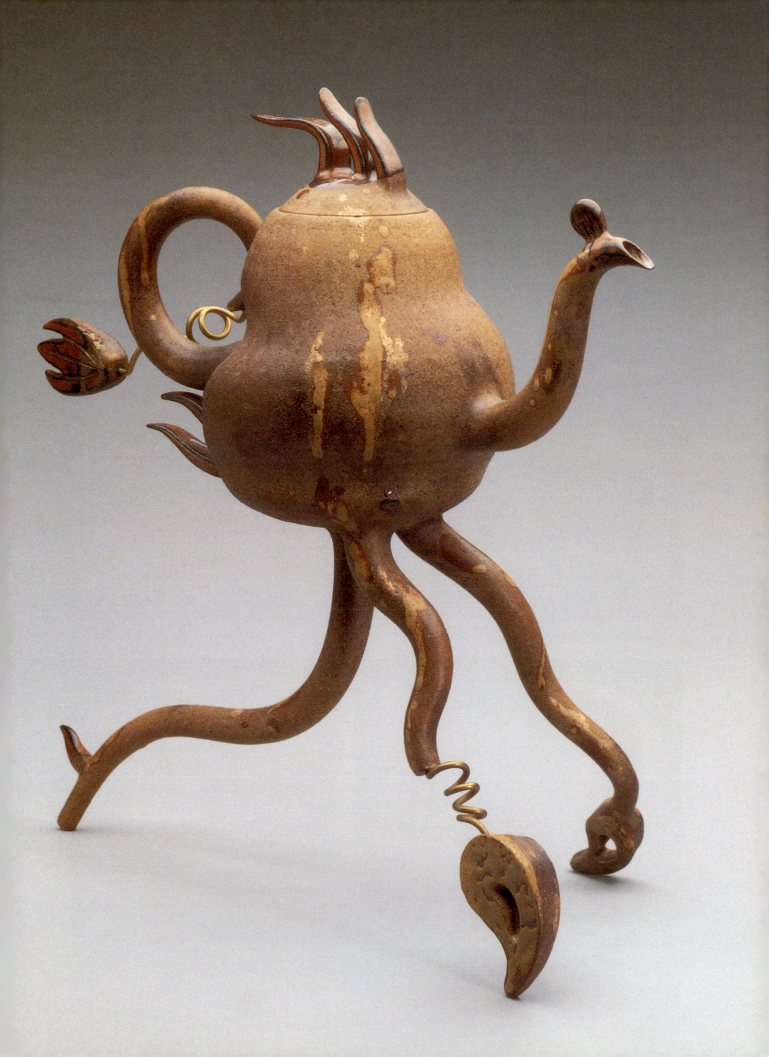

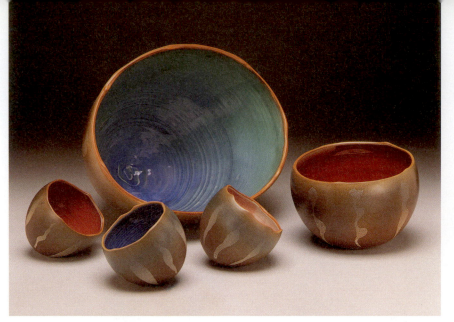

Don Davis' slanted bowl group, thrown and altered porcelain, is decorated with engobes, stains, resist patterns, glaze; tallest bowl is 13 ins. (33 cm) high

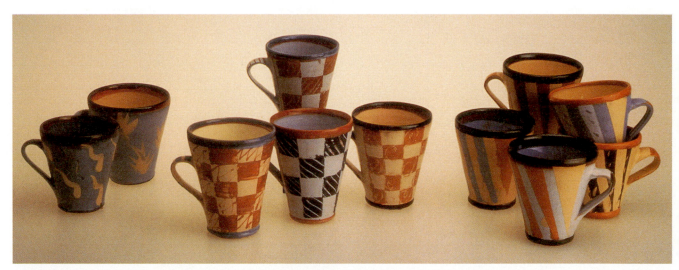

Nina Malterud (Norway), sets of cups, thrown, stoneware, underglaze stain decoration, 4 ins. (10 cm) high

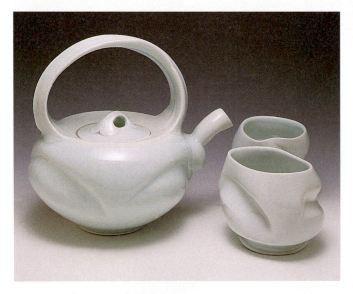

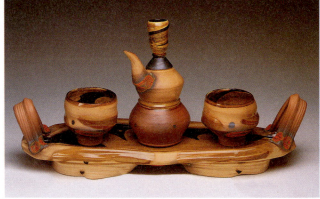

Thrown earthenware tray set, partly glazed with brush-strokes of commercial low-fire glazes, by Woody Hughes

Chris Staley's thrown porcelain teapot and cups were altered in the wet stage

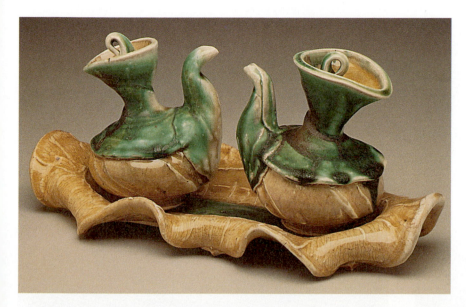

Josh DeWeese's thrown and altered oil and vinegar set is soda-fired stoneware

Jan Peterson's cast porcelain cups make a sculpture if grouped, or can be used individually; bisque fired c/10, glaze fired c/04; 6 x 5 x 4 ins. (15 x 12.5 x 10 cm) each

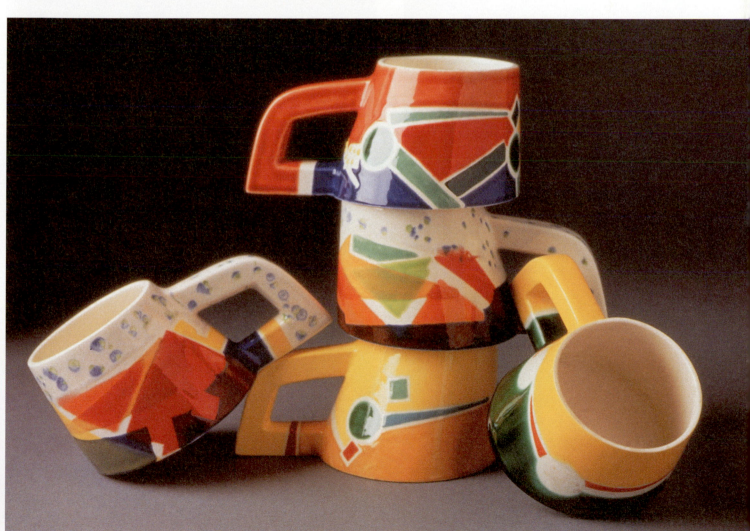

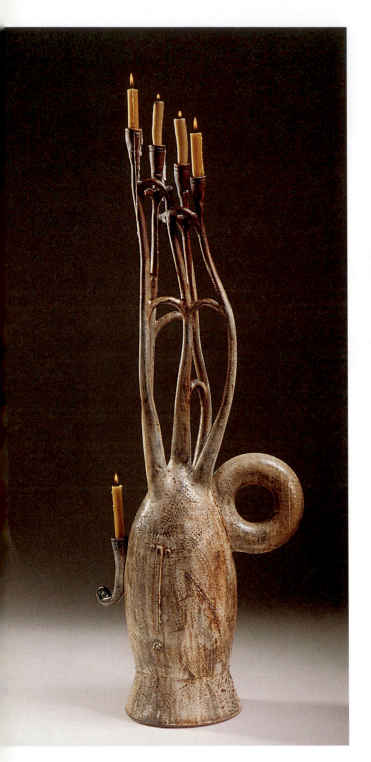

ALTERED FORM

Thrown pieces can be misshapen and changed into many other kinds of forms in the wet to leather-hard stage. Hand-built appendages are often added to thrown forms and vice versa

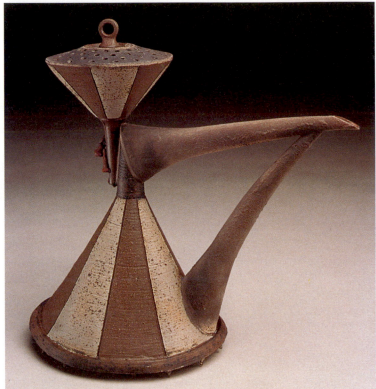

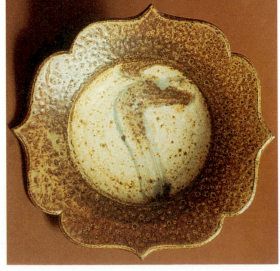

ABOVE Matthew Wilt's server is multicolored clays, reduction fired c/10 stoneware, 16 x 15 x 8 ins. (40 x 38 x 20 cm)

FACING PAGE Pat Kenny Lopez's earthenware cast bottle with hand-built additions is clear and matt glazed c/04; 10 x 6 ins. (25 x 15 cm)

LEFT Curtis Hoard's thrown stoneware candelabra, nearly 5 ft (152 cm) tall, is a tour-de-force of throwing and hand-building technique

RIGHT Tim De Rose's thrown stoneware plate with edge cut at leather-hard stage has been decorated with engobe and salt-glazed

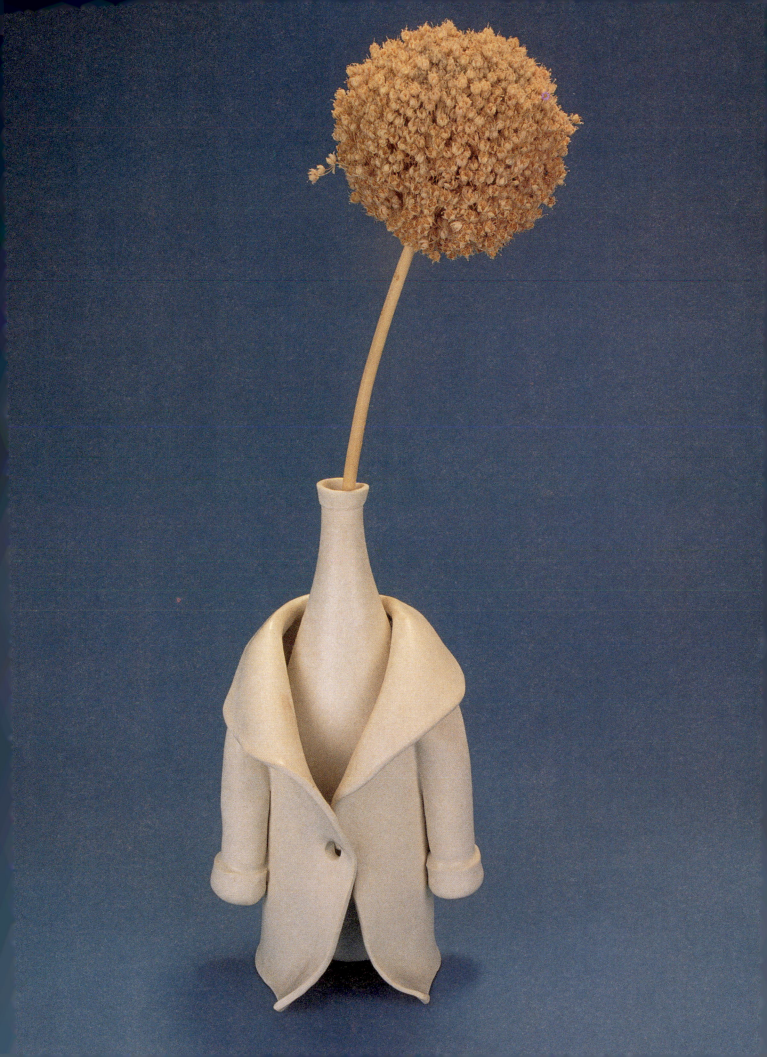

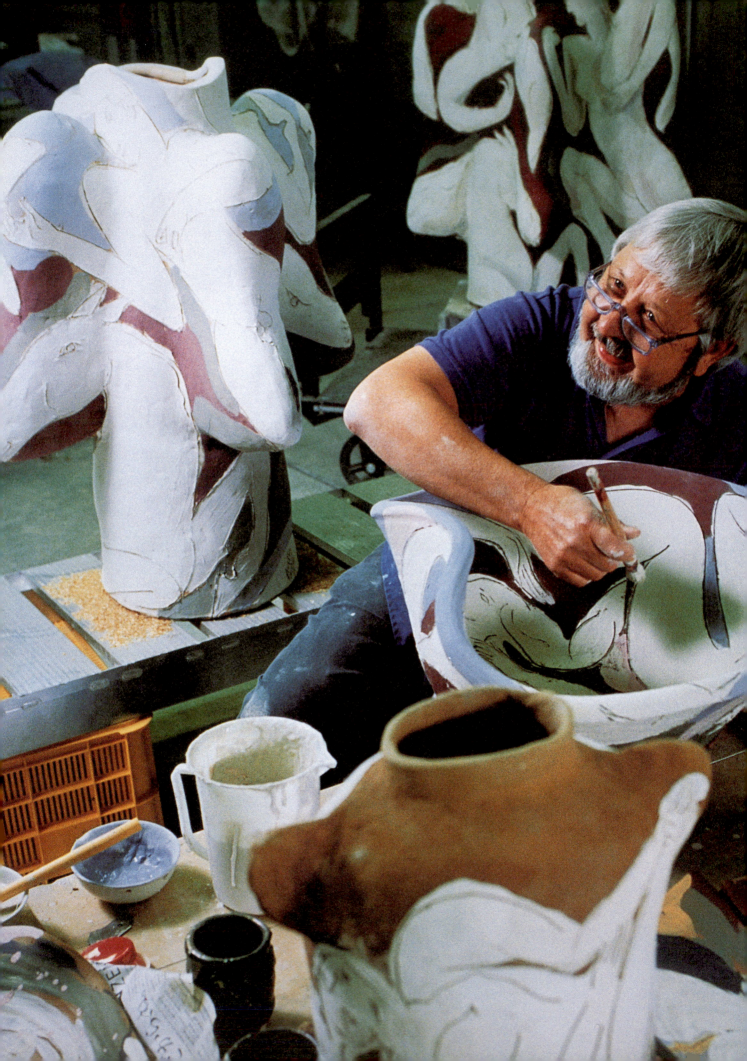

4

FINISHING TOUCHES

ENHANCING THE CLAY FORM

Since the beginning of time, human beings have felt a desire to embellish their claywork. Early in history, coiled pots were made with the coils showing, and perhaps stick-marks or indentations were made on them during fabrication. Often clays of other colors were added to the surface of a vessel and drawings were scratched through the added colors to the clay body. Sometimes clay cut-outs or decorative appendages serving no function were added to the surface. Many times, brush-strokes of a different-colored clay decorated the pot.

Thousands of years passed before glass and glaze were discovered, probably around 5000 B.C. With this achievement a variety of colors were possible and a shiny, easily cleaned surface was developed. More importantly, a transparent glaze could cover and protect the colored clays and textured surfaces with which primitive potters had been ornamenting their vessels.

Rudy Autio decorates a "fun" piece with vitreous engobes and stains, slab-built by mischievous students during a workshop at the Shigaraki Ceramic Center, photographed for a newspaper, Japan

The method of constructing the form does not matter: decoration of all kinds is possible on any clay shape. Industrial decorative processes do differ from hand processes, but some of those methods, such as the use of decals, can also be applied to handwork.

DECORATING WITH CLAY

Texture

The simplest method of decorating clay, from earliest times, is to pattern it in the wet or leather-hard stage with any tool or object pressed into the clay to various depths. This includes use of the fingers in a number of ways; pressing imprints of objects from nature – seed pods, rocks, shells – or "found objects" – nails, screws, wires, and so on – into the clay; using stamps you make yourself from clay, textured, carved, and bisque-fired so they can be pushed into wet clay for decoration; pressing wooden paddles or rolling castors that you have carved yourself against your pots or sculptures. Anything can be used to make impressions on clay in random or organized patterns.

TEXTURING CLAY

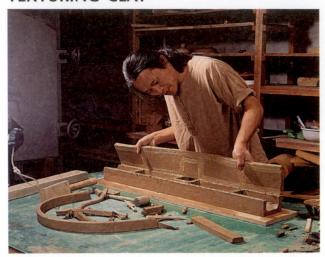

Ah Leon constructed his 60-ft (18 m.) long bridge in his Taiwan studio over a period of several years; each segment was slab-built hollow, with interior buttressing, and different colored clays were used

1

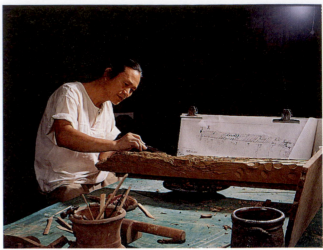

The artist meticulously textured the clay to resemble wood and fired in high-temperature reduction

2

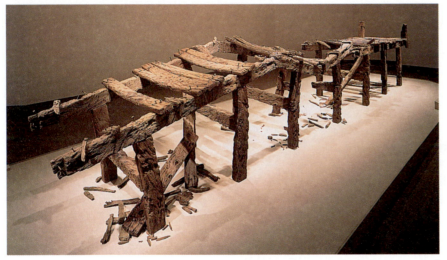

Section of Ah Leon's bridge; the entire piece was first shown at the Sackler Gallery, Smithsonian Institution, Washington D.C.

3

Texturing clay in the wet state gives a soft effect, as opposed to carving on the surface when it is leather-hard. After the piece is bisqued, colored metallic oxides can be rubbed into the indentations and wiped off, to highlight the patterns. This surface can be left unglazed to give a weathered or stony look; oxides without a glaze coating need firing at c/5 or above. Glaze can also be applied over the stained texture (not Ah Leon's style). Especially, transparent glazes will puddle in these indentations, which gives another quality to the texture.

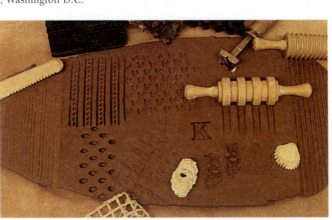

TEXTURING CLAY

Clay is so susceptible to marking that the simplest method of decorating it is to push something into it. Any number of objects or tools will leave an interesting decorative pattern

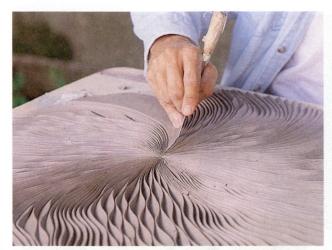

Marc Leuthold painstakingly carves from a flat slab a disk which will form the top surface of his sculpture   1

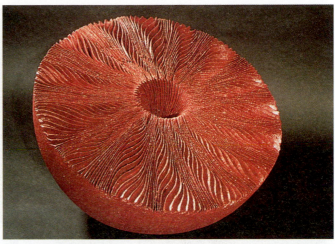

Leuthold's finished hemispherical sculpture is fired at cone 010 with a cadmium glaze   2

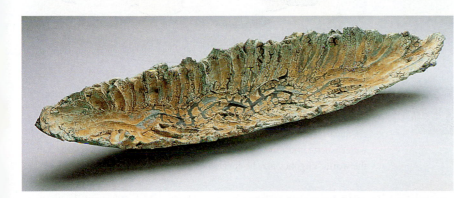

Gudrun Klix's (Australia) textured earthenware sculpture has been patinated with low-fire engobes and matt glaze to resemble bronze

Adding clay to clay

Clay forms of the same or different-colored clays can be appliquéd to the basic shape either wet or leather-hard; rolled, beaten, or torn slabs can be squeezed or pounded against moist clay forms; coils can be rolled into various shapes and added on, pressed flat or left to protrude; small balls of clay can be added in spots for emphasis; edges can be cut and folded to change the line. Experiment with many different additions to your forms – paddle, slash, and change the shape freely. Differing types of clays can be added to each other with varying results; shrinkage cracks are OK in "art."

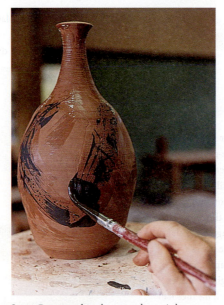

Susan Peterson brushes engobe to inlay a wax-resist pattern on leather-hard clay

Detail of a Katie Kazan tray made with her millefiore technique. Sections of different colored clays are laid and pressed together to form patterns, then wire-cut across the grain into slabs

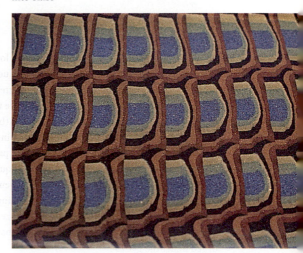

ENGOBES

Engobes are liquid colored clays, sometimes called slips, applied in coats, in patterns or all over a clay form, in its wet or leather-hard state. Engobes bond only on unfired, usually leather-hard clay unless they are specially formulated for bisque firing

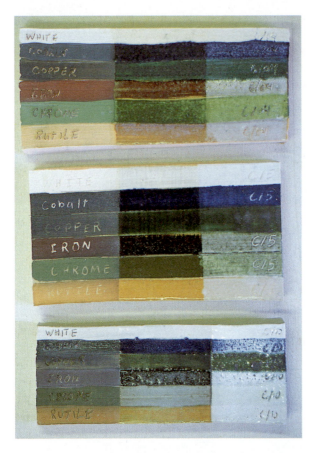

Basic engobe batch with 20% zircopax added for white, 20% cobalt oxide for blue, 20% copper oxide for blue-green, 20% iron oxide for brown, 20% chrome oxide for green, 20% rutile for tan, were each brushed across each of three tiles and bisque fired: cone 04 (top), cone 5 (center), cone 10 (bottom).
Each tile was left unglazed on the left, glazed in the center with the c/04, c/5, and c/10 transparent glazes (see page 108), and on the right side with the c/04, c/5, and c/10 opaque glazes (see page 108) and fired in oxidation at the three temperatures. Note the visual differences between the color unglazed, under the clear glaze, and under an opaque white glaze. If the tiles had been fired in reduction, the copper bar would have turned pink or red under the glazes

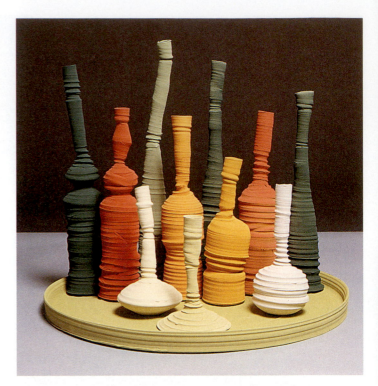

Engobes and glazes are colored with natural earth oxides such as iron, cobalt, copper etc; but commercial blends of these oxides with other chemicals, called "glaze stains," or stains, for short, will give the potter a wider palette and can be purchased from ceramic suppliers everywhere in the world. Engobes may be covered with a glaze, or left unglazed

ABOVE A porcelain sculpture by James Makins which was sprayed with stain-colored engobes and oxidation fired

BELOW Makins has added Mason stain 6005 to a basic semi-matt glaze to make a solid-colored glaze, cone 10 oxidation. Unglazed colored engobes and colored glazes are two different surfaces

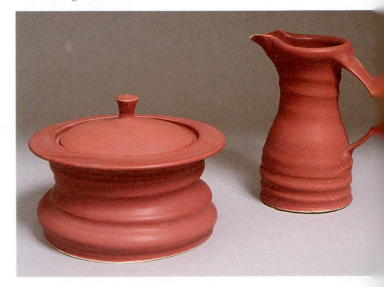

Engobes (slips)

Engobes are made of clay and other materials that fire to the same temperature as the clay body and fit the body without cracking off. Sometimes the base clay of the engobe is the same as the clay body, or at least a similar composition. Engobes with a major proportion of clay content will be applied to moist clay; engobes made with 50% clay plus other inert materials can be applied to dry or bisque clay; engobe compositions can be made that will become dense and almost glaze-like, and are called **vitreous engobes**. White engobes can be colored with various metallic oxides or stains (see page 107). Engobes are only clay, and will not stick to the clay kiln shelf or any other pot during firing. Add metallic coloring oxides or commercial stain colors to this batch in amounts of 20 to 50%; test the engobes on pots fired to your normal temperature with and without glaze until you reach the effect you want. This engobe is for use on wet to leather-hard clay.

An all-purpose engobe batch for bisque clay is:
    ball clay 50%
    talc 20%
    whiting 10%
    feldspar 10%
    silica 10%

An all-purpose vitreous engobe batch is:
    ball clay 40%
    whiting 10%
    feldspar 30%
    silica 20%

Terra sigillata is something like an engobe, but is never glazed. It is a very fine clay that has been ground in creek beds by nature (see ancient Greek red and black decorated vessels), or ground by you in a ball mill in an excess of water, then allowed to settle several days before use. Sigillata is best applied to leather-hard or bone-dry clay; the surface will be shiny when fired lower than or up to 1950° F (1050° C). The same effect will come from burnishing leather-hard clay or engobes with a smooth stone or with your fingers or a spoon. Sigillata made from white-burning ball clay can be colored with oxides or stains.

BASIC ENGOBE BATCH

An all-purpose engobe batch for raw clay is:
    ball clay 80%
    feldspar 10%
    silica 10%

Engobe techniques

1. **Sgraffito** Cover the clay body with one or more colored engobes and draw a design or carve away areas of the engobe through to the clay, to a desired depth. Use a variety of tools for different lines.

2. **Slip trail** Trail the liquid engobe with a syringe, a small bulb or a small ladle. Try this on the wheel too, allowing the design to go around with different speeds, with your marks.

3. **Combing** Draw a comb, a fork, a quill or a needle through one wet engobe to another one. This is a simple method that looks complicated, especially if several colored engobes are used.

4. **Marbleizing** Pour two or more colored engobes in layers on the piece, pick it up, and rotate it so the colors mingle. **Pattern pour** is similar to marbleizing; pour decoratively using several engobes but don't blend them. Different ladles, pitchers, and other pouring vessels will give different patterns as you pour, as will different speeds of pouring. **Dipping** a pot into one or more engobes is another way to achieve pattern.

5. **Brush, pour, dip, and spray engobes** Engobe consistency determines the look of the stroke: the thicker the more like oil painting, the thinner

Raw clay, unfired, engobe techniques. Top row, left to right: sgraffito; brown engobe brushed, wax covered, carved, white engobe inlaid; wax brushed pattern, white engobe over; engobes poured. Bottom row, left to right: mishima; combing; free brush; slip trail

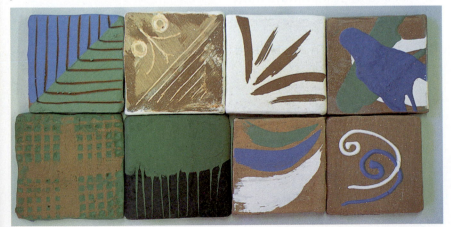

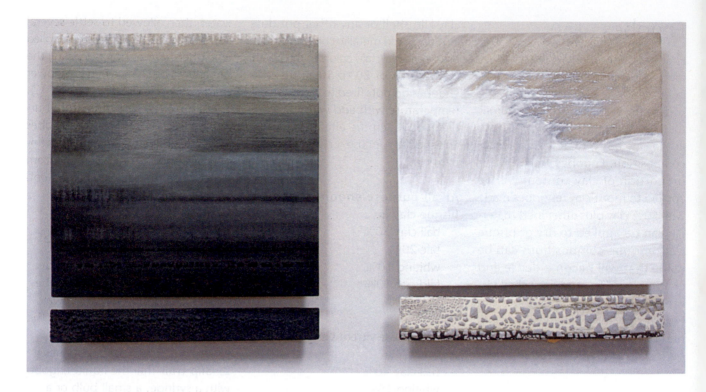

the more like watercolor. Spraying with a hand or an electric gun may require the engobe to be thinned to go through the nozzle.

6. Mishima A traditional Oriental technique used especially in Japan and Korea, which involves carving or texturing the clay surface, not too deeply, then applying an engobe over the whole surface and wiping it away with a cloth or rib tool, leaving the engobe embedded in the carving. The top surface can be wiped clean or some remaining strokes can be left.

7. Wax resist Wax resist technique is most common, but liquid latex, paper or cardboard, commercial labels, masking tapes etc will restrict the application of engobe or glaze. To keep a crisp line, paper and latex should be removed after the design is completed, although they will burn out. Essentially, resist is a stencil.

Wax resist is accomplished with water-soluble waxes, available commercially, or with melted paraffin,

to which benzine or turpentine is added to make the wax flow. (Great caution is needed when using these or any flammable solvents.)

Wax burns out at 300° F (150° C), leaving the blank spaces of the design. Water-soluble waxes do not resist as well as paraffin. Take care not to dissolve the wax when you cover the background with liquid engobe or glaze. Paraffin cannot be removed from a brush; keep separate brushes for wax and utensils. Always wash brushes with soap.

These techniques can also be used with glaze decoration.

LEFT Jeanne Otis's wall sculpture shows a variety of effects achieved with brushed and poured engobes, glazed and overglazed, accented with a thick white crawled glaze. 19½ x 39 x 1½ ins. (50 x 99 x 4 cm)

FACING PAGE **Hakami** is a traditional Japanese technique in which slip is applied with a huge brush, leaving the texture of the stroke or blob. This pot by Warren MacKenzie is reduction fired at high temperature and has an oatmeal glaze over the engobe; 14 ins. (36 cm) high

INSET Heavy engobe, laid on thickly with a big brush, engraved through to the earthenware body and left unglazed; bowl by Susanne Stephenson, 20 ins. (51 cm) high

Engobe decoration can be left unglazed, which keeps its clay texture and is a handsome finish. Or, covered with a transparent glossy glaze, engobe will show the design exactly and will be shiny; covered with a thinly applied opaque white or lightly colored glaze, the engobe will show through dimly; covered with a translucent matt glaze, it will be diffused and dull in surface

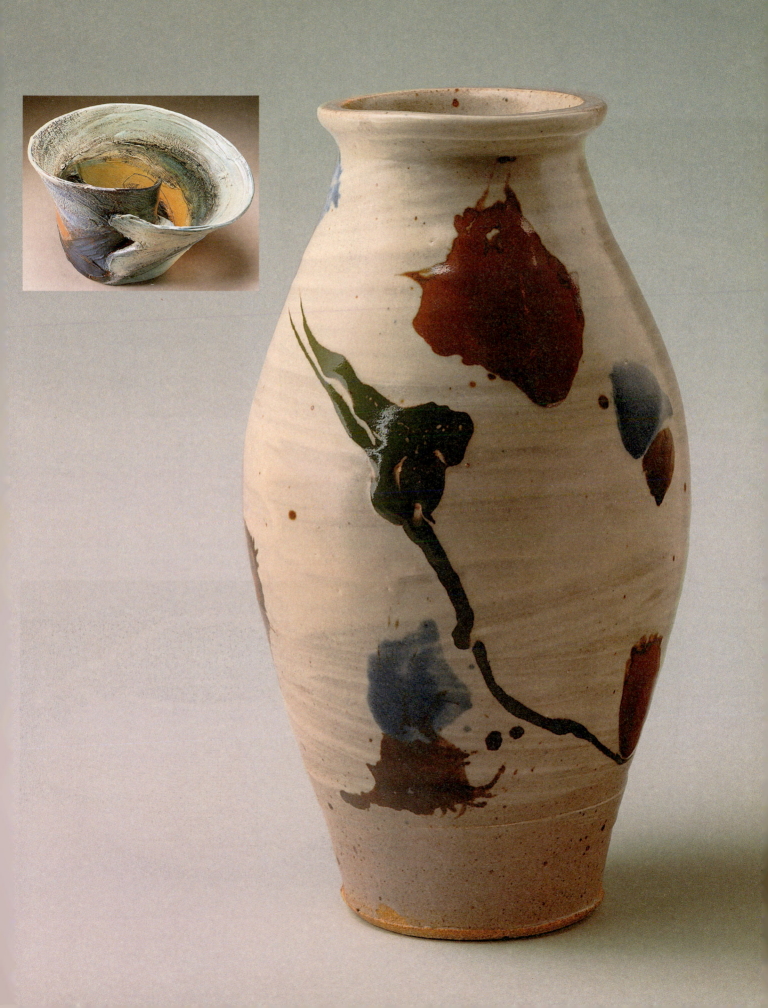

ENGOBE TECHNIQUES

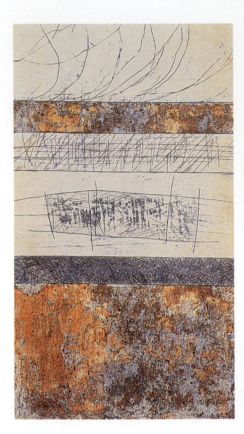

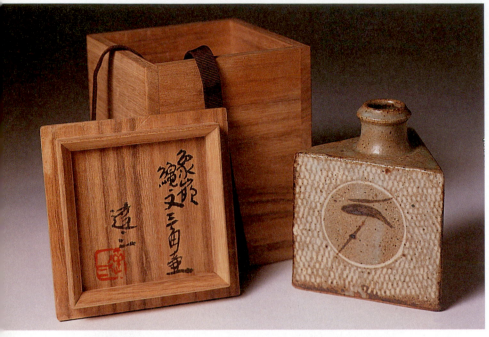

In the **mishima** technique, *raw clay is carved, then brushed over with wet engobe*; the surface is scraped clean, leaving the engobe decoration inlaid. This stoneware pot, 6 ins. (15 cm) high, by Tzaro Shimaoka, is high-fired in his hill kiln in Mashiko, Japan

This stoneware plaque by Cathy Fleckstein (Germany) illustrates the fine, crisp line that results from *a sharp tool being drawn through engobe*

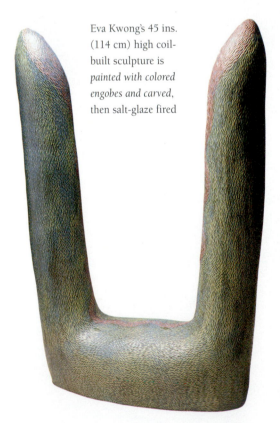

Eva Kwong's 45 ins. (114 cm) high coil-built sculpture is *painted with colored engobes and carved*, then salt-glaze fired

Richard Zane Smith's carefully coiled and textured pot is *painted with thin washes of colored engobes*, fired at low temperature without glaze; bamboo handle; 18 ins. (46 cm) wide

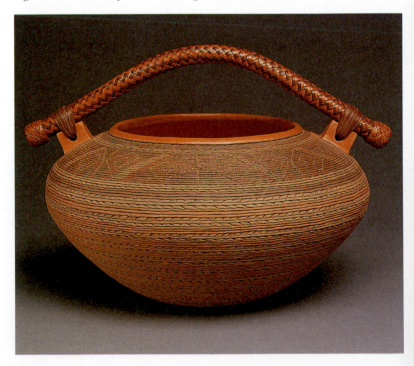

TESTING AND USING GLAZES

Glaze composition

Using glaze and glaze decoration techniques is similar to using engobes, but the materials are completely different. Engobe is clay, stays in place, and does not change in the fire; glaze melts to glass in the fire and, except in a matt form, will not hold its line

Glazes are made from several basic ingredients added to silica, the essential glass-forming oxide. Because silica requires 3000° F (1650° C) heat before it melts by itself, fluxes must

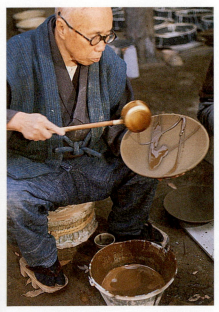

The late Shoji Hamada using a ladle to pour a pattern (which will come out black) on his famous kaki (persimmon color) glaze, pictured c. 1970

be added to lower the heat to regular glaze-firing temperatures for ceramics. Most glazes contain 50% silica, from various sources. The fluxes that lower the melting point of silica at low temperature – lead, boric oxide, soda, and potassium – and refractory fluxes – those that lower the melting point at higher temperatures, such as calcium, magnesium, barium, lithium, and zinc – are added to the silica in varying amounts according to the temperature to be fired. 10% clay is usually added for bonding.

The materials for glazes are dry powders, usually 200-mesh, mixed with water to a consistency measured by lifting your hand out of the glaze so that the liquid makes a long drool, then seven drops, and your hand is still visible through the liquid.

Calculating glaze formulas

Formulas of glazes for specific surfaces and temperatures can be chemically and mathematically calculated from the molecular formulas of all glaze materials, then translated into parts-by-weight batches.

Beginners will probably search books and magazines for glaze "recipes," or buy ready-prepared glazes for all temperatures, which can be purchased commercially in most areas of the world.

Lacking these aids and the will to learn glaze calculation, potters should know that all materials and minerals on the globe will melt at some temperature. Test what you think could make a glaze melt, add a 10% or so portion of white clay to each mixture for the bond, apply, and fire your tests. Weird and wonderful things may result!

WHY MAKE YOUR OWN GLAZE?

Compounding batches of glazes for yourself is not just fun, it is the beginning of creating your own style, in much the same way as compounding and mixing your own clay body. When you make your own clay and your own glaze, you are in control of your whole ceramic statement. In our view this is part of the process and gives you the utmost command.

However, many clay artists today buy ready-prepared clays and glazes, perhaps adding to them other materials, after making tests, for an individual emphasis. As well, there are hundreds of ways to handle glazes: decorative techniques, thickness of application, means of application, ways of firing, that make hundreds of differences, so that it may not matter where you get your glazes.

In the end you choose your own way, but we hope you at least try inventing your own glazes.

COLORING GLAZES

Glaze stains and oxides

As a start, color any basic glazes, or see page 108, with metallic oxides such as *2 to 4% copper* for green in oxidation or pink-red in reduction (see Chapter 5); *1 to 2% cobalt* for a strong blue; *1 to 4% chrome* for forest green; *10 to 15% vanadium* for

Basic glaze batches for low, medium, high temperatures

Here are some basic batches for mixing your own transparent glossy and opaque glazes and tests, to be fired at the three median temperatures: 1900°, 2150°, and 2300° F (1040°, 1180°, and 1260° C), or approximately Orton cones (see page 195) 04, 5, and 10.

Low-fire transparent glossy, *cone 04:*

Gerstley borate 55%
whiting 11%
soda ash 11%
china clay 11%
silica 12%

Low-fire opaque white, *cone 04:*

Add 15% zircopax to the 100-part batch of the transparent clear glaze above

Medium-fire transparent glossy, *cone 5:*

nepheline syenite 50%
Gerstley borate 25%
barium carbonate 5%
whiting 10%
china clay 5%
silica 5%

Medium-fire opaque white, *cone 5:*

Add 15% zircopax to the 100-part batch above

High-fire transparent glossy, *cone 10:*

nepheline syenite 40%
whiting 10%
Gerstley borate 20%
china clay 10%
silica 20%

High-fire opaque white, *cone 10:*

Add 15% zircopax to the 100-part batch above

Color any of these glazes by inserting natural metallic oxides or manufactured glaze stains in percentage amounts added to the basic 100% batch

CONE 04   **CONE 5**   **CONE 10 REDUCTION**

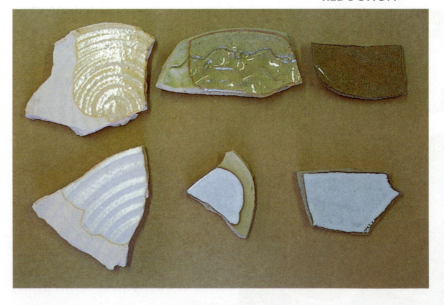

Top row: transparent glazes, batches above. Bottom row: opaque glazes, batches above. Shards are the same beige clay body; note the color changes at the different temperatures, and the darker color in cone 10 reduction

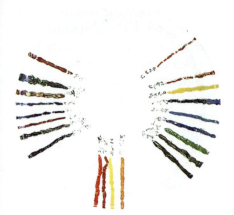

A variety of manufactured stains brushed *over* a transparent glaze, c/04 oxidation

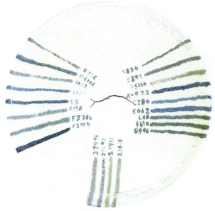

The same stains brushed *under* an opaque white glaze, c/5 oxidation

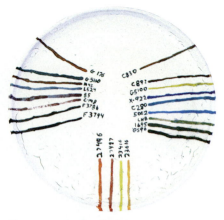

The same stains brushed *over* an opaque white glaze, c/10 oxidation

The clay body is beige-colored. Stains (or metallic oxides) can be applied under or over glazes with varying results, as you see in these tests. Many different companies in the world manufacture glaze stains. Buy samples and make your own tests.

Many ceramic suppliers throughout the world also make and sell their own commercial glazes, wet or dry, in small or larger amounts. The ingredients are secret; shelf life is limited.

Potters buy from color catalog pages which do not exactly correspond with the actual fired glazes.

---

yellow, best in oxidation; 10% rutile for burnt orange; 1 to 10% iron for amber to dark brown in oxidation, celadon to tenmoku in reduction; 2 to 8% manganese for tan to claret brown.

For a broader range of color, **buy manufactured glaze stains from companies around the world** such as Blythe, Drakenfeld, Ferro, Degussa, Pemco, Mason, and the like. Commercially prepared stains – basic natural coloring oxides combined with other ingredients to widen the palette, fired for stability, and ground again to powder – offer a broad selection of colors at most temperatures.

Glaze stains are manufactured from combinations of the basic metallic oxides – copper, cobalt, iron, vanadium, chrome, manganese, and a few others – plus added materials that stabilize them and widen the palette. Stains or metallic oxides do not melt by themselves within the ceramic temperature range. **They are the colorants for:**

• clay bodies;
• engobes;
• decorative techniques such as under- and overglaze;
• and glazes.

In addition, they are useful for:

• serigraph printing on ceramics: mix stains with silk-screen medium and hand-roll a design through a silk screen onto a ceramic tile;
• photo transfer or emulsion techniques;
• glaze stain crayons, made by adding coloring oxides to wax;
• decorating slumped glass at very low fire (1300° F, 700° C, or lower); or you can add stains to ground glass and cast it into a bisque mold;
• brushing or sponging over bisque to highlight a texture, with or without glaze;

• sprinkling dry over sand or grog on a flat surface – you then roll a slab of plastic clay over the sprinkles;
• making your own decals.

Reds, yellows, and oranges

Why are there no bright reds, true lemons, and oranges above 1900° F (1040° C)? Uranium oxide, which gave us those colors prior to World War II, was withdrawn, and reserved for the atom bomb. It is no longer considered safe for use on ceramics, although it is, surprisingly, available again.

Because cadmium and selenium oxides, which become red, orange, and yellow in chemically-specific glazes at low temperatures, burn out above 1900° or so F (1040° C), they are therefore useful to potters at low-fire temperatures **only**.

Cadmium and selenium reds, yellows, and oranges have recently been stabilized in a patented process for use at all temperatures and in all atmospheres, by Degussa in Europe and Cerdec in America. These stains work well but are expensive.

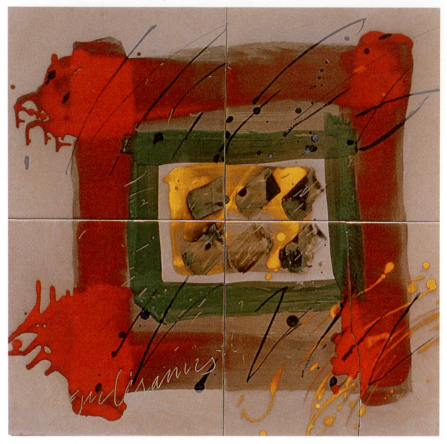

Marylyn Dintenfass's wall piece is a vibrant example of low-fire cadmium yellow, orange, and red glazes

ply the percentage weight for any quantity; 6½ lb (3000 grams) of dry material make approximately 1 gallon (4.5 litres) of liquid glaze.

Add the dry ingredients to a small amount of water to start with; add more water when necessary to make a milky consistency. Screen glaze through a window screen (minimum 20 mesh) or finer (60 mesh) if you want even color; if you want uneven color, don't screen. Store liquid glazes preferably in glass, stoneware, or oak containers, but most of us use plastic or metal buckets with lids. If glaze dries out, of course add water to the appropriate consistency.

GLAZE APPLICATION

Stir glazes with a gloved hand, or a stick, but only the hand can find lumps and feel the general consistency. It is a good idea to screen (strain) glaze before using it. Glazes tend to settle fast and need to be stirred often over prolonged use.

Glazes are not generally hazardous, but it is sensible to wear a mask, particularly if you suffer from asthma or another respiratory disease.

Methods

1. Dipping If the pot is to be all one color, dip it into the glaze container until the pot is covered and remove it quickly. Properly dipped, the piece will be glazed inside and out. Glaze dries almost instantly to a chalky powder. Touch up spots with fingers or a brush. Pots can be dipped in patterns, or dipped in several glazes.

Clay pieces can be bisqued and/or glazed at high enough temperatures to mature the clay body, then glazed with the usual cadmium low-fire reds, oranges, and yellows and fired a third time. There are other ways to achieve reds, such as with chrome and tin, and with copper in reduction atmosphere (see Chapter 5). The easiest way to get low-fire reds, oranges, and pure yellows is to buy glazes ready mixed.

The recent absence of raw or fritted lead from the catalogs of ceramic suppliers in the United States has made the particularly bright fire-engine reds, oranges, and yellows – as well as the brilliance of certain other colors – impossible to achieve today. Some countries still allow lead carbonate and fritted lead compounds to be sold.

Theoretically, fritted lead, such as lead silicate or other pre-melted lead combinations, is non-poisonous and insoluble when used in glazes. The new cadmium stabilized reds, yellows and oranges from Degussa (Cerdec) are less bright (see tests, page 116).

MIXING AND STORING GLAZES

Glazes should be listed as *100% basic batches* of materials, *plus* the colorant(s); color is always an addition to the basic 100% batch. You can easily multi-

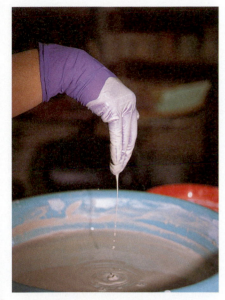

Stir glaze by hand (wear rubber gloves); adjust the viscosity by adding water until the glaze is as thin as cream and gives a long drool and several drops from your hand

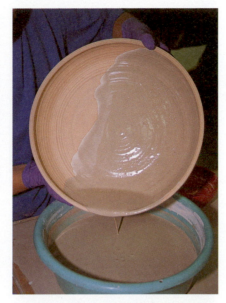

Pots are usually glazed inside first by pouring the glaze in, quickly rotating the vessel and pouring the rest out. Every overlap makes a mark; if you do not want it, scrape it down

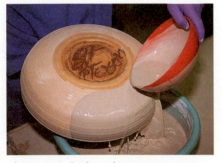

After waxing the foot of a stoneware pot, pour glaze on the outside, making a decision whether to keep the overlap pattern

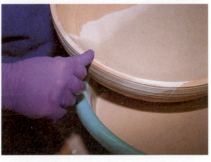

Scrape off the excess glaze to clean the lip; then spray, brush, or dip the lip last

stands from the piece, speckles may develop.

Fill the spray gun with glaze made more liquid than the consistency for dipping or pouring. Standing too close to the vessel while spraying results in runny glaze application – you could like that! Some potters use an air-brush type of sprayer for very controlled application and complicated shadings.

4. Brushing Painting is a good idea only when you want brush-strokes to show, because they do. It takes years of practice to learn to apply glaze evenly with a brush. Think of brushing as a means of getting variation and rhythm, according to the size of the brush and the manner of the stroke.

2. Pouring Always glaze the inside of a vessel first, usually by pouring. Fill a cup with glaze, pour it into the pot and roll it round up to the edge; pour the remainder out quickly. Turn the pot over and pour the other glaze over the outside. If the outside pouring is done on a rotating wheel the glaze will coat all round evenly. If you pour in overlapping patterns, generally all variations in application show after the firing.

Clean excess glaze off the lip with a wood knife and dip the lip in glaze, or brush the glaze on.

3. Spraying Using an atomized spray gun is a satisfactory method of applying glaze, but only if the potter sprays evenly. Usually the inside of the vessel is poured even if the outside is sprayed. Spraying different colors can result in highlights and shadows of color. Depending on how dry the glaze is when sprayed or how far the potter

Faith Banks Porter double-dips this stoneware vase in tenmoku glaze over her throwing marks, then ladle-pours a white glaze over. Note the color changes with thick and thin applications. 8 ins. (20 cm) high

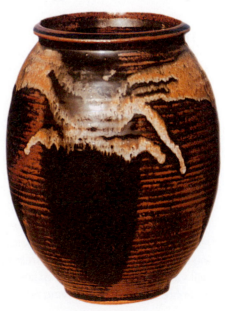

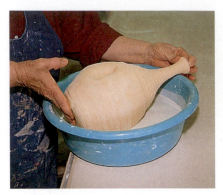

Patterns can be created by holding a vessel at different angles and dipping it into glaze

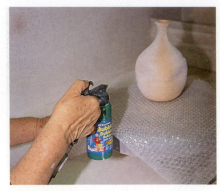

Spraying glaze adds variety of texture or color changes if you desire

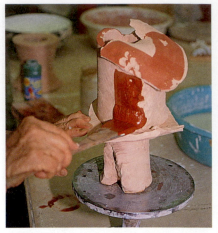

Brushing is not a good technique for overall glazing because all the strokes will show in the finished piece. It is better to brush glaze when you want the strokes to remain visible as a pattern

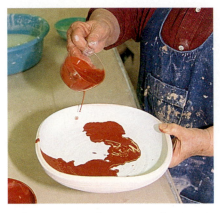

Ladle-pouring one glaze over another is an easy way of achieving decorative effects

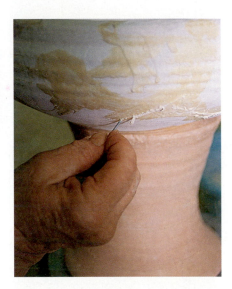

Resist pattern with wax. Put your pot up on a bisqued "chuck" or stand so you can see your design. Water-soluble wax or melted paraffin can make patterns over or between glazes, or on the clay before glazing. Here wax over glaze is being scratched . . .

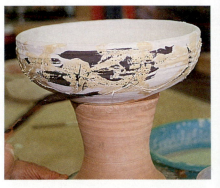

. . . and **liquid cobalt oxide** is being brushed majolica-fashion over and into the pattern

DECORATING WITH GLAZE

Usually pottery is bisque-fired at least to red heat (1300° F, 700° C) to make handling of the piece easier during the glazing, and then fired again to the glaze temperature. Once-fired ware implies that the work is glazed leather-hard or bone dry and fired to top temperature once only. Depending on which process is used, the results will vary. Drawing through glaze on an unfired vessel offers carving advan-

tages that would not be possible on a bisqued clay piece.

1. Dipping or pouring in pattern
Surely this is one of the easiest means of achieving decoration. Try dipping or pouring several colors with or without overlaps; try both matt and gloss surfaces; try leaving some of the clay body exposed. Pour from different containers to make different shapes and widths.

Dip into glazes at different angles. If you don't like something you've done, scrape it off and start again. All variations of glaze thickness will show up in the finished fired piece, which is part of the beauty of this method.

2. Decorative brushing
Stains or glazes can be brushed over or under each other. Brushing is a technique better known in the East

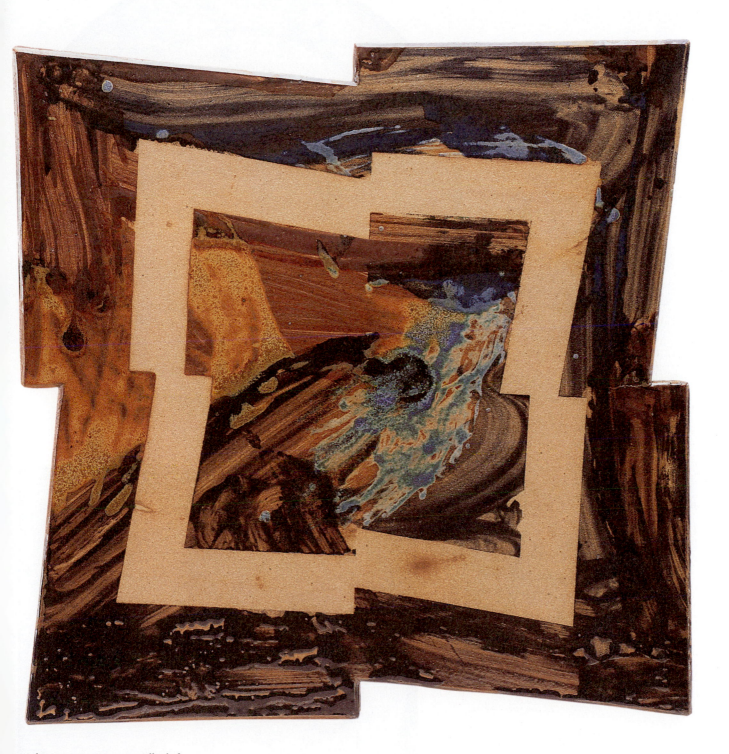

John Mason's stoneware wall relief
with resist patterns shows great
surface variety, accomplished by
differing thicknesses of brush-stroke
and exploiting the fluid quality of
glazes that meld with each other
during the cone 10 reduction fire;
24 ins. (61 cm) diameter

"Majolica," or *brushing oxides over glaze*, is a favorite centuries-old technique. If the glaze is glossy, the brush-stroke moves a lot; if it is matt, the brush-stroke holds, as in this stoneware plate painted by Seth Cardew (England), wood-fired at cone 10 in his anagama kiln; 14 ins. (35.5 cm) diameter

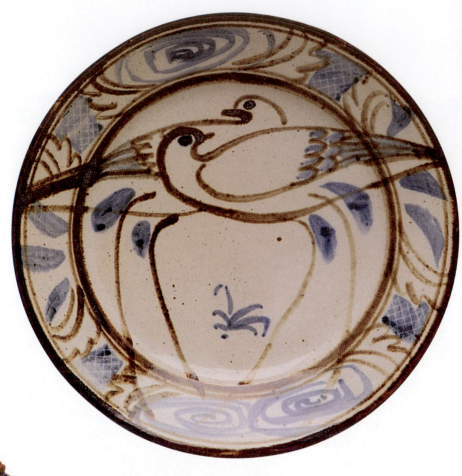

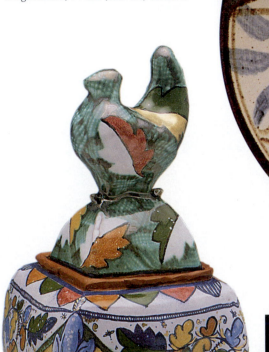

Liz Quackenbush's press-molded box has traditional Italian-style *majolica painting over the opaque white glaze* on an iron-red clay body, low temperature oxidation firing; 12 ins. (30 cm) high

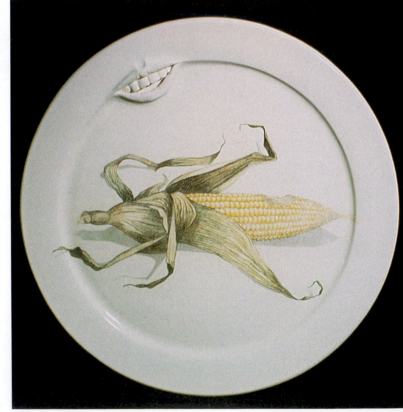

Verne Funk's delightful drawing is achieved with *underglaze pencils on the bisqued clay*, coated with a clear glaze, a technique possible at any temperature; 12 ins. (30 cm) diameter

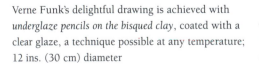

and better practiced over and over by us in the West.

3. Spraying one color over another

Colors will blend in this technique, but how depends on the firing, the thickness of application, and the consistency of the raw glaze. Keep records of what you do and analyze the results after the glaze firing.

4. Underglaze decoration

Just as this implies, metallic oxides or commercial glaze stains can be mixed with water and applied to the bisqued surface, then glazed over. As in watercolor painting on paper, the more water the lighter the color will be, the less water the denser. Potters can learn to achieve great subtlety of brush-stroke and nuance with this method. A transparent or translucent glaze should be sprayed – not poured – over this decorative application. Commercially prepared under-glazes have moisture and a bonding medium added in the jar. These colors usually come as liquid in small jars and are very expensive.

Underglaze pencils, crayons, and chalks can be purchased or you can make your own. Even spray cans with commercially prepared underglazes are sold by ceramic suppliers.

5. Overglaze decoration

Also called **majolica**, this technique is the opposite of underglaze decoration. Metallic oxides or stains mixed with water to watercolor consistency are applied over a dry glazed piece before it is fired. When the decoration is fired in the kiln it melts into the underneath glaze, causing a fuzzy or feathered line. The degree of fusion depends on the kind of glaze – some glazes are more fluid than others during the firing. If the glaze is very stiff, as a matt glaze is, the fusion will be slight. The characteristic melding of the design into the glaze is the trademark of majolica.

China paints and enamels are another form of overglaze decoration, but both are applied on top of a fired glaze and refired again at a low temperature, about 1300° F (700° C). Metals, such as gold and platinum, and lusters come in the same category. China paints, metals, and lusters require skill and experience in handling and patience in application. Brushes must be absolutely clean; painting must take place on an absolutely clean pot surface; firing is chancy (page 124).

6. Thickness of glaze

Normal thickness of application of a raw glaze is ½ inch (0.8 mm). Thinner than that is very thin, and heavier than that is a thick application. When placing one glaze on top of another, whether pouring, dipping, dropping, or whatever, you must keep in mind the total thickness of all the layers.

Too thick a glaze will crack as it dries and fall off the pot before it reaches the kiln. Test the thickness by placing the point of a needle or pin into the glaze; make a scratch, and estimate the depth. Your needle should feel as if it is going through a slim cushion of glaze; if the tool hits the pot right away the glaze is very thin.

Glaze on glaze effects are usually mottled or striated, with generally pleasing variations in color resulting from one glaze "boiling up" through another in the molten state. If you really want several colors to "run" together in a fluid manner, apply the colored glazes and then apply a coat of clear glaze over all.

7. Putting texture in glaze

Sand of varying sorts, dirt, tiny particles of grog (bits of ground, previously fired clay shards), or combustible materials such as coffee grounds can be added to glaze, or to engobe. In engobe non-combustible materials stay put, in glaze they move around during the firing.

8. Wax or tape resist

Wax on top of one glaze in a pattern, with another glaze applied over, burns out, leaving the second glaze in a design against the first. Tape works the same way but is pulled off before firing.

9. Sgraffito through glaze

Scratch through the raw glaze to the bisque pot (which may have been engobed). If the glaze is matt (matts do not run), it will hold your drawing during firing.

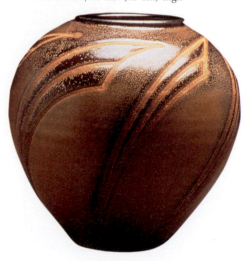

Rick Malmgren uses tape against the stoneware pot to make a resist glaze pattern, fired to cone 6; 10 ins. (25 cm) high

SAMPLE COMMERCIAL GLAZES

Commercial glazes are available from many companies in the United States and the rest of the world. The color quantity, shelf life of the glaze, and cost may vary. Most companies will send samples or sell groups of glazes for your own testing. The cone 05 and 6 samples on this page, from Georgie's Ceramic Supply, Portland, Oregon, were tested in my electric kilns. Color brochures of glazes from the manufacturer, produced in large quantity, may not be true to the actual fired glaze surface or color, but you have to buy from the catalog and make your own tests before using.

Two catalog pages from "Georgie's Ceramic and Clay Company," Portland, Oregon, USA, showing their prepared c/05 and c/6 glazes

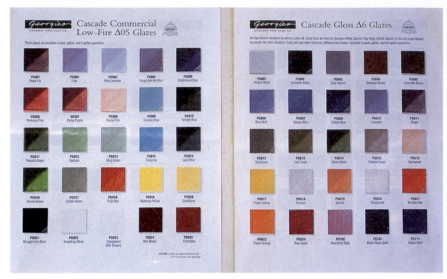

Tests of the same glazes (in the same order as the above catalog pages) were applied by dipping on bisqued beige-colored clay tiles, fired to c/05 and c/6 oxidation as stated in their catalog. It is impossible for the catalog to be as accurate as your own tests

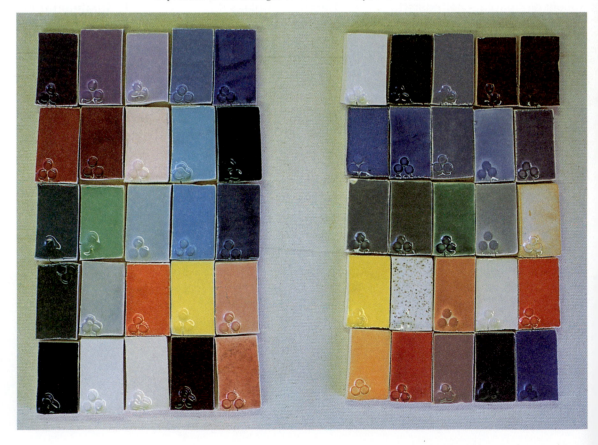

GLASS IS A CERAMIC MATERIAL

It is important to understand that glass is a large component of the ceramic industry and of the artist's ceramic vocabulary. Glass was probably discovered by the ancient Egyptians, about 5000 BC, and glaze was probably discovered simultaneously. Glass stands alone; glaze must adhere to something like clay or metal. It follows that glaze is a glass composition with a binder added – usually alumina in the form of clay – to bond the glassy surface to the pot. Simply said, the ▶ chemical composition of glass, with clay added, can make glaze.

Slumped glass in a clay mold. On the other hand, a glass object can be "slumped" in a bisqued clay mold by placing over the mold a sheet of glass covered with glaze or a low-temperature flux such as frit or ground glass, with oxides or stains added for color, fired to the point where the glass slightly melts into the clay form. The dividing compound to keep the two from sticking together is at least half an inch of powdered talc or powdered red clay.

Depending on the glass used, fire in an electric kiln with a door you can open periodically to watch the glass soften. When you see the glass edges shimmer like melting ice, turn off the kiln, which will probably be about c/1. Do not open the kiln until it is absolutely cold or your glass piece will crack. Shallow clay molds with no undercuts work best for slumping glass. Alternatively, glass can be blown with a pipe or cast in a mold.

Jun Kaneko, who usually works in clay, recently enlarged his huge ideas vocabulary to encompass cast glass at the Portland, Oregon, Bull's Eye Factory. There he was able to continue his emphasis on scale with their facilities and materials, and held an exhibition in their gallery.

Jun Kaneko's layered glass sculpture is 9½ x 19½ x 3 ins. (24 x 50 x 7.5 cm)

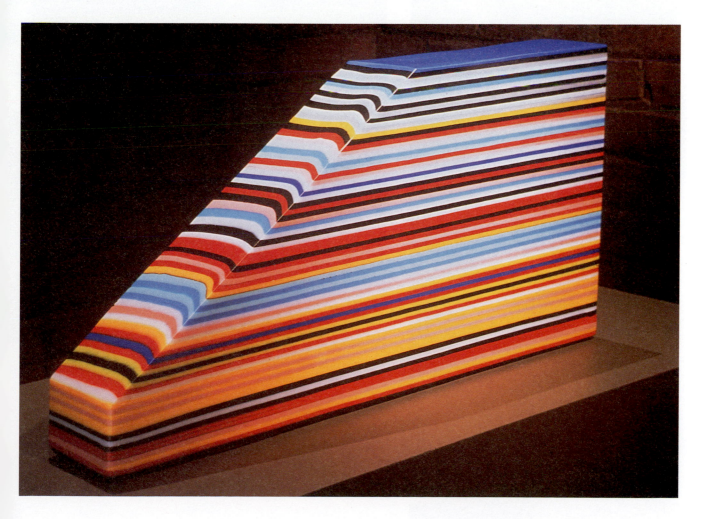

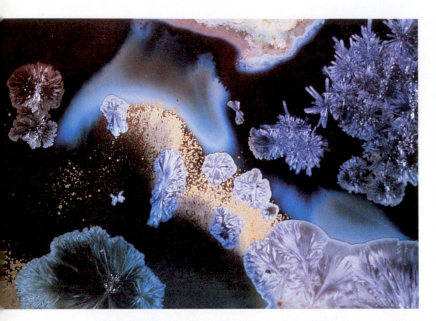

PUTTING TEXTURE IN GLAZE

Various chemicals (see below) can cause textural changes in glazes during firing. Alternatively, test additions to glaze such as sand, iron filings, dirt, and the like

Crystalline glazes are not exactly for beginners, because of the precision required to grow the crystals and catch them at the proper moment in the fire. Simply stated, add 20% or more zinc oxide to any high-temperature glaze; hold the kiln for several hours at cone 5 on the cooling side of the firing, and tomorrow you may have crystals. Detail of Sally Resnik's crystalline glaze

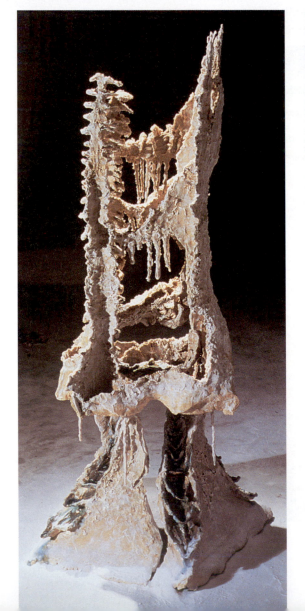

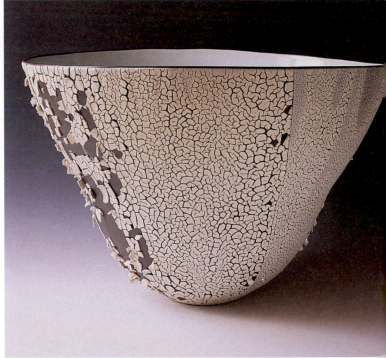

Cryolite can be very reactive during firing, and sometimes continues activity after it has cooled. Sally Resnik experiments with a thick application of 50% cryolite and 50% talc, which, after salt-firing at cone 4, will continue to grow crystals

Crawl glazes can be made with excess magnesium carbonate (20% or more), which causes the glaze to mound up during firing, or they can be made by applying a clay slip over a glaze: example above by Claude Champy (France)

Keep records

Do your own thing, but keep a record of everything you do. You think you will remember but you won't. Every overlap, every thickness of application, every glaze layer, in short, every nuance should be recorded. After every firing analyze your records and make notes. What you called thin may not appear thin after the firing, or what you thought was thick may not show thick. Perhaps the glaze disappeared because it was very much too thin or it ran all over the kiln because it was too thick.

When you have a number of records and many kiln firings, take the time to make a general analysis of them all, and write this in a separate place to refer to from time to time before you begin to glaze another kiln load. This is the way to teach yourself and to put your experience into intelligent practice.

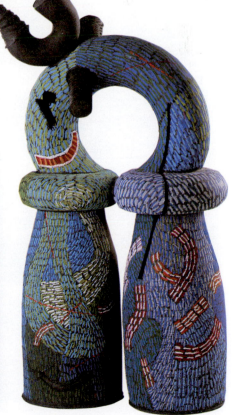

ABOVE Paul Berube's stoneware and unglazed bone china is *painted with acrylics*

"**Room-temperature**" **glazes** refers to ceramic coatings that are not heat-treated in a kiln. Usually, this implies that the clay piece has been bisque fired. These coatings can be house paint, oil or acrylic paint, poster paint, flock, fabric, crayon, or any other kind of pigment or material, but this may destroy the function of a vessel!

BELOW Lisa Wolkow's sculpture is coated with *colored wax crayons*

RIGHT Bill Farrell's stoneware sculpture is colored with *crayon and brushed pigment*

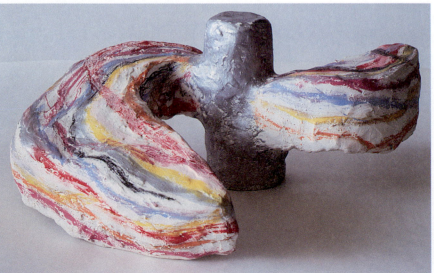

COLOR TESTING

These are examples of color line-blend experiments made by students of Jan Peterson at Phoenix College, Phoenix, Arizona. The top members of each test are the same, but each glaze batch varies. See Compendium, page 192, for explanation of how to make a line blend test with percentage additions of colorants to a basic glaze, and the following 50–50 mixtures.

Top member % additions to base glaze: (tiles left to right) 1. rutile 10%, 2. copper carbonate 4%, 3. red iron oxide 5%, 4. cobalt carbonate 1%, 5. manganese carbonate 5%

Clay bodies are different but all tests were fired at c/10 reduction. Note that the test in (4) shows the glaze over four clay bodies on each tile, indicating the amazing differences made to glazes by different colored clays.

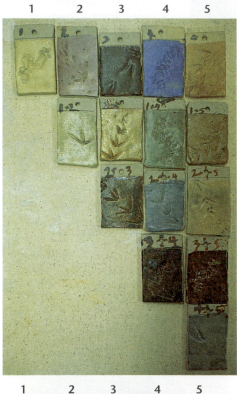

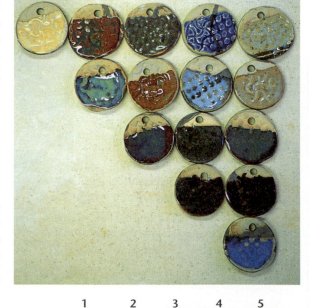

◄ Glaze batch 1

potash feldspar	50%
dolomite	22%
whiting	3%
china clay	25%
	100%

Glaze batch 2 ►

potash feldspar	77%
Gerstley borate	11%
whiting	11%
tin oxide	1%
	100%

◄ Glaze batch 3

soda feldspar	55%
(preferably nepheline syenite)	
spodumene	23%
Gerstley borate	5%
soda ash	3%
ball clay	14%
	100%

Glaze batch 4 ►

potash feldspar	36%
dolomite	18%
Gerstley borate	4%
whiting	4%
china clay	22%
silica	16%
	100%

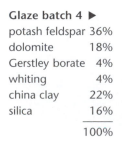

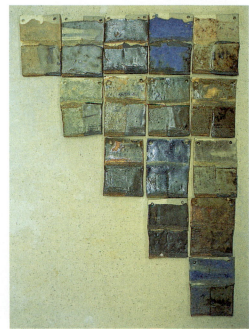

Experimentation

You can experiment with percentage or "part" additions to glazes with which you are already familiar, or you can run a line blend with five or more top members (see opposite) and make 50–50 mixtures. Color is always a percentage addition to a given batch. Always use parts of 100, or parts of 10; your base should always add up to 100 or to 10. If you make changes within the batch, keep it adding up to 100 or to 10; if you make additions to the batch, add them in percentage amounts on top.

Fusion button tests can be made of various raw materials by placing a thimble or crucible full of the dry material upside down on a fired clay tile which has raised edges to catch the melt if it occurs. After you see the results of the fired buttons you can begin to think of combinations from the visual look of the melts – or non-melts. At the same time you can mix each material with water, paint it on a bisqued test tile, and fire it at the same temperature as the fusion buttons. The buttons work like large amounts of a given material, the painted tiles show the effect of a smaller amount. When

you make 50–50 or 33–33–33 combinations, remember those facts.

Beginners especially need to make tests, but all potters experiment some of the time to add variety to their own work.

Line blends

Any known glaze, or any fusion button glaze, or any made-up glaze can be experimented with on a five-member (or more) "line blend," where the five top members are blended 50–50 with each other (see Compendium, page 192). You choose the percentages of colors you want to try, or you could choose to add percentages of other raw materials, to see how they would change the glaze.

GLAZE IMPROVIZATIONS

Try to think of everything that might melt at the temperature you fire. Or if the material didn't melt, would it be interesting to add it to a glaze or to a single material, such as ground glass, that will melt?

Below: garbage glazes. **Raw**, top row, left to right: green bottle glass, screws and bolts with blue plastic wire, dried lettuce leaf, crushed aluminum soda pop can, copper pennies, string soaked in salt. **Fired**, bottom row, **to c/5 oxidation**. At c/04 some "found objects" will melt, but at higher temperature the effects are more interesting. At c/10 most of the objects' shapes will be obliterated by the melt

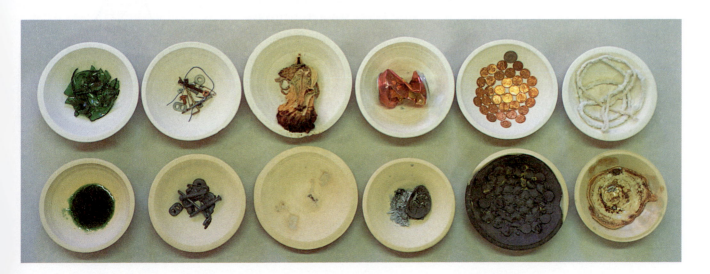

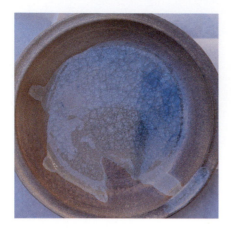

Fired broken glass

ASH GLAZES

Ash from any plant, vegetable or tree material, can make a glaze, or ashes can be added to known glazes to change the effect. Ash patina can also be created inside a kiln over a period of days in a wood-fire

"SLIP" GLAZES AND OVERGLAZE ENAMEL

Most low-temperature red clays and certain shales will form glazes when melted at temperatures from cone 5 to cone 10. One of the most famous "slip" glazes from crushed shale is the so-called kaki, showing brown here among the overglaze enamels on this bottle by Shoji Hamada (Japan). The overglaze enamel colors were painted on the already fired kaki and clear glazed stoneware bottle; the pot was refired to a much lower temperature, cone 013, just to melt the enamels but not to melt the previously fired glazes

Crushed rocks such as granite, stones such as agate, broken glass bottles, pieces of metal such as copper, should be tested alone on dog-dish-shaped bisque tiles, and in combination with known glazes.

Various plant materials have always been glaze materials in the Orient. The most notable is *wood ash*; the ashes of some woods will melt at 2300° F (1260° C); most ashes will definitely melt when mixed 50–50 with clay, feldspar, soda ash, or borax. In addition other ashes such as those of seaweed or flowers, and volcanic ash will give appealing results.

Some flowers and plants will make their mark, if placed in or wrapped round a clay vessel, in a high-temperature firing for stoneware or porcelain. Plants contain at least soda, potassium, calcium, and silica – all glaze ingredients. Such things as seaweed, rice straw, wheat, ferns, and the like will volatilize during firing and will leave the imprint of their shape in a sheen on the clay below.

It is important to test and keep testing. Artists continue to grow by trying new things

The metal wire found in copper, stainless steel, and brass kitchen scrub pads can be pulled apart and wound round a clay piece, then glazed over or left bare. Glaze will melt the wire more and will bring out its true color. If left unglazed, the wire will probably melt into a feathered line on the vessel and will have a metallic black color. Alternatively, the wire can be placed over an unfired piece that has been glazed, and in the firing it will melt down into the glaze.

Low-fire common surface clays will usually become glazes when fired at 2100° F (1150° C); we call these "slip" glazes. In the United States the most famous clay for this purpose was named Albany Slip and was mined near that city in New York State. The supply has run out, but other similar clays are being mined that give the same result. It is easy to prospect your own surface clay from a creek bed or near a lake, or in the desert in a dry lake or riverbed. You could try clay from a brickyard or from a sewer-pipe or brick plant; fired high enough, a glaze *will* result from a low-fire clay.

Shoji Hamada, the famous potter and National Treasure of Japan, used a crushed shale from Mashiko, his pottery village, which when melted at 2300° F (1260° C) was, as he said, the color of ripe persimmons on the 24th day of October. His name for the glaze was Kaki, the Japanese word for persimmon, and he dubbed it the "specialty of the house" from his studio because the color quality and surface luster were so popular.

Shoji Hamada's "kaki" slip glaze made from local shale ground fine and applied over a clear glaze, wood-fired c/10 in his noborigama; later his painted overglaze enamel decoration was wood-fired to c/013

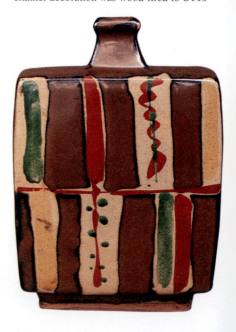

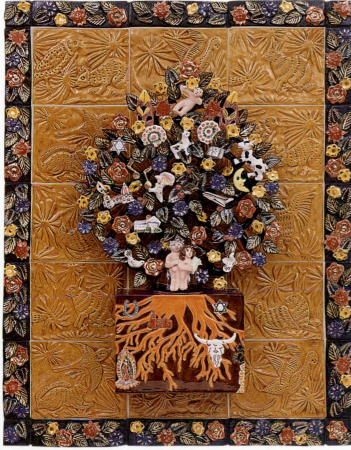

Karen Koblitz's piece uses commercial underglaze heavily painted under clear glaze; the gold luster detailing is accomplished in a final, lower-temperature fire, 1300° F (690° C), 36 x 24 ins. (91 x 61 cm)

DECORATION

Commercial pigments, glazes, and china paints can be used alone or in conjunction with your own glaze batches

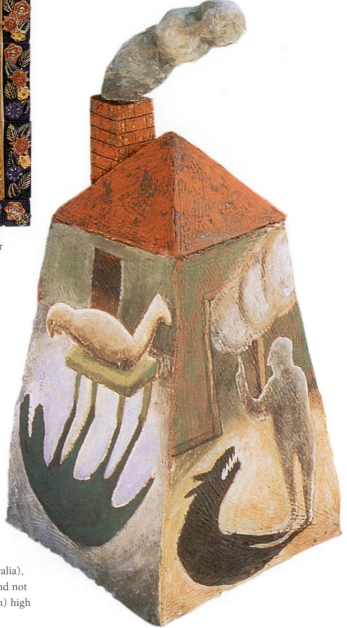

A sculpture by Sandra Taylor (Australia), is painted with commercial stains and not glazed, fired cone 04; 18 ins. (46 cm) high

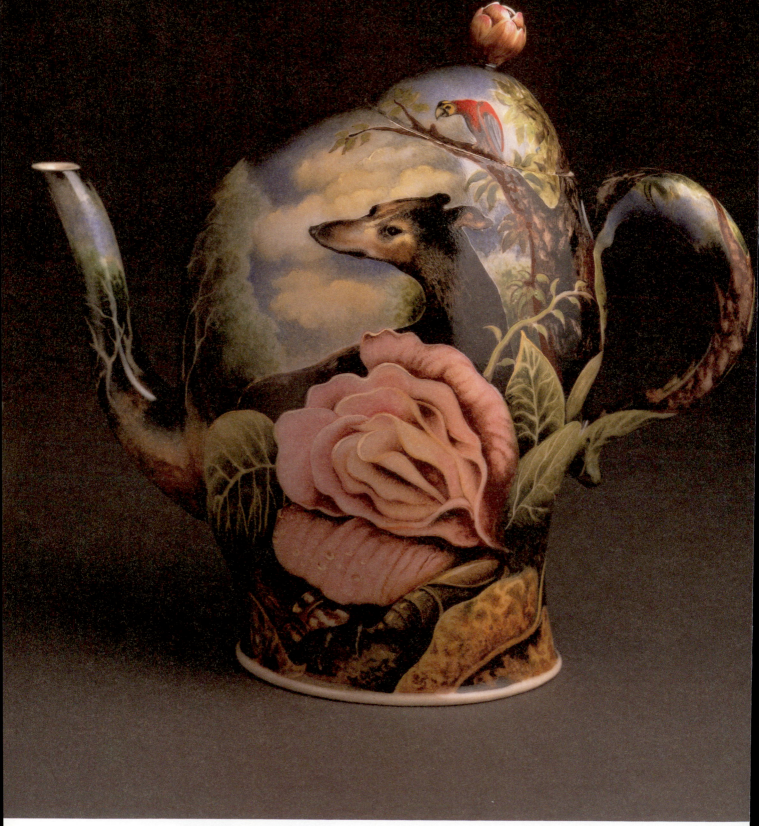

Kurt Weiser makes his own molds, casts his porcelain, glazes, **china paints**, and fires his work
several times. This teapot is a fine example of virtuoso china painting; 12 x 12 ins. (30 x 30 cm)

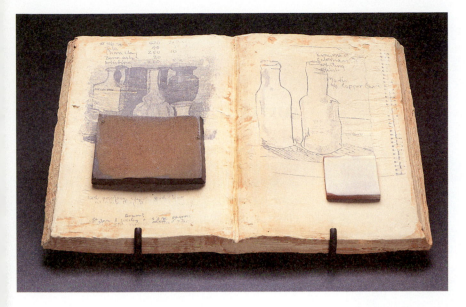

LEFT Nancy Selvin's sculpture is made by xeroxing images from her own journals onto transparent film. After reversing the film and copying the reversed image on regular xerox paper, she transfers it onto a finished ceramic piece with a non-toxic solvent; the reversed image now reads correctly

BELOW Two illustrations of decal overglaze technique (decal is a commercial process for applying the same decoration to hundreds of pieces):

To make a ceramic decal for his sculptures Les Lawrence (1) **uses a magnetic laser printer** with iron oxide in the toner, printing onto decal paper and fixing with a clear lacquer spray. (2) **The decal design is soaked in water** to loosen the image so that it and its coating can be slid onto the glazed piece. (3) **The color variation** resulting from different firing temperatures: below cone 010 is insufficient for a secure image; at cone 04 the decal fuses into the glaze and at cone 1 the color bleaches out

Charles Krafft silkscreens ceramic pigments onto flexible decal paper and applies the transfer onto earthenware, as in this plate

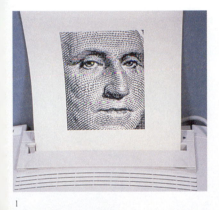

1

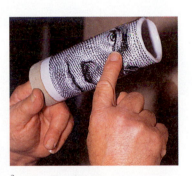

2

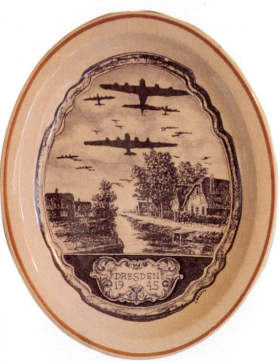

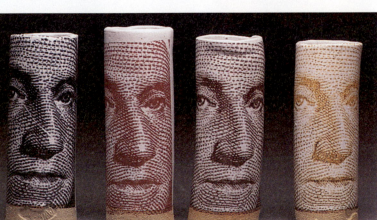

3

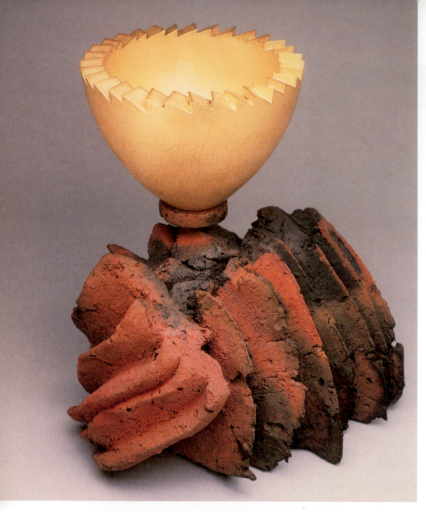

LUSTER GLAZES

Lusters and china paints are usually purchased commercially to be painted on bisque or glazed ware and require a final low fire from cone 022 to 013 depending on the desired effect. In fact, you can fire a piece very many times with different glazes, beginning at the top temperature and coming down every cone if you want. Eventually the piece will break from stress

Adrian Saxe's assembled sculpture includes a porcelain cup with gold luster on a base raku-fired with a cadmium red glaze

Elena Karina's handbuilt porcelain shell form is bisque fired at cone 10 and refired with platinum luster at cone 013; 24 ins. (61 cm) high

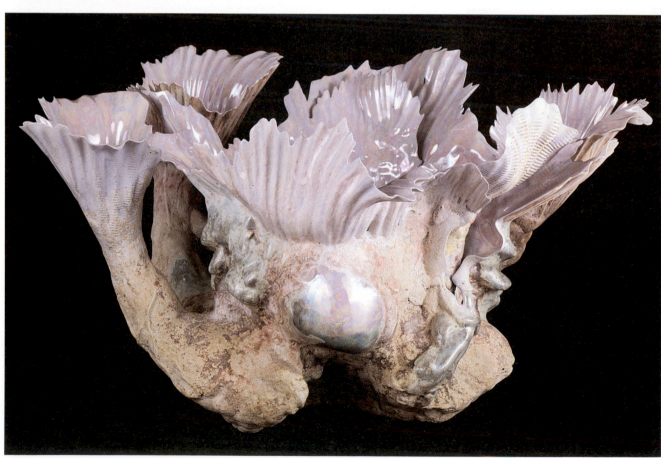

RIGHT Joan Takayama Ogawa's sea urchin cup is thrown, hand-built, and fired to cone 08 for the copper glaze, china painted and fired to cone 013, and finally gold luster fired to cone 019

BELOW Regis Brodie's porcelain kaki glazed bottle is refired at cone 019 with platinum luster

BELOW RIGHT Ralph Bacerra makes his own molds, casts porcelain, and fires in high-temperature reduction. In this piece the celadon glaze has crazed, perhaps due to the many subsequent low-temperature firings for the multicolored and gold lustered surfaces

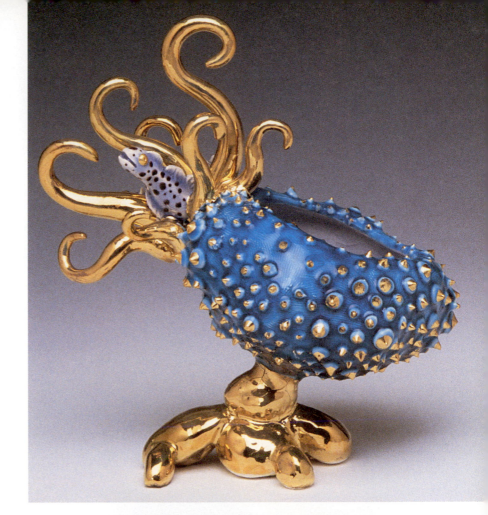

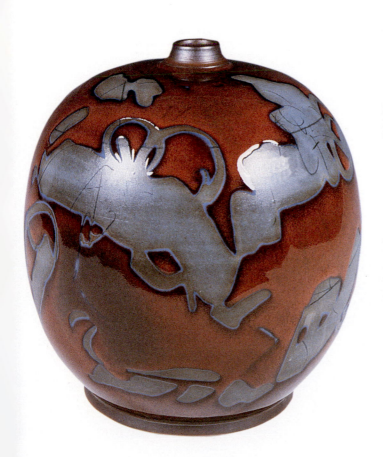

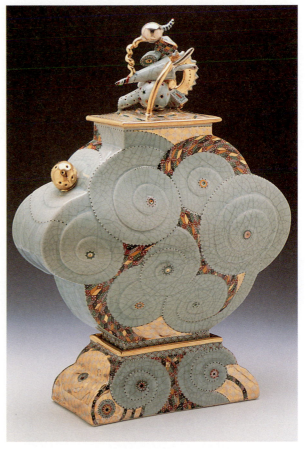

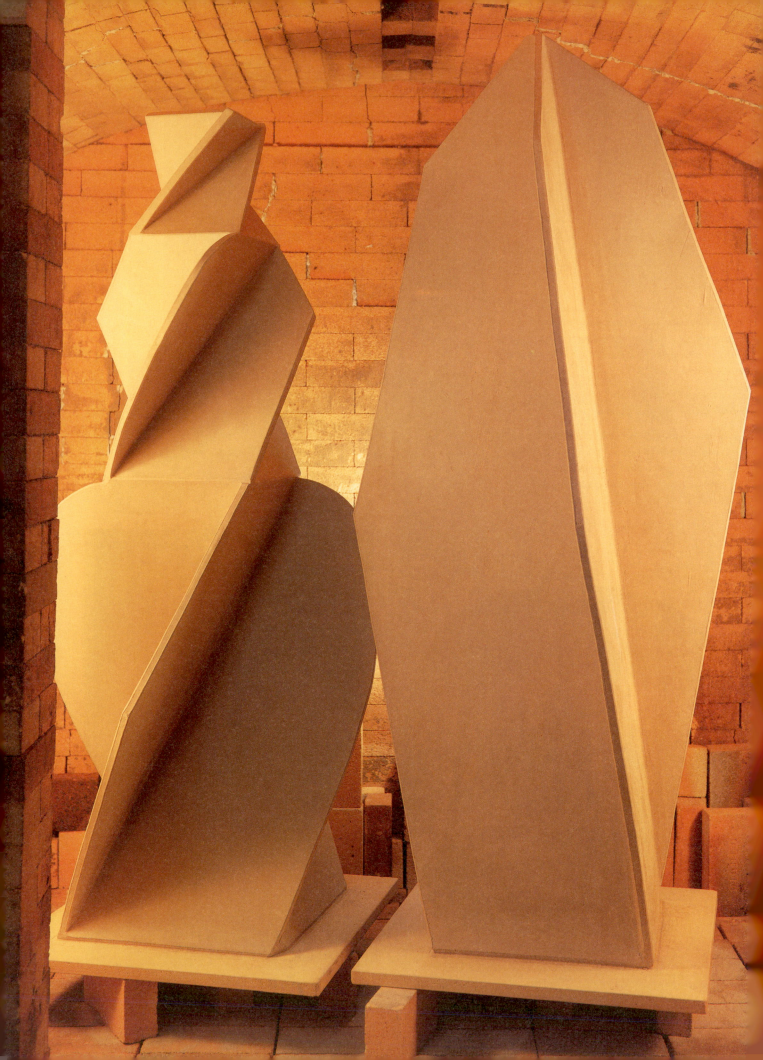

5

FIRING CERAMICS

HEAT PRINCIPLES

Ancient peoples fired pottery on the ground, with twigs and other combustible materials between and over the work. In some societies the mound of pots was covered with earth to give some insulation. In China, where huge figures have been excavated in recent years at Xian, archaeologists surmise that they were probably bonfired lying horizontally in a pit, or possibly hand-made bricks were piled over the sculptures to retain heat; the bricks would have been removed from round the figure when the firing was over.

Native Americans fire one or a few pots at a time, in an open bonfire fueled with wood, or with organic material such as cow, sheep, squirrel, or deer dung.

A bonfire reaches red heat, 1300° F (700° C), the lowest temperature at which clay will become chemically hard enough to be somewhat durable. Common surface clays, found everywhere in the world, become more dense at low temperatures than other clays and are the most widely used by tribal peoples.

In most parts of the ancient world, firing was accomplished in caves, or pits in the ground, or in bricked-up cylinders with fire underneath and a lid of some sort on top. In India and Nepal, many "kilns" are piles of bricks or pots interlaced with combustible material

Two huge slab-built sculptures by John Mason have been loaded into his kiln ready for bisque firing: Figure 60½ x 28 x 25 ins. (154 x 71 x 63.5 cm); Spear 66½ x 29 x 29 ins. (169 x 74 x 74 cm)

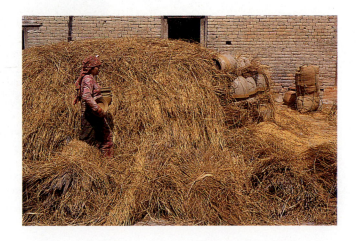

In Nepal, pots are stacked amidst heaps of combustible straw for fuel. This huge mound will be covered with clay and ash, lit, and allowed to smolder several days

such as twigs and brush, then an overlay of insulating clay is added, with more brush. This is lit to become a large and fast-burning fire, then allowed to smolder for a few days. Astonishingly, such methods of firing are still the norm in many parts of the world. Many contemporary potters enjoy experimenting with these primitive techniques in a quest for unusual effects.

The important point is that clay needs at least red heat to become durable enough to use. Anything that burns can be used as fuel. Various woods are preferable for ceramic firing in countries where trees are plentiful, or where they are planted in a sustainable program. Engineering charts will give you the BTU (British Thermal Unit) rating of different woods, dungs, petroleum fuels, and kinds of electricity; but red heat is the highest temperature that open-fire wood and dungs can yield.

Fossil fuels – such as gas, oil, kerosene, and coal – and electricity produce higher temperatures when contained. Historically, as soon as petroleum fuels were discovered they were used to fire claywork in pits in the ground, a method that can still be witnessed, particularly in the Middle East. Most cultures use these fuels today in kilns.

KILNS

When the first "kilns" or enclosures around the ceramic bier were developed, perhaps in about 5000 B.C. in China, heat could be contained, reflected, and refracted, making possible the attainment of still higher temperatures. Eventually the Chinese became the first to learn to fire at a high enough temperature to turn a

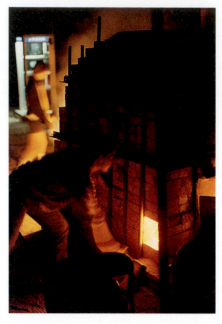

Throwing salt into a downdraft outdoor kiln in a night-time firing at Idyllwild School of Music and the Arts, California, where Susan Peterson taught for 30 summers. Firing salt or soda at night helps you monitor the flames and see the volatilization. Firing in the dark for a reduction atmosphere helps monitor the color of the flames and the back-pressure

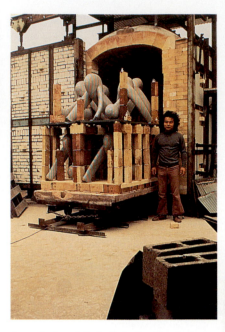

An updraft car kiln built by Jun Kaneko in Los Angeles c. 1965

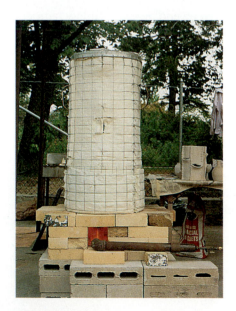

Rick Hirsch has constructed a tall ceramic-fiber kiln for his raku ware which can be fired with natural gas or propane

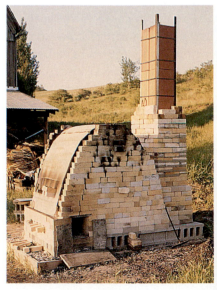

Robert Turner's downdraft wood kiln; the wood goes into the large hole at the front, while the smaller holes control the draft; Alfred, New York, c. 1980

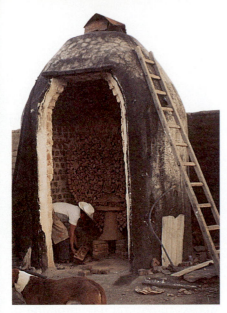

A very tall kiln in Metopec, Mexico, for firing large "trees of life"

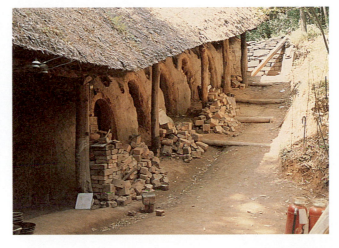

The five-chamber woodfired noborigama kiln that Shoji Hamada used to fire; bricks for closing each chamber are piled in front. Mashiko, Japan, c. 1970

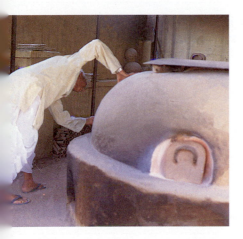

Kripal Singh, the well-known potter of Jaipur, India, tending his updraft kiln

Kilns can be built of refractory brick or any other insulating high-temperature material, such as the space materials "kaowool" or "fiberfax," or they can be natural caves or holes in the ground

RIGHT AND BELOW Susan Peterson's 1955 updraft kiln, still in use. Twelve burners are under the kiln; center four control bottom of chamber, eight outside control heat at top – these are on separate gauges; pilot has a separate valve; excess gas jets to aid reduction are next to inside burners and also controlled by a gauge, below

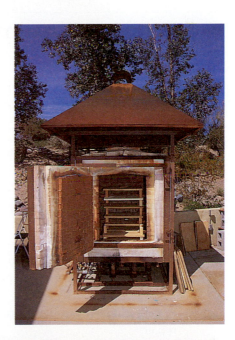

china clay body into fine porcelain. Porcelain-making temperatures could not have been attained without the development of kilns – or enclosures – to retain the heat.

Kiln design is ancient but has hardly changed today: there is the single chamber hill-kiln called an anagama, the multi-chamber hill-kiln called a noborigama, and variations; the box or round structure with a side or top-loading door that can have fire under, around, or above the ware; the "tunnel" kiln, through which pottery

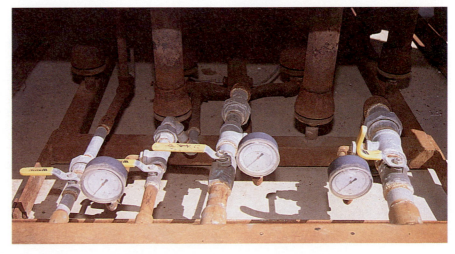

moves on a firing and cooling temperature curve; the "envelope" kiln that moves over the stationary ware; and many other shapes and types.

Most furnaces that potters use today are fueled with natural gas or propane, or oil. Electricity is also used to fire kilns, although it does not offer the possibility of different atmospheres, as do petroleum fuels. And firing with wood has become very popular for the fun of it – camaraderie builds up in a team that must almost continuously stoke the kiln to top temperature over a period of several days and nights. Such a lengthy period is needed in order to achieve the fascinating colorations and flashings that develop from the build-up of wood ash and the play of the fire.

The kind of fuel and the way a kiln is designed make quite a difference in the firing. Certain glazes are more affected than others. Oil and coal are "dirtier" fuels than gas or propane; electricity gives only a neutral atmosphere – neither oxidizing nor reducing (see page 138) – which makes certain metallic oxide glaze colorants impossible. Some potters build and use several different types of kilns to exploit the different effects obtainable.

Gas kilns

Many areas of the world do not have access to natural gas; propane or bottled gas is the alternative. Gas is

ELECTRIC VERSUS GAS-PETROLEUM KILNS	
Electric	**Gas**
1. Can be plugged into household current up to cone 04; needs 220–240v for high temperature	1. Is best installed in the open or in an outside building. Optimum requirement: 8 ins. (20 cm) of water-column (¼ lb./250 gm. equivalent) gas pressure at the kiln, but 2 or 3 ins. (5 or 7.5 cm) will do; pipeline size up to 3-inch (7.5 cm) diameter, depending on distance from natural gas meter or propane tank
2. Easily moved; doesn't take much room	2. Not easily moved; gas should be installed by a licensed plumber; generally kiln size is large
3. Low temperature and high temperature require different elements; specify	3. Burners can blow out during firing; buy safety features
4. Initially cheaper but wants frequent repair	4. Costs more but almost never needs repair
5. Top load is cheapest, easiest to make yourself; hinged lids and doors cost more	5. Catenary or sprung arch kilns are easily built by you; gas kilns, larger and better insulated than electrics, cool slowly
6. Can be made of lightweight "insulating" firebrick, or entirely of ceramic fiber; fiber does not hold heat, kiln cools fast	6. Updraft, downdraft, crossdraft kilns are variations that can be designed with refractory hard brick or soft brick, or brick lined with fiber
7. Firing atmosphere is neutral – for more oxygen leave peeps out, and leave lid or door cracked; reduction atmosphere is possible with mothballs or other carbon-releasing materials	7. Fires easily any atmosphere, oxidizing or reducing; this perhaps most important difference is easily controlled and easily changed

the cleanest, probably the easiest to control, and the fastest-firing fuel. The first precautionary rule is always to light a gas kiln with the door or lid open, and with the damper, wherever it is, open. Do not let the fire blow out; if it does, open the kiln again to relight the burners. Gas provides you with complete control of the kiln atmosphere: fully oxidizing, in-between neutral, or partial reduction of oxygen.

Electric kilns

Firing an electric kiln is relatively easy compared with firing wood or petroleum. Electric kilns, as manufactured everywhere in the world, can be purchased with additional gadgets that will turn the kiln on and off, devices that can be programmed to turn it up, or thermostats that hold the heat at a given temperature. Small electric kilns can be installed on regular household current; larger ones require more volts.

Electric kilns are available as top-loading models with a lid, or side-loading with a door, in virtually any size. The simplest and cheapest are built of lightweight refractory brick or ceramic fiber, in a circular design, and with rings that stack for easy loading and for adding on when extra height is needed. More expensive models are square or rectangular, with hinged or guillotined doors. Today fixtures are available that will vent an electric kiln, which can be a help in gold and luster firings.

In the photographs, a Skutt kiln is shown whole and with the rings removed. It is interesting that Carlton Ball and I, teaching at the University of Southern California many years ago, were the first to test the previous generation of kilns and potter's wheels developed by Jim Skutt's father.

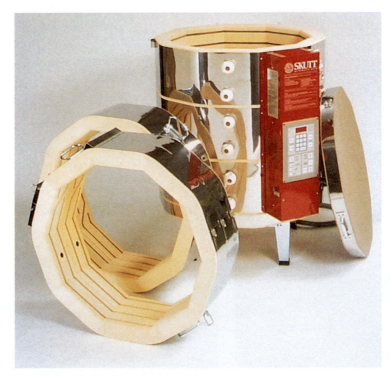

Many companies in the world manufacture commercial electric and gas kilns. Today gadgets for computerized firing control are available from simple to complicated and from inexpensive to very expensive.

Electric kilns, such as the Skutt Kiln (Portland, Oregon) pictured here, are particularly useful for artists firing sculptures of varying scale; unlimited rings can be added to increase height

COMMERCIAL READY-MADE KILNS

Manufactured kilns are available in most parts of the world. In general the differences are few: gas, wood, or electric; side loading or top loading; round, oval, square, or rectangular; size varying from one to 60 cubic feet or more; refractory brick or ceramic fiber; in sections or one-piece; with pyrometric instrumentation or without; with computer controllers or without; with "kiln sitter" turn-offs (never to be trusted) or without.

For gas or wood-fired commercial kilns, choose updraft (burners on the bottom, flue at the top), downdraft (burners at front or back, flue opening – damper – at back) or crossdraft (burners on two sides, flue opening – damper – at back). I like updraft.

Kilns do not exactly wear out, but they mellow, and firings may change with age. Bricks do erode after many years of use, or after salt or soda firings, and may need to be repaired or replaced; soft-brick kilns are more fragile than hard-brick, but hard brick takes longer to heat up and cool. The choice of fiber as opposed to brick is controversial. Some potters like a fiber lining over one course of brick; some potters are addicted to ceramic fiber bricks; some

BUILDING A WOODFIRED ANAGAMA KILN

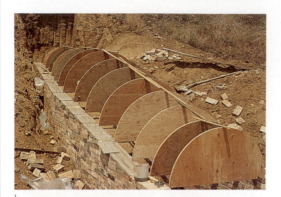

John Balistreri building an "anagama," Japanese-style single-chamber climbing kiln, in Ohio:

1. **Plywood ribs** make an arch support for the plywood form of the kiln

2. **Brick is laid over the form**, which can be burned out in the first firing or can be pulled out after the bricks are mortared

3. John, Ken Ferguson, and a group of students **fire the kiln**

4. **Looking through the door** of the kiln while a log is inserted during firing

5. **This exhibition piece** by John Balistreri documents with slabs and pots an entire firing in the 60 ft (18.3 m.) long anagama kiln

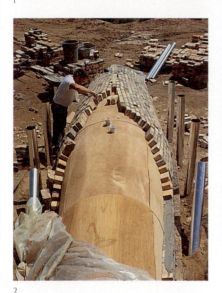

2

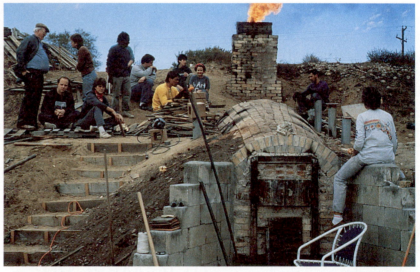

3

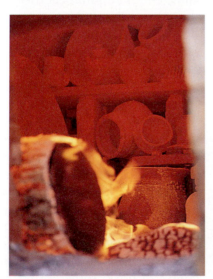

4

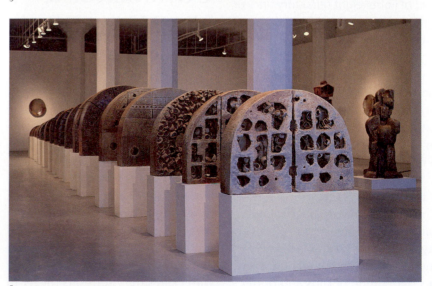

5

potters drape a blanket of fiber over a load of pots and put a burner into the interior. Paperclay kilns (see p. 26) provide an experimental toy for some artists.

Electric kilns are more problematic. Europeans, especially Scandinavians, probably have the most experience with them because electricity has been their basic fuel for such a long time. Electric elements give out quickly and deteriorate over successive firings. Globar and other esoteric elements have a better survival rate, but are costly. Where electricity and natural gas or propane are available, electricity is often more expensive.

For certain kinds of glaze firings – such as colored lusters, gold and platinum, low-temperature bright reds, yellows, oranges (these colors need lots of oxygen) – in electric kilns leave out the peeps and the lid or door cracked for air; for china paints and crystalline glazes, electric kilns may produce a cleaner, more controllable firing. Any fuel will work, but the results may vary.

You certainly can build your own kiln, in which case you need Fred Olsen's *Kiln Book* (see Bibliography). Fred is the only potter we know who makes and sells kiln kits all over the world, along with complete instructions.

Cone and firing charts are at the back of this book (pages 143, 195).

WHY BUILD YOUR OWN KILN?

Like making your own clay body and concocting your own glaze, to build your own kiln is a similar triumph.

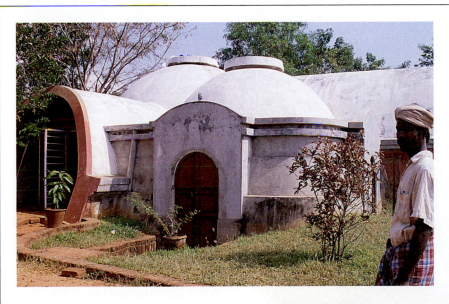

FIRED HOUSE

Ray Meeker has been building fired houses for the past fifteen years in the area of Pondicherry, South India. This staggering feat is accomplished by building vaults and domes with handmade brick and firing with wood inside the structure for many days. The house-kiln needs to be full of claywork to hold the heat, so bricks and other clay products are stacked inside. After firing, the house is plastered. Recent tests with coal dust as fuel, mixed into the clay-mud brick, have greatly reduced fuel consumption

After firing, the house is plastered. Meeker originally conceived the idea as a solution to the low-cost housing problem in India, but unfortunately wood is too rare and costly to make it practicable

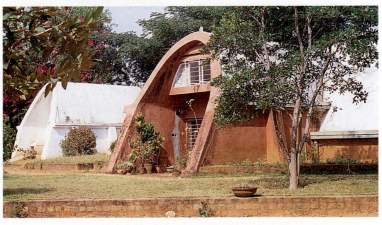

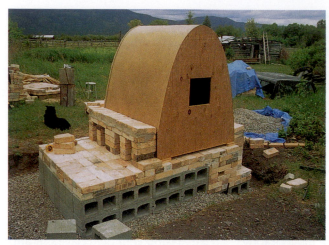

Catenary arch form constructed of plywood will support the brick arch for this wood-burning downdraft kiln; exit flues begin the stack on the left

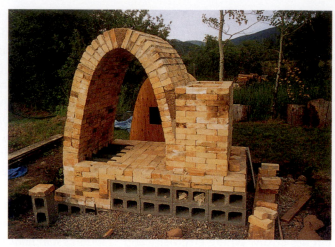

After bricking the arch and building up the stack, the wood form is removed

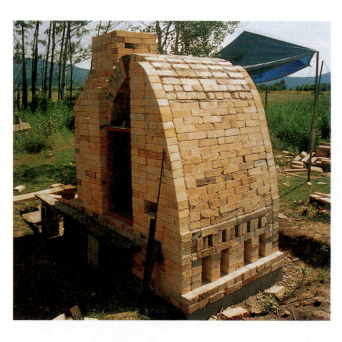

The nearly finished kiln, with door opening, which will be bricked up for firing, shows height of stack and stokeholes for wood fuel. Note: use refractory bricks that will be stable at higher temperatures than you need, such as "K26" bricks for a cone 10 kiln. Two courses should be enough

FIRING PRINCIPLES

1. Clay bodies shrink as they dry, and in the early stages of firing; they become more dense as the fire gets hotter, and finally warp or melt if the heat is too great for that particular clay.

2. The rate of heating and cooling is determined by the volume of the load in the kiln: the more ware, the longer it will take to fire and cool.

3. How the ware is distributed in the chamber, evenly or not, makes a great difference to the atmosphere and reaction to heat in a kiln. Most potters endure a long series of mistakes before coming to an understanding of the importance of how the kiln is packed.

> It is important in stacking a kiln to leave enough spaces everywhere for even heat distribution during the firing

Most kilns are built of commercially purchased "soft brick" graded for specific temperatures; hard brick is cheaper, takes longer for heat absorption, withstands wear, and is essential for wood, salt, and soda fires. Books will help you – see the Bibliography.

If natural gas is your choice, the gas provider will furnish you with the amount of gas you need and tell you what size line from the meter will deliver that. If the kiln is electric, the type of service you have determines the size and temperature.

In the United States there are no rules about kilns, as there are for water heaters, boilers, stoves, and the like. Safety tells you to install a gas kiln 4 feet from any existing wall, with plenty of space for you to move about and for ventilation.

Here, potters Matt Sleightholm and Julie Wills build a downdraft kiln in Montana.

4. Ceramics fire by heat radiation from the walls of the kiln and from the other surrounding pots.

5. Clay pieces must be properly structured in the first place, to withstand the weight and shrinkage movement that takes place during firing. Every different clay body will react differently.

6. A kiln should be fired slowly up to top temperature and allowed to cool down slowly. How a kiln is fired has many variations and the right degree of control can be discovered only through many trials and much practice. In general, let the kiln cool before opening it at least as many hours as it took to fire it.

For firing curves see page 143.

TEMPERATURE INDICATORS

The color of the heat changes in a kiln as the temperature goes up. Most of us are familiar with the orange flame of a bonfire, which reaches a maximum of about 1300° F (700° C). As the temperature rises above that, the color becomes cherry red, then lighter red, until finally at 2300° F (1260° C) the color in the enclosed kiln chamber is nearly white, hence the term white-hot. In China and Japan, where the first stoneware and porcelain products were made, "reading the fire," that is, reading the color of the fire to gauge the corresponding temperatures, became a special profession. Fire readers were hired by potters when it was time to run a kiln.

About one hundred years ago Seger in Germany and Orton in America,

SET CONES CORRECTLY

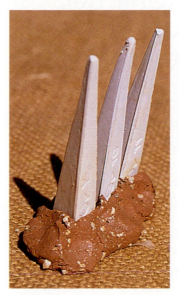

WRONG   RIGHT

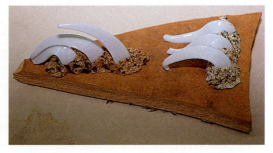

LEFT Cones should be properly set in a pack of clay laced with grog and with holes punched in. Face the cones forward, so that they will fall without touching each other

ABOVE Wrong setting on the left: cones fall against each other. Correct setting on the right: cones fall free to provide accurate temperature measure

more or less simultaneously, devised a system of temperature measurement based on the slumping of certain clay body compositions at certain temperatures. Both men used **cone** shapes, narrow triangular forms of clay-glaze mixtures, to indicate their temperature scales.

These cones are now commercially manufactured, numbered according to the melting temperatures on the Orton or the Seger scale (see page 195). 2000° F (1095° C) is the mean heat, the melting point of cast iron. Cone 1 and cone 01 are designated immediately on either side of the mean temperature. So above 2000° F the cone numbers have no zero in front; below 2000° there is a zero in front of each number. Below 2000° the numbers run downwards, from 01 (hotter) to 022 (cooler); above 2000° they run up in ascending order. So 022 is cooler than 010; 010 is cooler than 1; 1 is cooler than 10.

Because each cone is made of ingredients similar to the ware and glazes in the kiln, it is the best direct measurement of the heat treatment of the

ware during the fire. At least one cone should always be used in every firing – take a new one out of the box each time. Generally potters use three cones, one lower and one higher than the middle cone indicating the desired firing temperature, which act as a warning as well as a check to see if over-firing took place.

Cones should be set in a very small amount of groggy clay and placed opposite the vantage hole inside the kiln, so they can be watched. When a cone has bent to the 3 o'clock position, it has reached its temperature. Cones must not touch each other and must be placed in the cone-pack so that they can fall free as one after the other they slump at the end of the firing.

There are approximately 32° F (18° C) of difference between cones, and about twenty minutes of firing time between cones at the end of a normal cycle; this helps you to know when to keep a constant vigil. If the atmosphere is to be controlled at specific points during the firing, cones for many temperatures can be placed in the kiln. If your kiln has a mechanical thermocouple and pyrometric measuring device – which all potters should own and use for efficient firing – **always** include and watch cones inside the kiln.

Small cones for a "cone sitter," often used to shut off an electric kiln, are not the same as regular-sized cones placed inside the kiln, and will not do as a substitute.

Guide-posts for temperature

It is useful to remember some guide-posts for temperatures and cone numbers for special bodies, glazes, or effects, as follows (Orton scale):

> **cone 10**
> 2350° F (1290° C)
> stoneware and porcelain
>
> **cone 5**
> 2150° F (1175° C)
> stoneware
>
> **cone 1/01**
> 2000° F (1095° C)
> melting-point of cast iron
>
> **cone 04**
> 1922° F (1055° C)
> earthenware
>
> **cone 010**
> 1700° F (930° C)
> normal bisque
>
> **cone 013–022**
> 1300° F (700° C)
> lusters, gold

PYROMETRIC TEMPERATURE DEVICES

> The intelligent kiln firer always uses a pyrometer-thermocouple, records a temperature curve during the firing cycle, and analyzes each kiln load's firing curve; this enables the potter to duplicate a good firing or change the curve to improve a bad one

With energy conservation an issue, as well as the price of fuel per firing, it is important to know exactly at what temperature the kiln is at all times, the length of time it has taken to get wherever it is, and what the settings on the kiln were. Some commercial electric kilns have only numbers of hours that can be set, some have just one or two switches that allow little control; commercial gas kilns usually have no instrumentation, but it should be added.

Inexpensive pyrometers can be purchased, with inexpensive chrome-alumel thermocouples, ordinarily usable only for low temperatures. High fire requires a more costly thermocouple, made of platinel or platinum-rhodium. However, the cheap low-temperature chrome-alumel thermocouple can be covered with an 8-gauge, 1-inch (2.5 cm) diameter protection tube made of the nickel alloy inconel, which will protect the couple for many years' use at high fire. Any pyrometer must be calibrated to match the type of thermocouple to which it is attached.

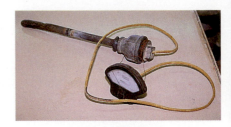

Pyrometers gauge temperature during the firing of a kiln. Heat is registered on a two-wire thermocouple in the kiln and is transferred to the pyrometer. Inexpensive thermocouples for low temperature can be used at high temperature if covered with a nickel alloy protection tube as shown here. Today digital pyrometers are also available

Instrument companies or ceramic suppliers may help you make a proper purchase. You should definitely use a pyrometric measuring device each time you fire, as well as cones in the kiln.

OXIDATION AND REDUCTION ATMOSPHERES

An oxidizing atmosphere is one in which all the molecules in the clay and the glaze have an opportunity to pick up as many oxygen molecules as they need to complete the chemical reaction. Some potters call this a "complete burn." Simply stated, in an organically fueled firing this means a blue rather than an orange flame. Each metallic earth oxide we use for ceramic pigments has an oxidized hue after firing, which can vary according to the oxidized temperature.

Reduction firing means that the amount of oxygen in the atmosphere

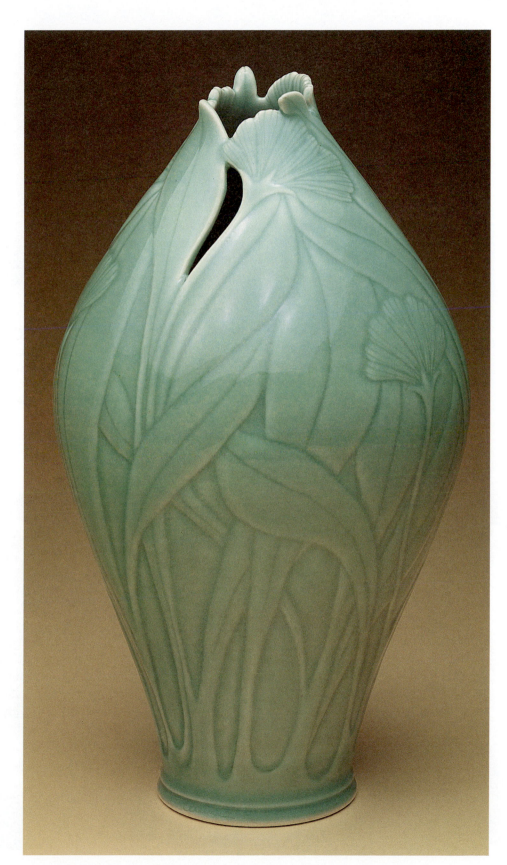

CELADON IN REDUCTION

The beautiful sea-green or jade green glaze color, called **celadon**, developed by the Chinese about A.D. 900 in the Sung Dynasty, still holds mystery for contemporary potters. One quarter to one per cent iron oxide added to a clear glaze, fired in an atmosphere of reduced oxygen, will yield light to dark celadon. Here Elaine Coleman uses a transparent reduction-fired celadon glaze to enhance her design; the glaze flows to puddle in the carvings and break over the smooth surfaces of her thrown porcelain vase.

You must monitor your reduction firings and keep good records, to duplicate results

is reduced. The oxygen supply to the firing chamber must be cut down by:

- inserting more fuel to increase the carbon ratio;
- cutting down the air supply;
- literally smothering the fire.
- Reduction works best from cone 5 to cone 12, but is possible at low fire too.

In a gas or petroleum-fueled furnace, or in a wood fire, reduction is usually accomplished by cutting down the air supply through means of partially closing a damper on the flue. Increasing the amount of fuel to the chamber will increase the proportion of carbon to oxygen. Primitive potters often smother an open fire with wood ash or cow dung to create a black instead of an oxidized red clay color.

Copper reds

The Chinese discovered that a small amount of copper oxide in a glaze, which customarily yields a grassy green or turquoise color in oxidation, would produce an "oxblood" red in reduction.

Since the Chinese Sung dynasty (A.D. 900–1200) potters have continued attempts to achieve orange-reds, pink-reds, purple-reds, in this manner. However, copper oxide is fugitive, that is, flies around in the kiln, and even if once reduced, tends to re-oxidize. It is difficult to capture copper reds, and it is imperative to keep complete firing records for any chance of duplicating good results. If a copper red

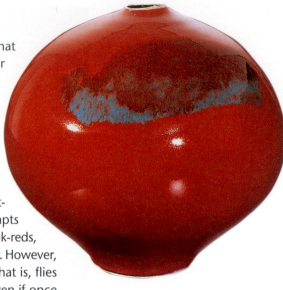

COPPER RED

Greg Daly's (Australia) porcelain vase with a brush-stroke of copper over the glaze has been post-reduced on the cooling side at 1300° F (700° C) to achieve this color

A group of porcelain bottles by Susan Peterson illustrates tiny variations of percentage amounts of copper carbonate in the high-fire reduction base glaze

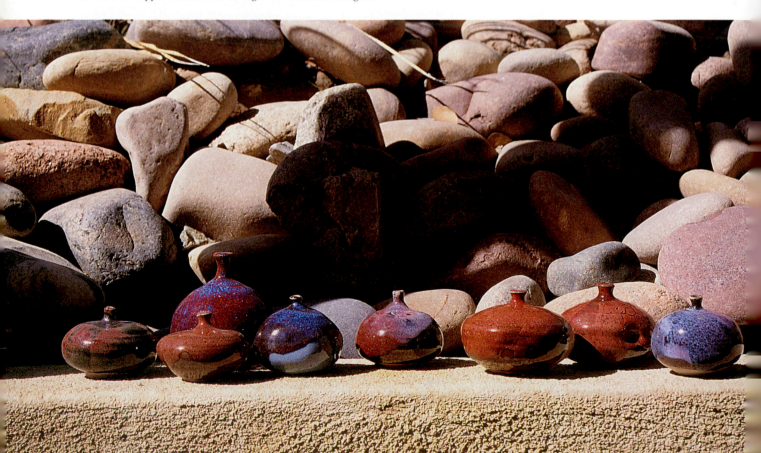

glaze turns out white it has fired in a neutral atmosphere, if it turns out light turquoise it has fired in an oxidizing atmosphere. Some kilns have uncontrollable spots, try as you might.

Iron celadons and tenmokus

The Chinese also discovered that a small amount (¼ to 1%) of iron oxide in a glaze, which usually results in an amber color in oxidation fire, would become jade green in reduction; this color is called celadon (see page 139). A larger amount of iron in a glaze yielded the well-known tenmoku black-brown colors, famous from the stoneware and porcelain of the Tang and Sung dynasties. Most other coloring oxides are not affected by a change in atmosphere.

Electric kilns have a neutral atmosphere; no air circulates, causing a not quite oxidizing situation. Reduction is not easily feasible unless a reducing agent is present (such as oil of lavender in commercially manufactured luster glazes), or if the potter adds silicon carbide to the glaze. However, combustible organic materials such as oil-

soaked rags, new-mown grass, rubber tires, asphaltum, and the like, can be injected into the electric kiln at red heat and above, to burn and therefore reduce what little oxygen is present in the chamber. It isn't easy, but low-fire Persian-style lusters and high-fire Chinese reds and celadons can be produced this way.

STACKING AND FIRING KILNS

Bisque firing

Bisque or biscuit is the term given to a clay body fired without glaze. It can imply either low or high temperature. Most potters bisque-fire at low temperature – red heat or a bit higher to cone 010 – to facilitate handling, and glaze at a considerably higher temperature to make the body more durable. Commercial porcelain manufacturers bisque high to support each piece to density, and glaze much lower. Some artists fire high for the body and low for the brighter-colored glazes.

In any case, in a bisque kiln wares can be stacked together, touching, sideways or upside down; yet the weight, volume, and design of the pieces must be thought about for support as well as even distribution of heat. Stack askew, lid sideways on the pot, bowl lip off bowl lip, plate edge off plate edge, so that air can circulate inside the pieces; if such forms are stacked with lids or edges fitting tight, a huge air pocket is formed, which causes probable blow-up of the piece.

> Damage in a greenware to bisque firing is almost always caused by improper packing or improper firing. Stacking greenware too tight, packing the kiln too full, asks for trouble

Bisque firing in six to eight hours
Fire carefully, so as not to blow up the ware from the evaporation of the physical and chemically combined moisture content. Go up to a pyrometer reading of 1100° F (600° C), making a gradual temperature rise over about six hours. At this point the clay will have passed through the "water smoking" period, when the water that made the clay plastic is driven off, and through the "dehydration" period, when the hygroscopic water combined in the clay molecule is driven off. If the ware is large it is a good idea to leave the door or the lid of the kiln open a crack, so that the moisture can escape, and to slow down the heat.

After 1200° F (650° C) close the door if it is still open, and go as fast as the kiln will go to the desired bisque temperature; well-built kilns – electric, gas, oil, or wood – should reach cone

Supports for kiln shelves should be as broad and sturdy as possible; three-point stilts or bar stilts are used for stacking greenware in a fast bisque firing or for stacking low-temperature glazed pots (stilts do not withstand high firing)

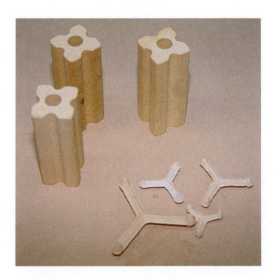

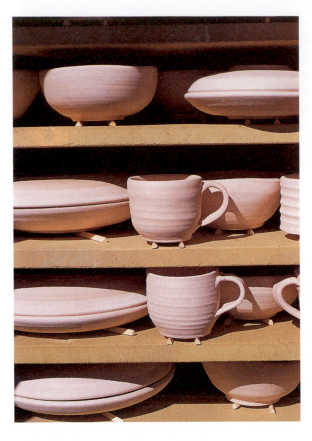

Susan Peterson's bisque fire stacking shows each pot elevated on stilts to allow even heat circulation, and air space between lip-to-lip plate stacking. This method of stacking allows for a relatively fast bisque firing, four to six hours, following the curve (see opposite) but shortening the time

Glaze firing

Glazed wares fire at the temperature necessary to mature the clay body, or at the temperature necessary for the glaze itself

I have explained the definition of earthenware, stoneware, and porcelain (pages 17–21), the making of which may determine your firing temperature. The body can be bisqued low or high and glazed at some other temperature. Think of maturing the clay body and firing the glaze as two different things, not necessarily linked.

Stacking the kiln for a glaze firing is perhaps the most important single act of the firing process. How the kiln is stacked determines the color and surface quality of the glazes as well as how comfortably the kiln will fire.

Glazed wares must be placed at least an inch apart. Glaze bubbles like boiling water during the firing and can attach itself to nearby wares, or to the kiln wall or the shelf. Use kiln wash on shelves to prevent glaze sticking if it drips. Large and small pieces should be placed randomly but evenly. Even heat distribution during firing is actually the result of even kiln stacking.

In a gas kiln keep at least a 4-in. (10 cm) open space – called flue space, or combustion space, between the wall and the work – all around the group of wares. In an electric kiln stack wares at least 2 inches (5 cm) from the elements. Electric atmospheres produce no movement like the turbulence that transpires during firing with wood or gas; leave several inches more room between each piece and each shelf for

010 in another hour or two. Large kilns holding hundreds of pieces will take at least twice as long to fire. Huge hill-style wood kilns can take days and nights of stoking.

When the firing is finished, the kiln should be closed and left untouched until it is cool, for at least as long as it took to fire, but usually for 24 hours. If you have a pyrometer, it should register at or below 400° F (210° C) before the kiln lid or door is opened a crack. Wait until the temperature shows 100° F (38° C), or even room temperature, before removing the ware.

Bisque firing for large wares
If the pots are excessively large or heavy, the bisque firing will take much longer. For instance, for sculpture that may be as tall as the kiln chamber, it is wise to move the firing up a maximum of 50° F (29° C) per hour until

past 1200° F (635° C) – this takes at least 24 hours. The pyrometer is measuring the heat at the point the thermocouple reaches into the kiln, not the heat that the pots have actually absorbed, which always lags behind the instrument reading. When the pyrometer registers a certain number of degrees on a kiln full of large pots, you need to allow a bit more time for the interior of the work to become as hot as the pyrometer says.

After reaching 1200° F (635° C) slowly, with vents open, you can close the kiln and proceed as rapidly as your kiln will go under oxidizing conditions, to the desired bisque temperature. Time and fuel are the costs of firing a kiln; to fire efficiently you must use your watch and a pyrometer and thermocouple, as well as the indicating cones inside the chamber to read the final temperature.

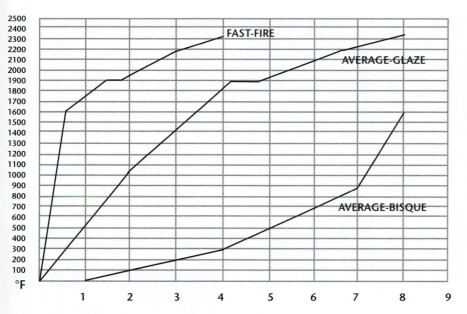

Fast fire and average glaze firing curve for cone 10 and average bisque firing curve for cone 010 in a gas kiln. Damper, burner settings, and other information such as weather conditions can be written in. Plot your own curve each time you fire with any fuel

air circulation in an electric kiln. Only petroleum or organically fired kilns can be fired easily in reduction atmosphere, remember – electric kilns are basically limited to slight oxidation or neutral atmosphere.

The glaze firing starts fast, just the opposite of the bisque firing, and slows as the temperature goes higher. The last 100° F (60° C) of any glaze fire should take one hour to mature and soften the glazes, no matter what the temperature. This is an important point often ignored, which produces immature glaze surfaces and undeveloped colors.

A reduction firing requires a proper balance between the fuel and the air to provide the required atmosphere for the desired glazes. Reduction firings are always problematic and frequently yield surprises instead of expected results.

Most glaze firings to stoneware or porcelain temperatures take eight to ten hours, although I fire to cone

10 in four to five hours. During this time a complete record should be kept of burner and damper settings in a gas-fired kiln, and of time and temperature. An electric kiln offers fewer options, but keep a record of the switches, time, and temperature. Records should be compared with results every time you fire, and analyses made.

All kilns are individual. Even kilns made by the same manufacturer to the same specifications will not be the same. Kilns built alike sitting next to each other will not fire the same. No matter what, your results will not be the same as mine or anyone else's. Therefore potters can work and learn best with their own kiln. **Firing is an extremely personal matter; if it is recorded and analyzed over and over, doing it satisfactorily will become second nature to the artist**.

ALTERNATIVE FIRINGS
Pit firing

Pit firing has many connotations: an actual pit in the ground, a built-up pit made of brick, a metal garbage can, paperclay formed like a pit, a sand pit, or a sagger. The wares in the pit are usually laced with combustible material such as vegetable garbage, twigs, brush, straw, paper, rags, or sawdust, which will fire and smolder; more fuel can be added to achieve more heat and a longer time, or the firing can be consummated in a few hours.

Low-fire glazes or frits can be applied to the raw or bisque pieces for coloration, or chemicals can be sprinkled in the mixture: for example, silver nitrate for silvery luster, potassium bicarbonate for yellows, potassium dichromate for yellow-greens, bismuth subnitrate for goldish color. Experiment with the chlorides and nitrates of all the metallic oxide ceramic coloring agents.

Raku firing

Raku is a special kind of ware, with a good deal of Japanese folklore attached, developed by Zen monks in the sixteenth century and made famous by a family dynasty named Raku. The firing is akin to the Native American or any primitive bonfire technique, but not the same. The theoretical idea is to pull a burning glazed pot from the hot fire, at about 1800° F (980° C), and smoke it to develop black lines in the crackles that open up in the thermal-shocked glazed surface. Artists have elaborated on this idea, as have the Japanese tea

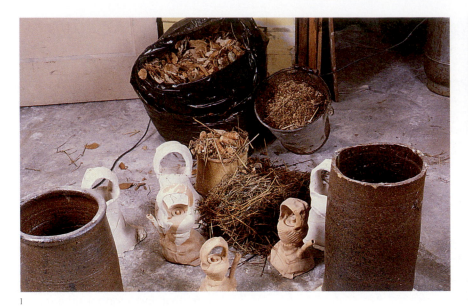

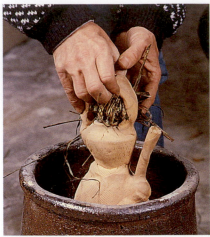
2

SAGGER FIRING

Chuck Hindes's combustibles for sagger firing include (1) corn cobs, straw, woodchips, and leaves, (2) placed in the container around the pots. (3) Some saggers can be fired by themselves for low-temperature smoldering, but Hindes is placing the sagger in a kiln for high-temperature firing. The finished look of saggered claywork at low fire is usually pale and chalky but hard and dense at high fire; either can become gray or black due to the combustibles in the container, or colored if there are pigments in the mix

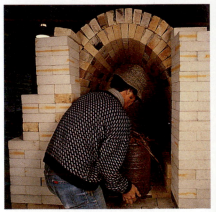
3

MARIA'S BONFIRE KILN

This pot decorated with a polished *avanyu* (rain god) by Maria and Julian Martinez is an example from a black firing, c. 1920

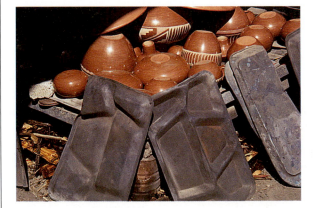

American Indian bonfiring: Maria Martinez and her daughter-in-law Santana, c. 1975, stack their burnished red pots on a grate over juniper wood, which will be covered by old metal trays and dried cow dung to insulate the bonfire; the fire is smothered with fresh horse manure and ash to turn the red clay black

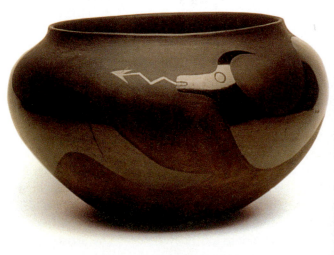

LUCY FIRES WITH COW CHIPS

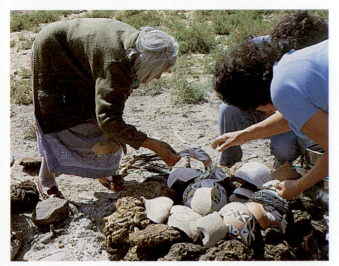

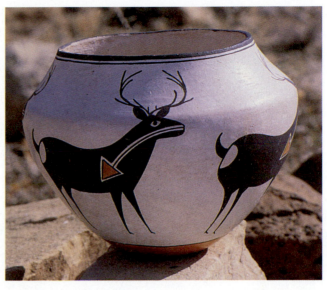

Lucy Lewis and her daughters Emma and Dolores set their pots among protective shards surrounded by a mound of dried cow dung, which provides the fuel for the fire, c. 1984

Dung-fired burnished vessel decorated with hematite and red iron oxides by Lucy Lewis, c. 1980

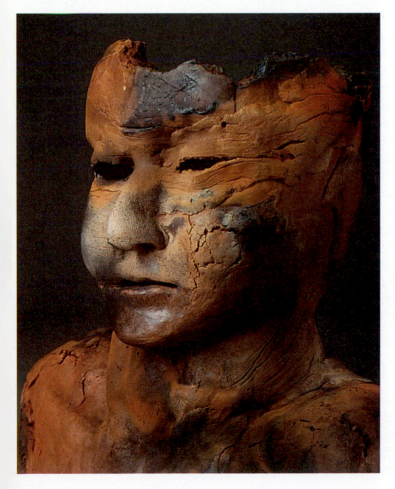

PIT FIRING

Detail of Paula Rice's pinched and slab-built pit-fired figure; the smoking enhances the iron, rutile and cobalt engobe decoration

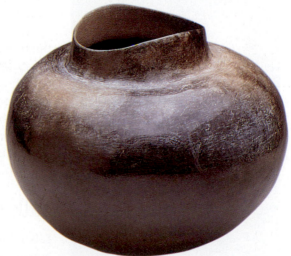

Jimmy Clark's hand-built, burnished, pit-fired and smoked jar shows the markings from the organic matter he used to fuel the pit

RAKU

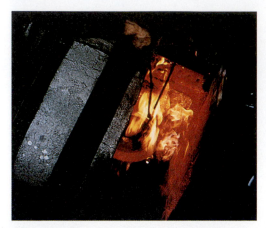

ABOVE Paul Soldner, probably the most famous exponent of raku technique in the West, pulls a pot out of the fire with a raku tong

RIGHT A Paul Soldner raku sculpture

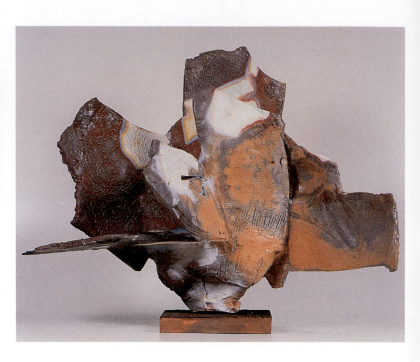

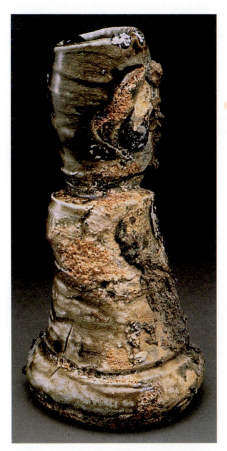

Rick Berman has coined the word "salku" for his wood-firing with salt using the raku technique

ceremony bowl-makers. Some potters use cold water to quench the piece, some thrust the hot pot into combustible materials such as leaves and straw that burn again, some add salt or the chemical salts of metallic coloring oxides to the post-firing for a lustrously fumed surface, some just use smothering of the hot unglazed piece in the combustibles to totally reduce and therefore blacken the work.

Raku is only a decorative technique; the temperature is so low that pots will not hold water, and fear of bacteria in the porous clay body should keep food out of raku containers. The "happening" quality of the firing makes it experimental and joyful, which is a possible meaning of the word *raku* in Japan.

Salku firing

Salku, or saltku, firing is a combination of salt and raku or salt and higher-temperature glaze tumbled firings. Many combinations of all kinds of alternative firings are being coined by pot-

ters today, and are highly experimental, often not to be repeated.

Salt firing

Potters experiment with many different types of firings, but usually decide on just one or two for their own work. Add chemicals for effect.

Salt, sodium chloride, one of the most important catalysts that can be added to the fire to change the surface of claywork, causes a pock-marked kind of clear glaze on unglazed ware, and was developed in Europe, notably Britain and Germany, during the sixteenth century. Throwing rock salt (sodium chloride) into the fire **at the maturing temperature of the clay body** results in an orange-peel, glossy texture, that takes on the color of the clay or engobe decoration underneath. In Europe and later in America this became a relatively inexpensive method of achieving a durable glazed surface on utilitarian wares such as crocks and mugs, and also for roof tiles and water pipes.

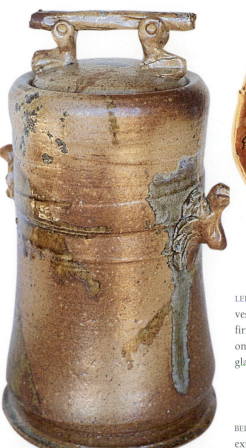

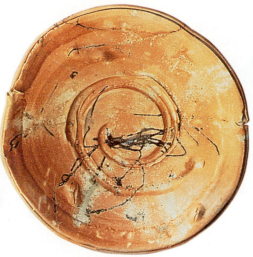

LEFT Marie Woo's wall piece was covered with straw and placed in a soda fire, leaving markings from the grasses and color from the sodium

LEFT A typical example of Don Reitz's large vessels, glazed by high-temperature salt firing. Don Reitz has for many years been one of the foremost exponents of the salt-glazing technique

BELOW In recent years Don Reitz has explored low-fire salt glaze over vitreous engobes, as in this platter

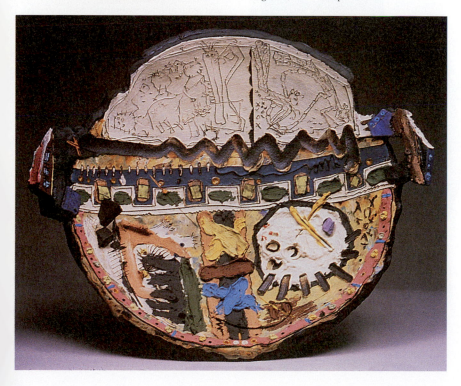

Soda firing

Sodium bicarbonate or **soda ash** can be substituted for the usual rock salt used in a salt firing. Soda vapor enhances the color of stains and oxides but usually does not develop the orange-peel glaze texture characteristic of salt firing. Adding soda ash to the fire at any temperature, not necessarily the maturing temperature of the clay body, is a similar treatment to salt glazing, but mainly enhances engobe and clay colors and does not yield the heavily pock-marked glaze quality of salt. Soda ash may be less hazardous than salt to the environment. However, most chemists will state that sodium is not dangerous when volatilized above red heat; potters use soda and salt at much higher temperatures.

Wood firing

A kiln can be fired with wood purely as a fuel for bisquing and glazing clay-wares. In contrast, wood and its ashes can become the principal means of coloring and partially glazing the work inside the kiln as it is stoked over long

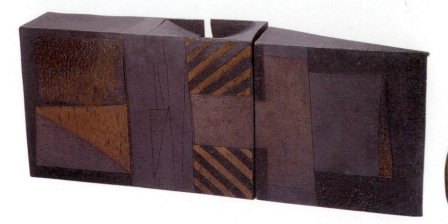

ABOVE Robert Winokur's hand-built sculpture, made of Pennsylvania brick clay and decorated with engobes, is salt-glazed

duration – several days and nights – according to the desired build-up of patina on the ware. Wood ashes from firing can be used as actual glaze fluxing ingredients, similar to the mineral feldspar, but with quite different effects. Japanese potters have long been addicted to the look of wood-ash firing, mainly in folk-pottery villages such as Shigaraki. A number of other clay artists have adopted wood firing as a principal aesthetic of their work.

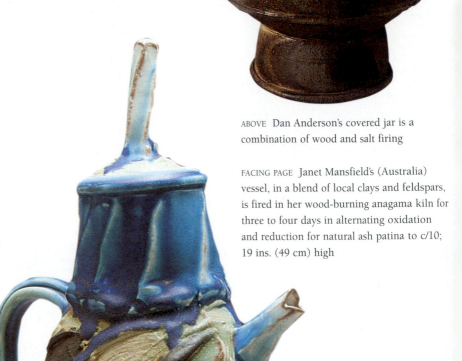

ABOVE Dan Anderson's covered jar is a combination of wood and salt firing

FACING PAGE Janet Mansfield's (Australia) vessel, in a blend of local clays and feldspars, is fired in her wood-burning anagama kiln for three to four days in alternating oxidation and reduction for natural ash patina to c/10; 19 ins. (49 cm) high

RIGHT Jay LaCouture has improvized a blower system to augment the heavy deposit of soda ash vapor, which yields enough sodium during the firing to turn his copper engobe to turquoise color on his thrown and handbuilt porcelain teapot

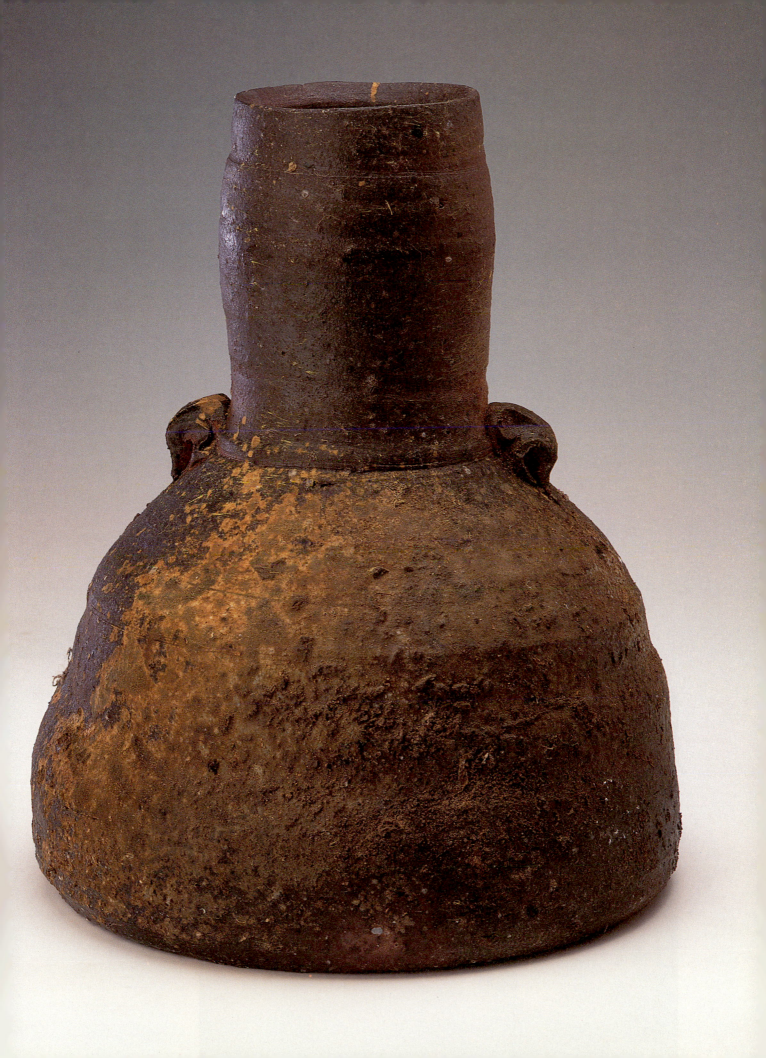

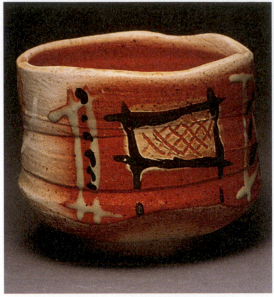

Sometimes wood ash reacts on porcelain to give vibrant colors, as in this wood-fired pot by Don Reitz

RIGHT Unglazed wares are fired with wood especially for the ash patina, but many potters use wood as the most readily available fuel for glaze firing. Goro Suzuki (Japan) uses a traditional green oribe glaze for his wood-fired chair sculpture

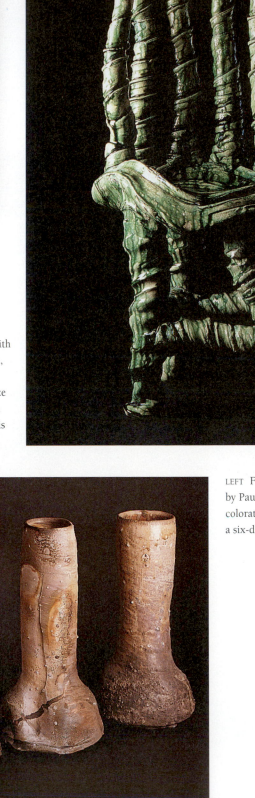

LEFT Four long-necked vase forms by Paul Chaleff show the colorations of the ash deposits from a six-day wood firing

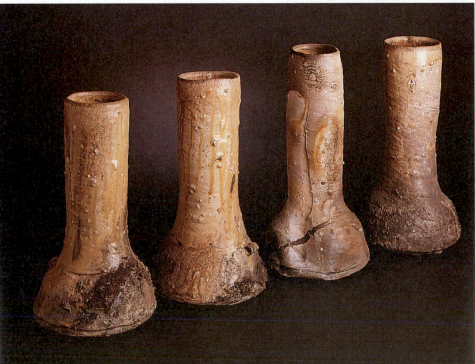

GLAZE AND FIRING PROBLEMS

1. Glaze runs off the pot onto the kiln shelf

• Too much glaze was applied. Remember that the recommended thickness of any glaze application is ¹⁄₃₂ inch (0.8 mm). If several layers have been applied, scrape to dry underlayers thinner toward the bottom. Glaze should be the consistency of milk or thin cream in the container; usually studio potters need to add water to glazes that have been standing between uses.

• Glaze runs too much due to long firing, or firing too slowly as top temperature is reached; remember to take **only** the last 100° F (38° C) in one hour.

Earthenware vessels fired at low temperature can be glazed all over and supported on three-pointed ceramic "stilts" that can be knocked off when the piece is removed from the kiln. Stoneware and porcelain should have no glaze on the foot and for at least ¼ inch (0.6 cm) above it – we call this "dry footing." These wares become so dense in the firing that stilts would warp the piece.

2. Glaze appears bubbled or blistered after firing

• Air was trapped during the glazing application. You can learn to note these bubbles as you work. Glaze dries instantly, so you can rub bubbles down with your fingers before putting the pot in the kiln.

• Specific bubbling material has been added to the glaze.

• The glaze is overfired or underfired; either can cause blisters.

3. Glaze drops off the pot and fuses to the kiln shelf during firing, leaving unglazed areas on the piece
Probably the glaze application was so thick that bonding could not ensue, hence in the initial stages of firing some glaze fell off.

4. Glaze "crawls" away in spots, revealing unglazed clay in some areas
The answer can be the same as above, too thick an application. Or the potter may have used hand lotion before glazing and touched the pot – lotion or oil prevents the glaze bonding properly.

5. A glazed piece that has been bisque-fired blows up during the glaze fire
The kiln was stacked and fired immediately after the pots were glazed. Always let the pieces dry a day after glazing before packing the kiln.

6. Several pieces have stuck to

Firing is the proof of the pudding. After all the work that has been involved in preparing the claywork for the firing, this is the test. Losses occur during the fire from improper stacking or handling of the kiln and its fuel. The potter should concentrate on the firing during the whole sequence and not do any other tasks

each other during the fire Ware was placed too close; allow the space of at least two fingers between each work.

7. Pieces fell over during the glaze firing
Wrong construction, bad support, or improper loading.

8. The fired glaze is harsh and dry to the touch
The glaze can be immature for various reasons:

• the glaze batch could have been improperly mixed;

• the firing temperature was wrong or no cone was in the kiln;

• the kiln fired in minutes during the last 100° F (38° C) instead of approaching the peak slowly. Each glaze requires different handling, which is one reason potters limit themselves to a few types of glaze in order to learn and appreciate all the nuances.

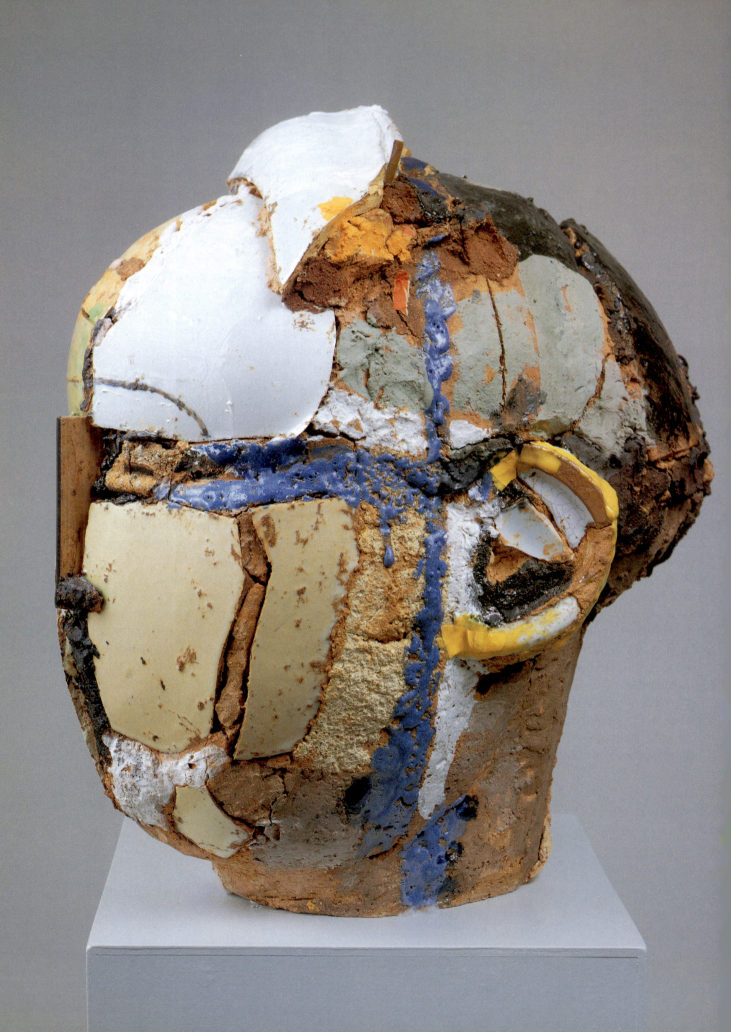

6

THE ART OF
CERAMICS

FROM IDEA TO ART

Having an idea in mind and being able to execute it in clay are two different things until you gain a certain amount of expertise. Knowing what is or isn't art, or if art is craft or craft is art, may not occupy your thinking in the beginning, but later on these questions are of some concern to the clayworker. Philosophically such questions always spark heavy discussions among collectors and purchasers of ceramics. The trick is to know when a piece is good, no matter what it is or how it was made. The artist or the collector tries to develop an eye for what the sense of passion brings.

Learn to see line and space everywhere, in nature and natural settings, in architecture, in city streets. Practice making decisions intuitively about what you like and don't like. Eventually, when working in clay or when buying clay objects, you will see line directions and define shapes and planes automatically. Always be aware of our colorful world; color often supersedes line and even space.

Make judgments alone, so that they are personal and meaningful to you. Today no one emits adamant statements about what design is or what art is; no one can tell you that. You tell yourself through constant observation and silent pro and con discussions with yourself, refining your judgment as you go.

The remarkable assets clay has – surface, color, scale, unlimited shape – have been incredibly exploited in the last 50 years. Clayworks overlap with sculpture in all media, with shaped canvas and off the wall painting, and functional ceramics in many cases become objects of art. As well, we are looking at historical ceramic objects with a new realization of the remarkable contributions of all cultures to the art of today.

As this book goes to press, we have lost the artist who provided the most impetus for the growth of ceramic art over the past 50 years. Peter Voulkos (1923–2002) led us, guided us, took us by storm, with his bravado, his innovations, and his personal magnetism. His memory lives.

I show you the stunning international portfolio that follows so that you will have a small understanding of the larger ceramic picture, from all areas of representation to installation and conceptual art. Use the work of these clay artists as a springboard for your own discoveries.

Gertraud Möhwald (Germany), *Head with Orange Earring*. Stoneware, glaze and added broken bits, 15 ins. (39 cm) high

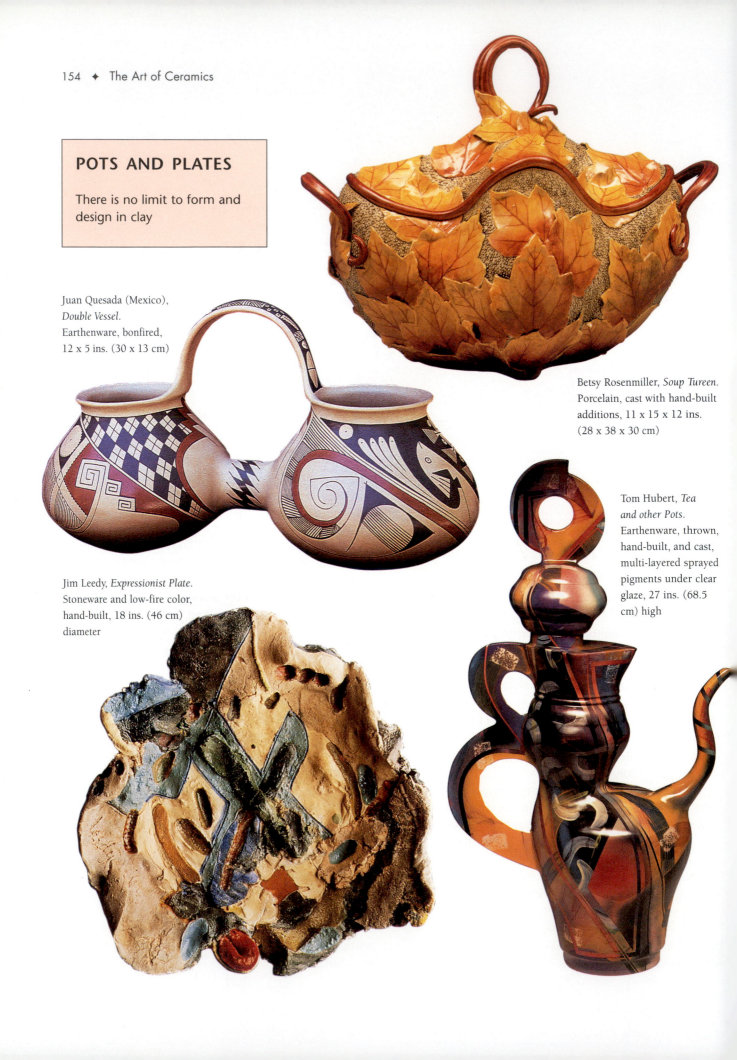

POTS AND PLATES

There is no limit to form and design in clay

Juan Quesada (Mexico), *Double Vessel*. Earthenware, bonfired, 12 x 5 ins. (30 x 13 cm)

Betsy Rosenmiller, *Soup Tureen*. Porcelain, cast with hand-built additions, 11 x 15 x 12 ins. (28 x 38 x 30 cm)

Jim Leedy, *Expressionist Plate*. Stoneware and low-fire color, hand-built, 18 ins. (46 cm) diameter

Tom Hubert, *Tea and other Pots*. Earthenware, thrown, hand-built, and cast, multi-layered sprayed pigments under clear glaze, 27 ins. (68.5 cm) high

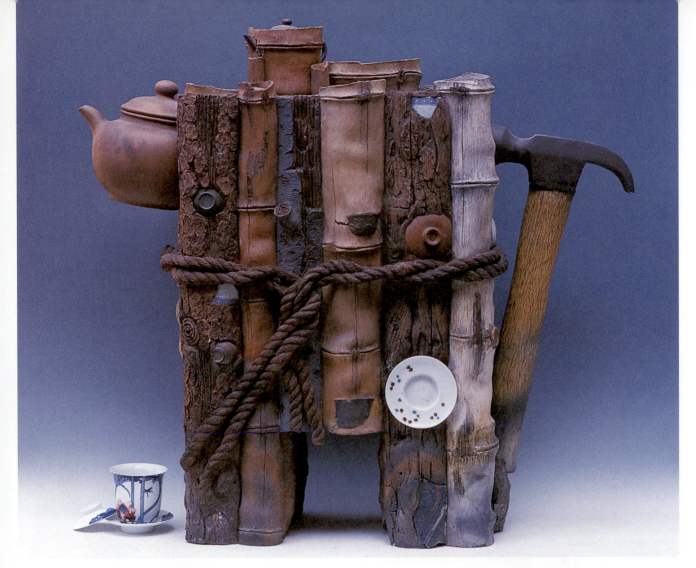

Luo Xiaoping (China), *Teapot Ramifications*. Vitreous YiXing clay
and porcelain, slab-built, 34 x 16½ x 31 ins. (86 x 42 x 79 cm)

Ron Nagle, *Cup Metaphor*. Earthenware,
cast and mounted, 12 ins. (30 cm) square

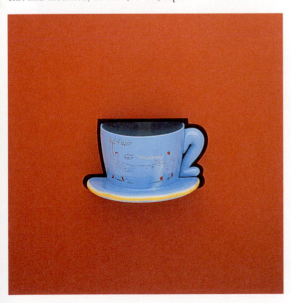

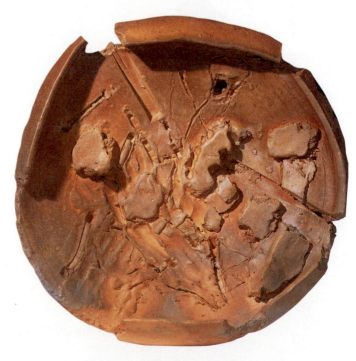

Peter Voulkos, *Untitled*. Thrown and altered stoneware,
wood-fired, 24 x 24 ins. (60 x 60 cm)

BIRDS AND ANIMALS

Hollow-building ceramic sculpture with reference to birds and animals is currently very popular

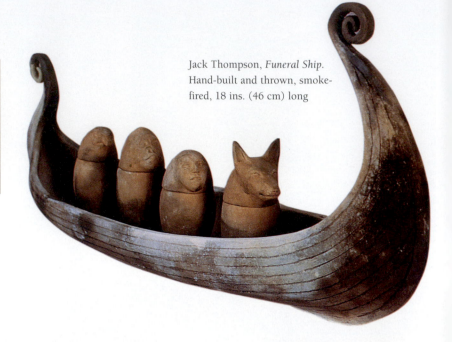

Jack Thompson, *Funeral Ship*. Hand-built and thrown, smoke-fired, 18 ins. (46 cm) long

Ann Adair Voulkos, *Pope-Alligator*. Earthenware, slab-built, 18 ins. (46 cm) high

David Smith, *Waiting*. Stoneware, thrown and hand-built, 15 ins. (38 cm) high

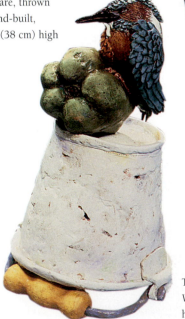

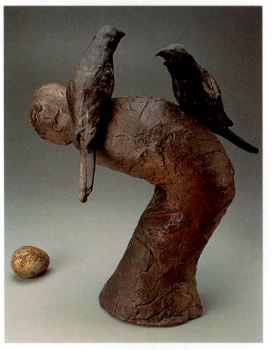

Jolyon Hofsted, *Pig*. Stoneware, thrown and altered, oxidation fired, 12 ins. (30 cm) high

Tom Supensky, *Where is the Water?* Stoneware, press-molded, hand-built, 24 ins. (60 cm) high

Etta Winigrad, *The Guardian*. Earthenware, smoke-fired with newspapers, hand-built, 30 x 14 x 5 ins. (76 x 35.5 x 13 cm)

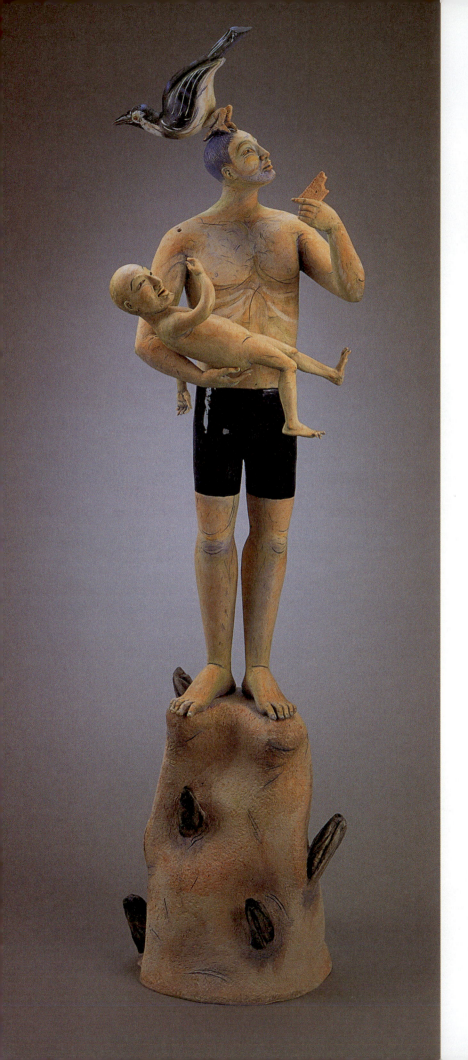

FIGURES

Large-scale sculpture is hollow-built in a similar manner to coil, pinched or slab vessels, or it is cast, or a combination. Some of the most exciting work being done in ceramics today is figurative

Patti Warashina, *Feeder*. Stoneware, hand-built and cast, underglazes, some glaze; 68 x 17 x 18 ins. (173 x 43 x 46 cm)

Cara Moczygemba, *Princess*. Stoneware and porcelain, cast and hand-built, smoke-fired

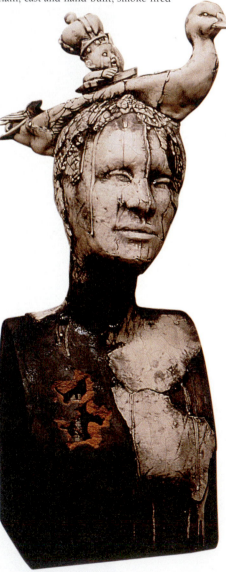

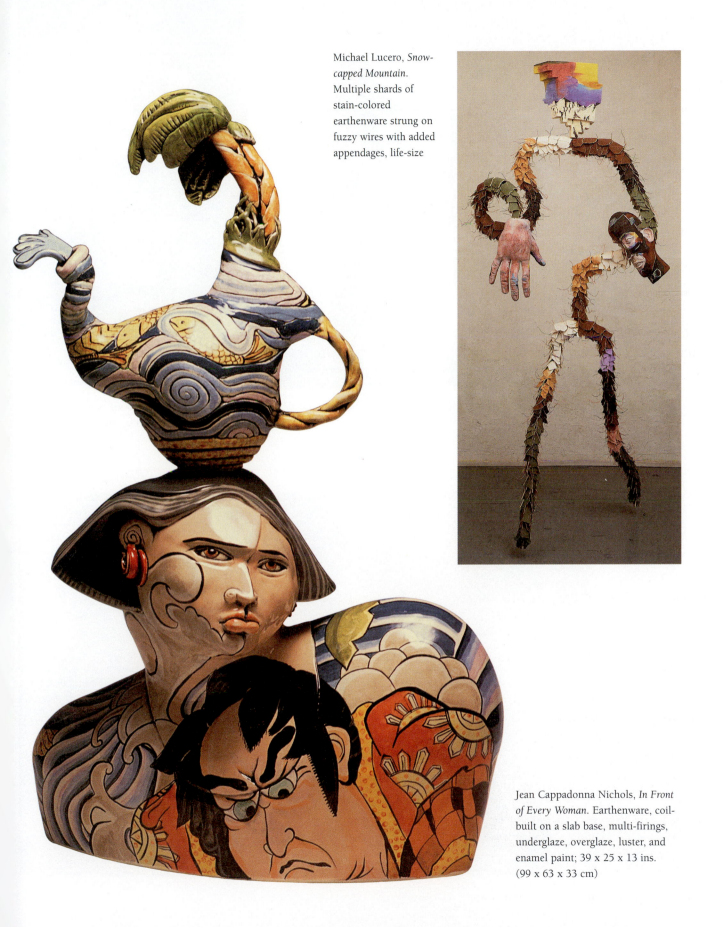

Michael Lucero, *Snow-capped Mountain*. Multiple shards of stain-colored earthenware strung on fuzzy wires with added appendages, life-size

Jean Cappadonna Nichols, *In Front of Every Woman*. Earthenware, coil-built on a slab base, multi-firings, underglaze, overglaze, luster, and enamel paint; 39 x 25 x 13 ins. (99 x 63 x 33 cm)

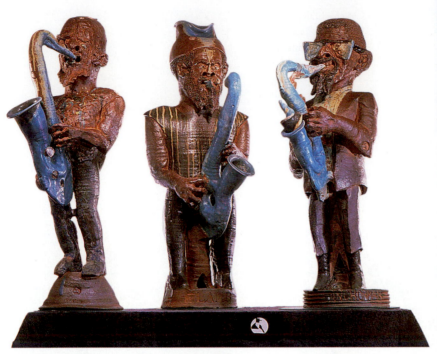

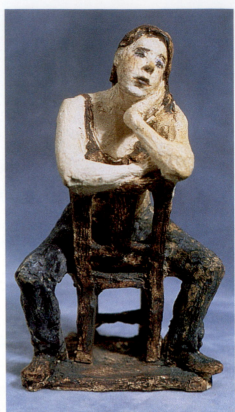

Jeff Schlanger, *Three Tenors*. Stoneware, thrown and altered from live concert sketches, glazed c/10; 36 x 42 ins. (91 x 106 cm)

Claire Clark, *Lila Sitting*. Stoneware sculpted solid, stains, 12 ins. (30 cm) high

Ingrid Jacobsen (Germany), *Ein Mann sucht was* (A man seeks something). Stoneware hollow-built figures, with stains, unglazed, life-size

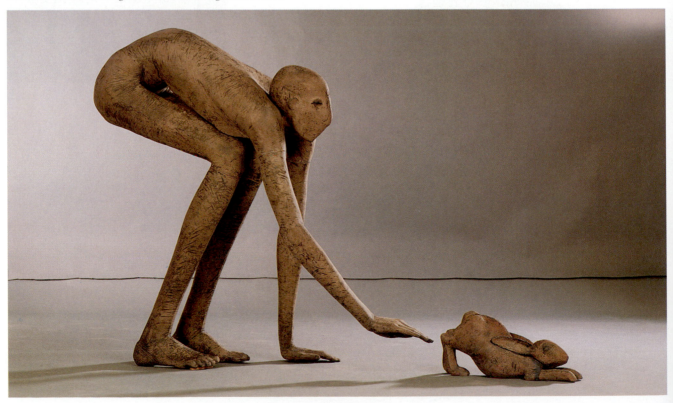

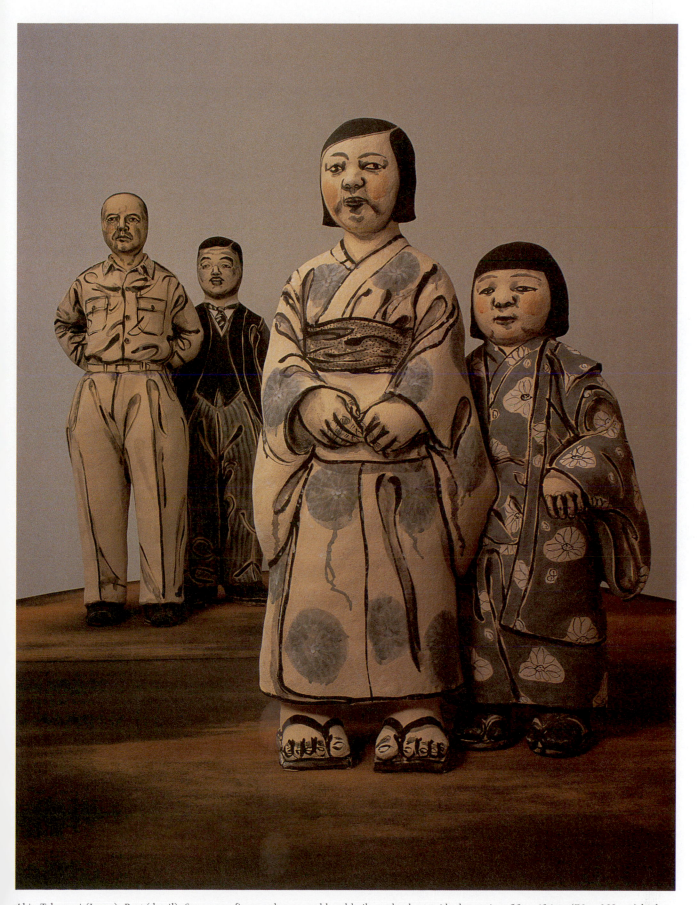

Akio Takamori (Japan), *Boat* (detail). Stoneware figures, thrown and hand-built, underglaze oxide decoration, 30 to 40 ins. (76 to 102 cm) high

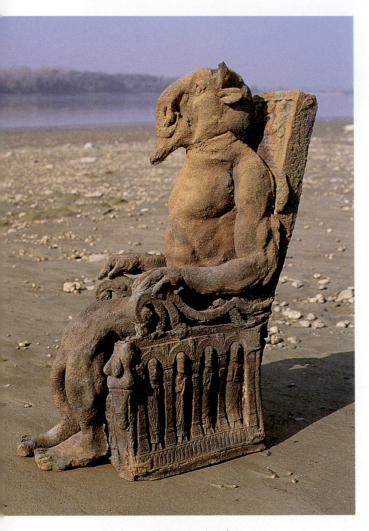

Imre Schrammel (Hungary), *Lifesize Figure*

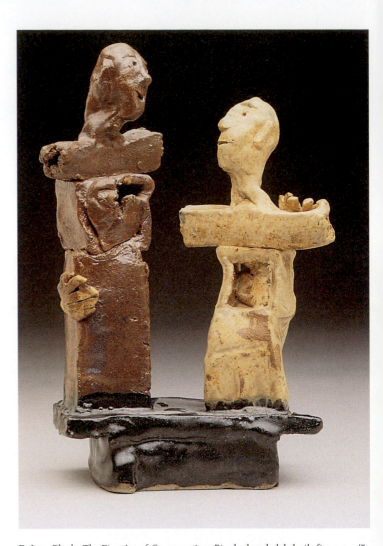

E. Jane Pleak, *The Fine Art of Conversation*. Pinched and slab-built figures, c/5 stoneware

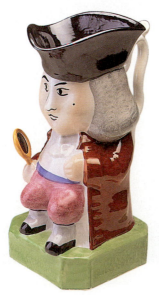

Richard Slee (UK), *Young Toby*. Cast porcelain, glazed at lower temperature, 10 ins. (25 cm) high

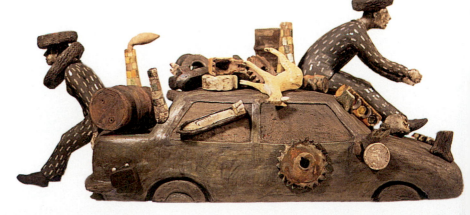

Stephen Braun, *Out of Gas*. Hand-built stoneware, stains and paint

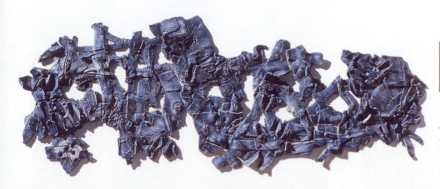

WALLS

John Mason, *Blue Wall*. Mason was one of the few ceramic artists in the 1960s to fabricate and install large wall constructions. The 21 ft x 7ft x 6 ins. (6.4 x 2.13 m. x 15 cm) wall is one of his best-known

Henry Pim (Ireland), *Grid Piece 2000*. Stoneware and paperclay hand-fabricated tiles make a wall unit, 45 x 45 ins. (114 x 114 cm)

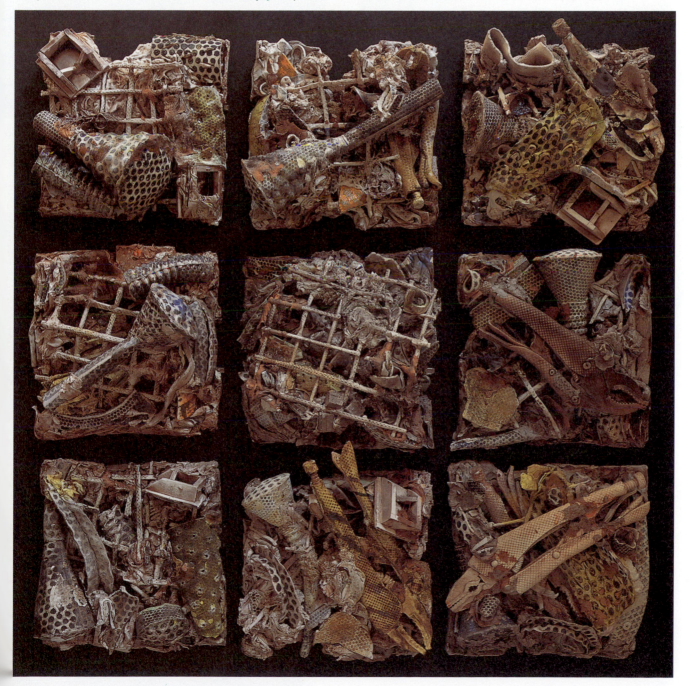

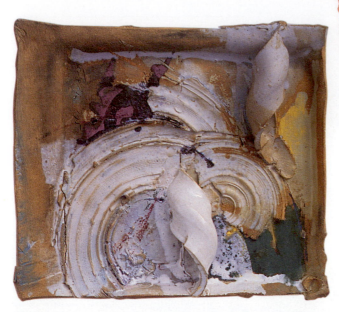

Vaslav Serak (Czech Republic), *Wall Piece*. Porcelain, thrown and altered forms, 24 x 24 ins. (60 x 60 cm)

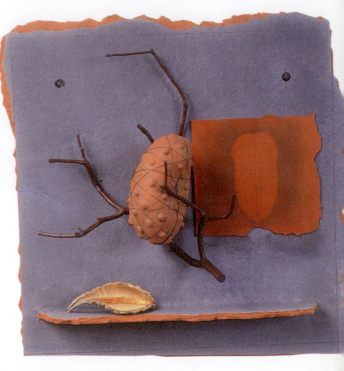

Carol Aoki, *Pod Collage No.1*. Paperclay body wall collage, 28 x 30 ins. (71 x 76 cm)

Marit Tingleff (Norway), *Wall*. Porcelain and stoneware, 8 ft (2.4 m.) high

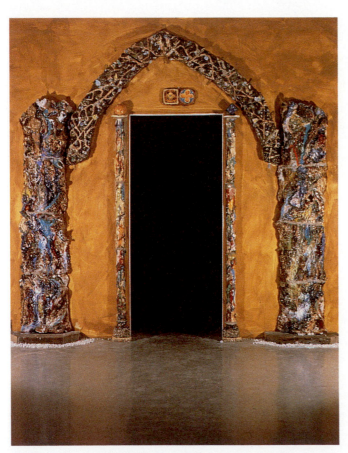

Anthony Rubino, *Ovid's Threshhold*. Room-sized stoneware door with arch and ornaments, multi-glazed, c/10

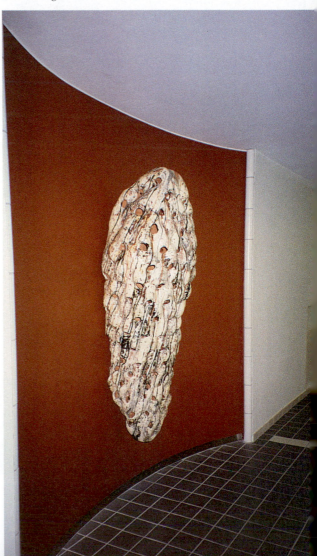

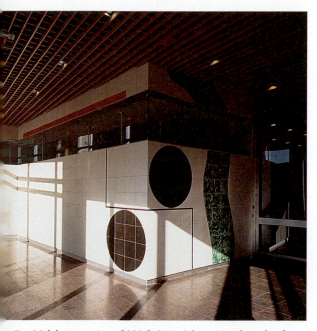

Jim Melchert, section of 220-ft (67 m.) long *Mural*, made of hundreds of hand-decorated and glazed tiles

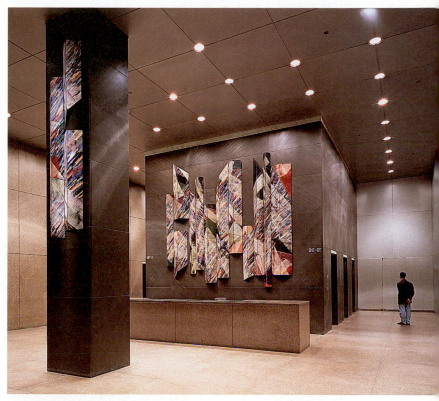

Jale Yilmabaşar (Turkey), *Eyes*. Hand-built, building-sized earthenware wall installed in Istanbul

Dale Zheutlin, *Archisites*. Earthenware and stoneware tile pictographs mounted on lobby walls

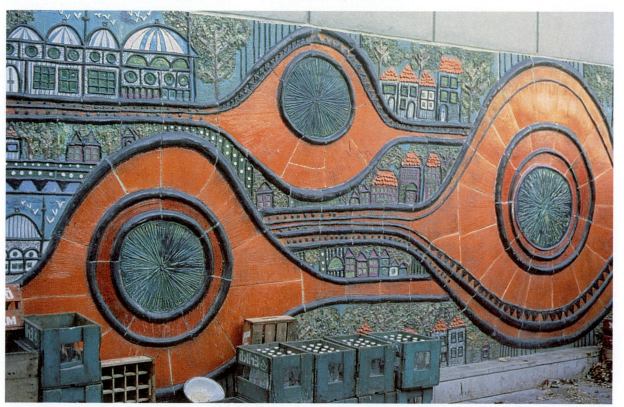

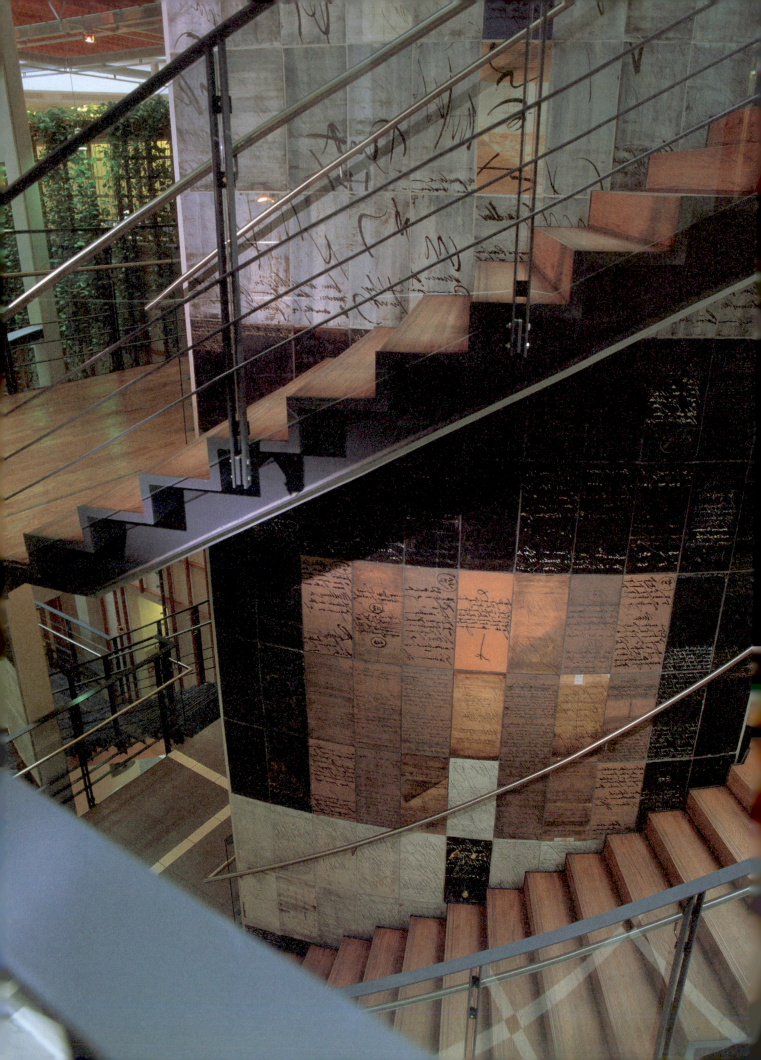

FACING PAGE Ole Lislerud (Norway), *Oslo Supreme Court Building*. Detail of staircase with cast porcelain wall panels with symbolic calligraphy and writing as metaphor for this public site

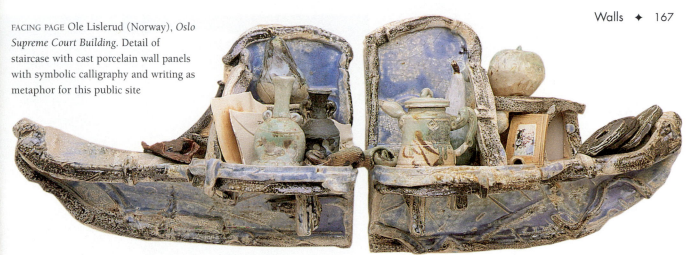

John Glick, *Mantel Diptych*. Engobes, stoneware and porcelain, soda-fired, c/10 reduction, 3 ft (91 cm) long

Paula Winokur, *Entry III, Boulder Field*. Room-sized porcelain portal, slab-built with pinched-out accessories

Wayne Higby, *Intangible Notch*. Thousands of raku-fired shards augment the glazed earthenware tiles in this wall-sized installation

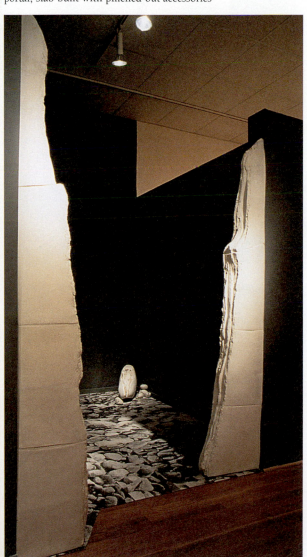

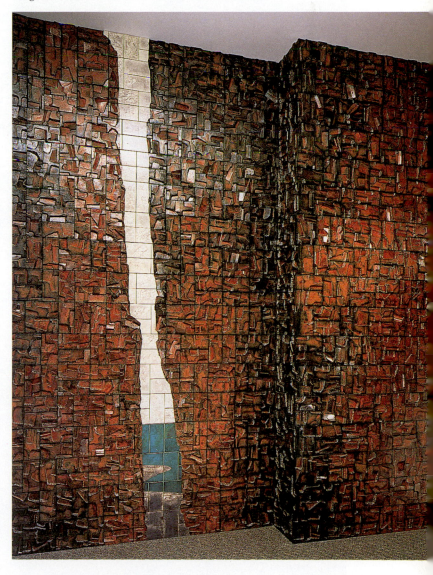

MIXED MEDIA

Ceramic materials are often combined with one or a variety of other materials, for aesthetic or structural reasons

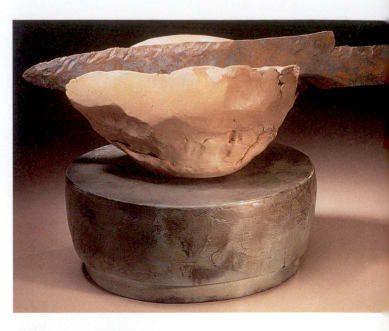

Rick Hirsch, *Altar Bowl with Weapon*. Raku-fired with forged steel base, 18 x 9 ins. (46 x 23 cm)

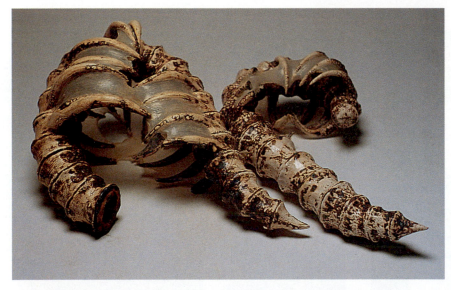

Nori Pao, *Two Generations*. Stoneware with poured latex segments, 12 x 18 x 7 ins. (30 x 46 x 18 cm)

Elisabeth Langsch (Switzerland), *Garden Balls*. Concrete, clay, glaze, largest 36 ins. (91 cm) diameter

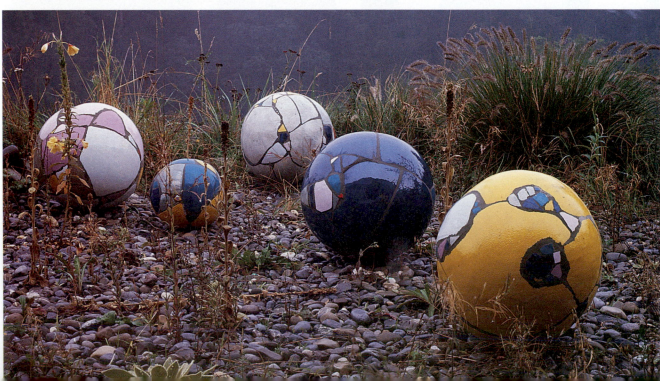

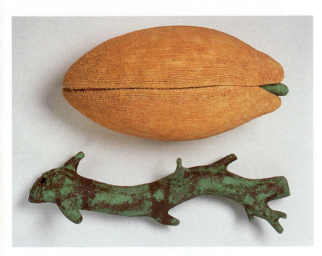

Juan Granados, *Growth*. Earthenware, copper, and glaze, 29 x 23 x 20 ins. (74 x 58 x 51 cm)

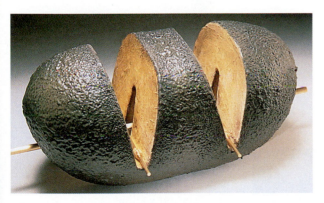

John Stephenson, *Isolator*. Wooden dowels and stoneware clay, 18 x 7 ins. (46 x 18 cm)

Nora Naranjo-Morse, *Mother*. Hand-built micaceous local clay from Santa Clara Pueblo, New Mexico, wood-fired with cedar, wire wrap, 4 x 12 ins. (10 x 30 cm)

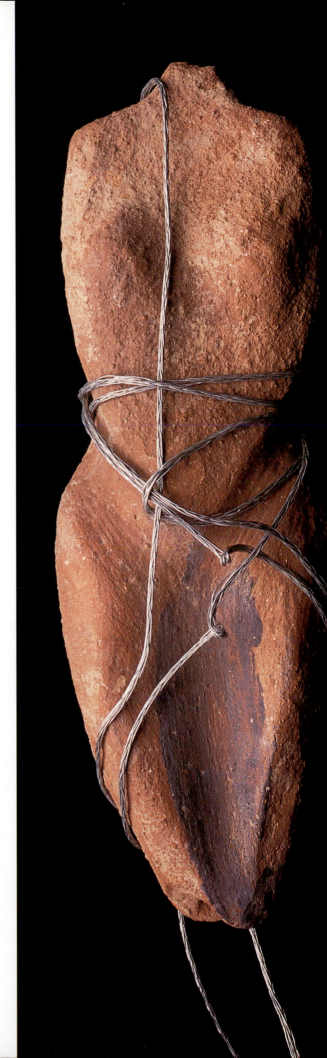

SCULPTURE

Sculpture is a nebulous term. Often it applies to abstract work with no realistic meaning. Sometimes sculpture is allegorical or metaphorical, or even humorous. Recognizing that all three-dimensional pieces can be called sculpture, we have chosen a few representative images here

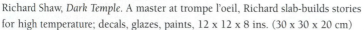

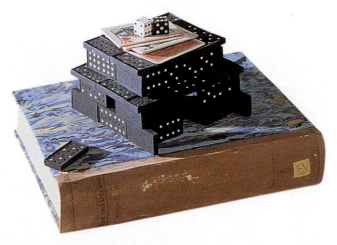

Richard Shaw, *Dark Temple*. A master at trompe l'oeil, Richard slab-builds stories for high temperature; decals, glazes, paints, 12 x 12 x 8 ins. (30 x 30 x 20 cm)

Bill Stewart, *Doodad*. Earthenware, wheel-thrown, pinch and slab; engobes and glaze, 6 ft (182 cm) high

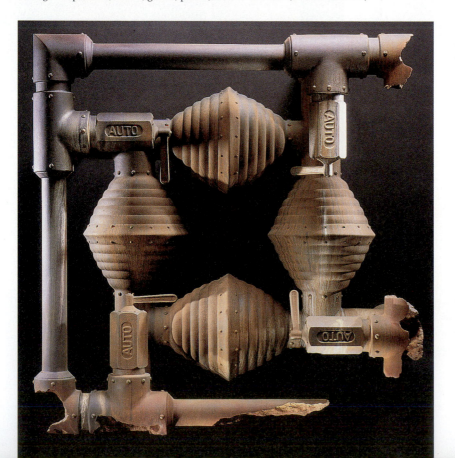

Steven Montgomery, *Quadrus*. Stoneware, wheel-thrown, press-molded, hand-built; 36 x 36 ins. (91 x 91 cm)

FACING PAGE Øyvind Suul (Norway), *Dive*. Stoneware, cast and hand-built sections, wall size, unglazed

INSET Angel Garraza (Spain), *Sitios y Lugares* (detail). Huge wall piece, fabricated in sections and mounted, vari-colored clays

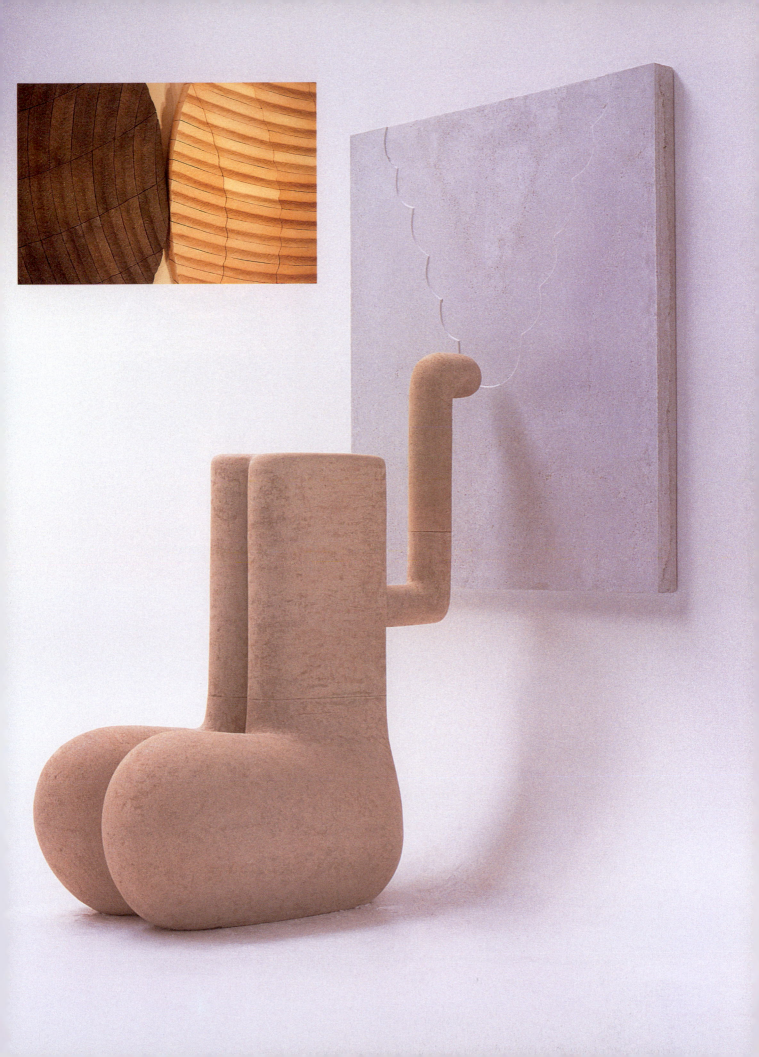

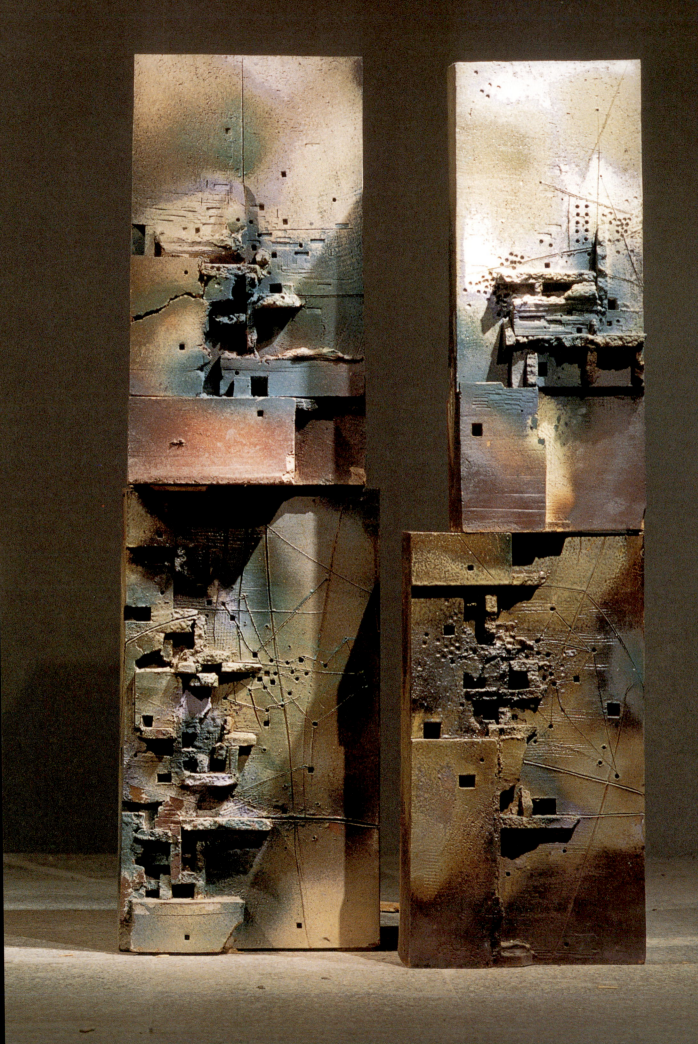

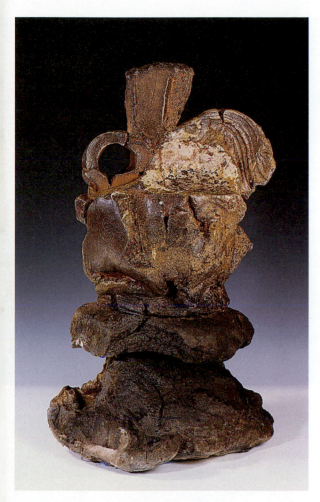

Peter Callas, *Sculpture*. Thrown and squashed stoneware, wood-fired ash patina, 36 ins. (91 cm) high

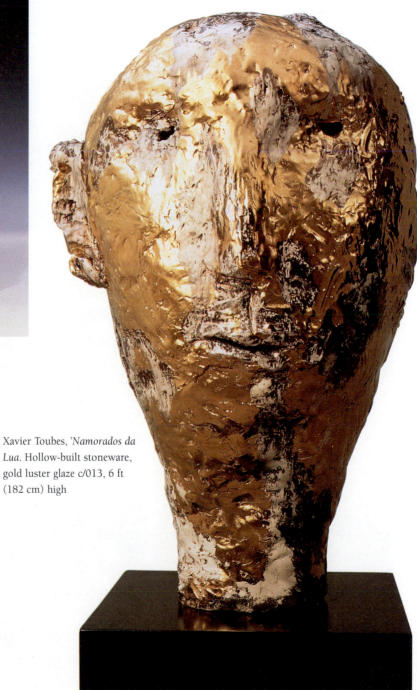

Xavier Toubes, '*Namorados da Lua*. Hollow-built stoneware, gold luster glaze c/013, 6 ft (182 cm) high

FACING PAGE Lu Pin-chang (China), *View of Relic No.1*. Stoneware, hand-built, smoke-fired in wood kiln, c/10, unglazed; 16 x 14 x 67 ins. (40 x 36 x 170 cm)

INSTALLATIONS

Ceramic installations are increasingly important as outdoor public art statements, as accessories to architecture, and in large public spaces such as lobbies, subways, hospitals, stations, and so on

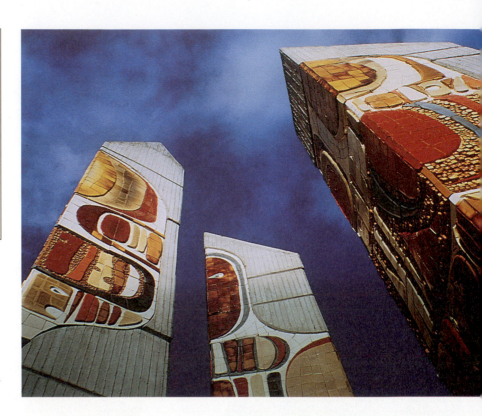

Edoardo Vega (Ecuador), *Los Totems* (detail)

Patricia Lay, *Mythoi*. Black clay with colored inlay, steel pole installation, 10 ft. (300 cm) high, installed in Denmark

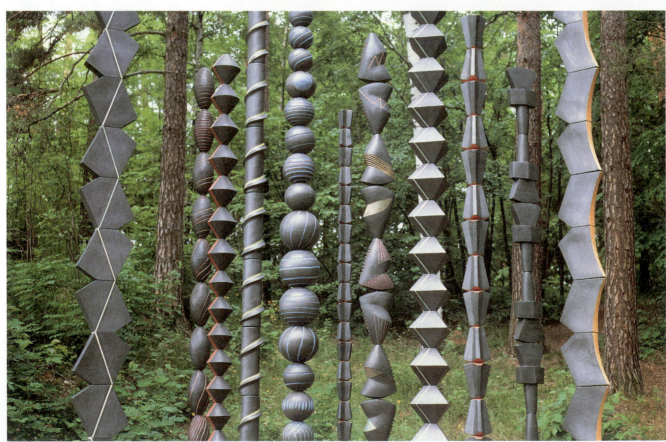

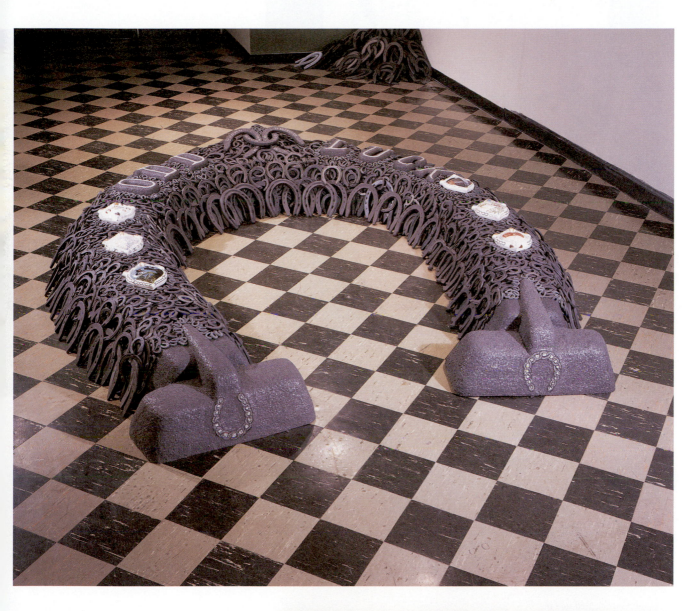

Mary Jo Bole, *Odd Luck*. Black porcelain, bone china, decals, hand-built hollow with additions and photo silkscreen, 12 ft x 8 ft x 16 ins. (3.6 x 2.4 m. x 41 cm)

RIGHT Berry Matthews, *White Space*. Installation of metal and ceramic tiles coated with wax to be set on fire; room-size

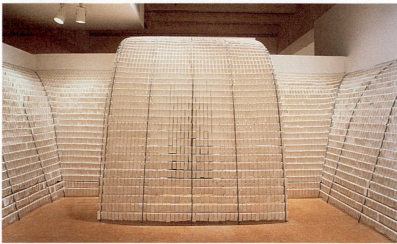

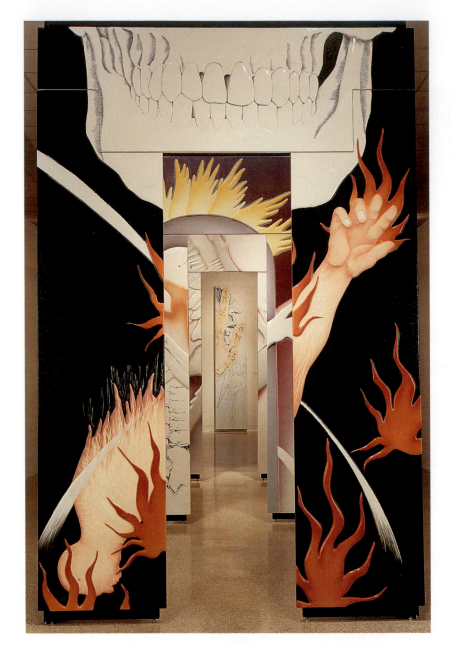

Deborah Horrell, *Hell and In Between*. Multiple arches fabricated at Otsuka Factory, Shigaraki, Japan; room-size

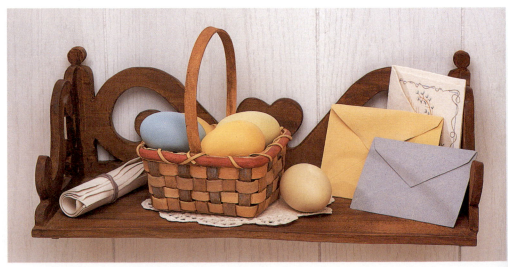

Sylvia Hyman, *Still Life no.5*. Stoneware and porcelain, 8 x 17 x 6 ins. (20 x 43 x 15 cm)

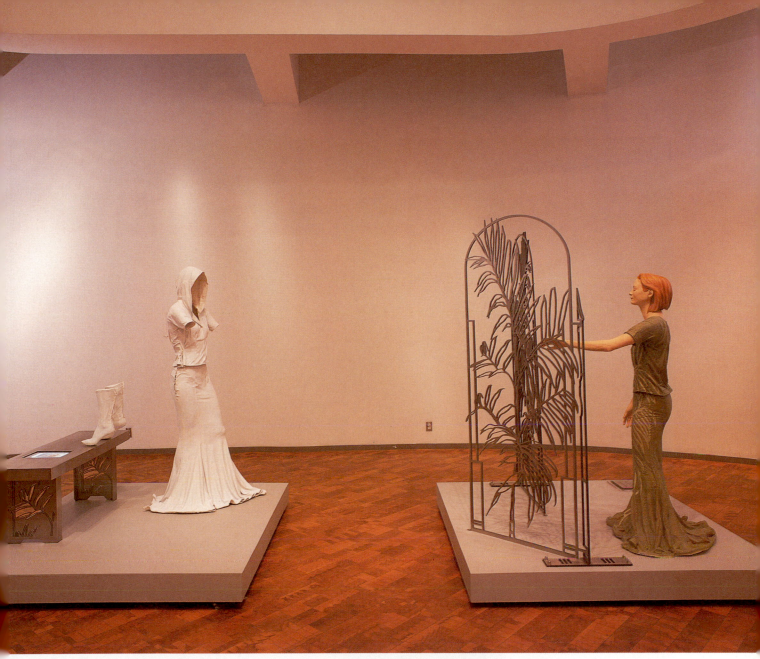

Nan Smith, *Beyond Illusions*. Life-size figures constructed with latex and plaster molds plus modeling and carving; steel gate; commercial stains and glazes airbrushed over stencil decoration, c/04; 92 x 72 x 192 ins. (2.33 x 1.83 x 4.88 m.)

Bernard Kerr (Australia), *Throne*. Earthenware, stoneware, and porcelain, exhibition installation, thrown, cast, and hand-built, unglazed; 10 x 8 x 4 ft (3 x 2.4 x 1.2 m.)

Nedda Guidi (Italy), *Limerick*. Terracotta-colored earthenware slab construction, 8 x 8 ft (2.4 x 2.4 m.)

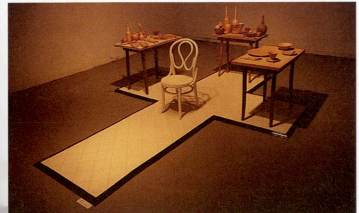

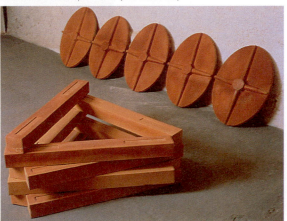

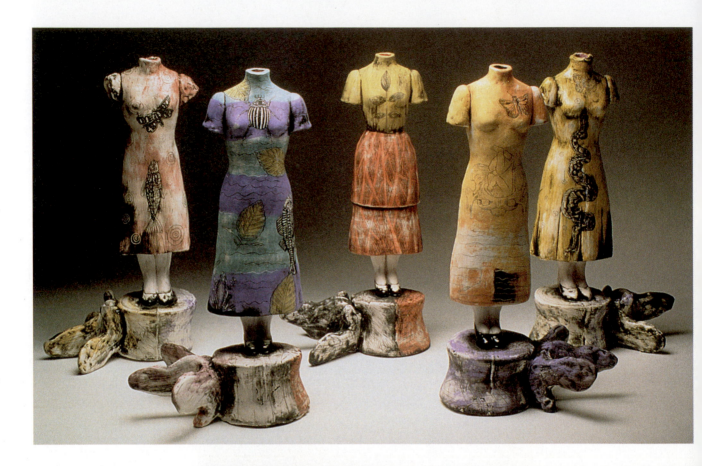

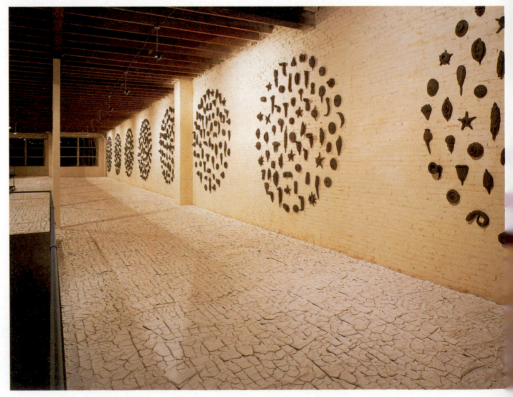

ABOVE Marilyn Lysohir, *Tattooed Ladies*. Hollow-built stoneware, sprayed and brushed stains and oxides, oxidation fired; each figure 26 x 11 x 9 ins. (66 x 28 x 23 cm)

RIGHT Sadashi Inuzuka, *Wall-Mounted Installation*

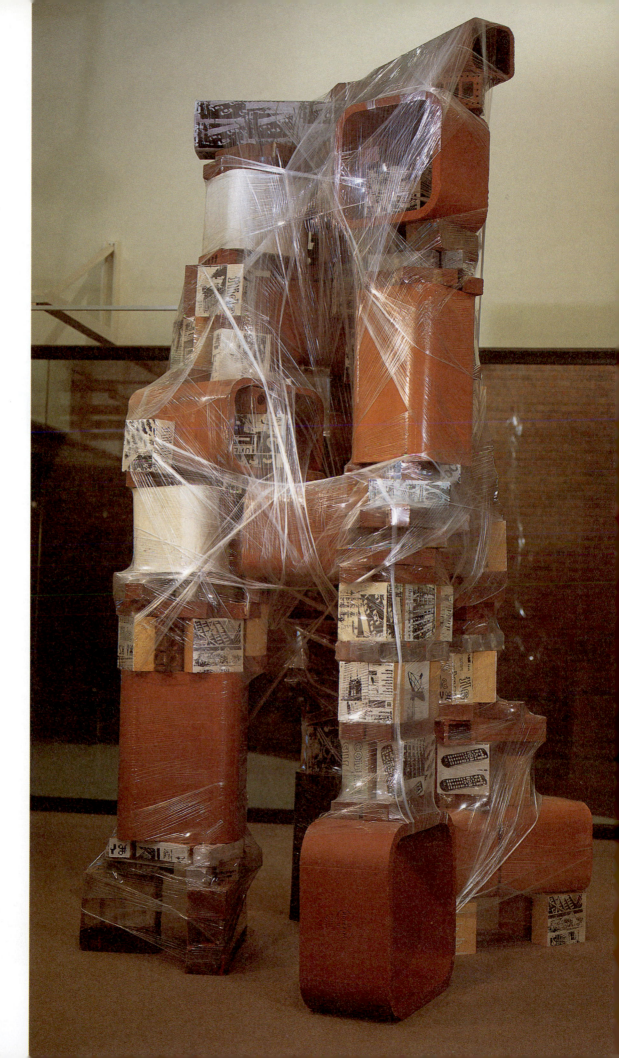

Fred Spaulding, *Shrink-wrapped Brick Sculpture*. Arbitrarily arranged and moveable shrink-wrapped manufactured brick, photo silkscreen engobe and majolica decoration with some glaze; bricks can be reconstituted; 10 ft (3 m.) high

7

THE TIMELESS WORLD HISTORY OF CERAMIC ART

What seem to be the earliest glazes were discovered in Egypt, dating from about 5000 B.C. At the same time, the Egyptians mixed clay and glaze into "Egyptian paste," a self-glazing clay body, to make small ushabti figures to be buried with the dead

Jomon ("cord pattern") large jar, coil built, with characteristic impressed surface decoration, from prehistoric Japan; 10,000 B.C.

Prehistoric Chinese pot, one of the earliest examples from the long tradition of Chinese pottery unbroken until this century; c. 5000 B.C.

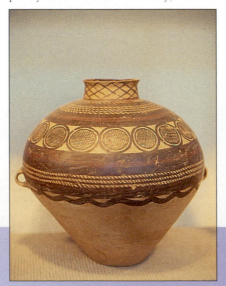

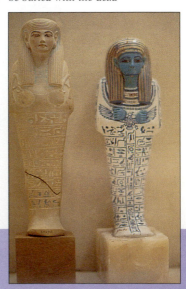

Fragments of clay vessels and objects have been the chief and sometimes the only remnants left from prehistoric human activities. Ancient peoples are studied mainly through the clay artifacts that remain in tombs and excavations all over the world. From the ceramic fragments that survive we draw inferences about cross-cultural borrowing, trade, migration, lifestyles, and the degree of sophistication of various societies according to their art forms. Clay was such a universal, easily obtained and moldable material that – more than rock art or marble sculpture – its remains supply countless ways to determine an intimate picture of ancient life, albeit without language.

Decorative motifs often seem to be similar and timeless. Perhaps the motifs that we see repeated time and again, simultaneously in different cultures or progressively through the ages, occur because processes are parallel and because the universal forms demand certain kinds of graphics. Or perhaps, as some leaders of surviving tribal groups maintain, there were long-term, long-distance migrations, exchanges, and communications of all sorts among distant peoples.

Tradition prevails in ceramics more than in other arts, because there are so many variables to be controlled in the materials and firing. Potters tend not to change anything for fear of having to change everything. Families and dynasties continued secret processes for generations and knowledge was refused to outsiders. All the same, new ways developed and some traditions were lost.

It is interesting to speculate why certain cultures were ceramic pioneers and others were not. For instance, why did only the Chinese develop porcelain, when the natural china clay plus flux and filler combination existed in the ground in Japan and Korea as well? Why did it take several thousand years for Europeans to develop porcelain, when they had the same ingredients but deposited separately? Why did North and South American societies burnish clay and never discover glaze? Why was the wheel used historically by potters only in the Orient, Middle East, and Europe, never in the so-called West? The answer probably lies in the fact that, if the societies did not invent or pick up from each other, their attention was focused elsewhere – on warfare, for instance.

The art of ceramics has the longest and most varied history of any of the arts. Neanderthal hunting and gathering groups roamed across Eurasia 70,000 to 35,000 years ago at least. Those early people had fire and probably made clay pots.

The first evidence of carving and the artistic employment of clay for ritual and functional use occurs about

The early Minoan culture on the island of Crete made very sophisticated pottery, thrown on the wheel, unglazed and decorated with various clays; 2500 B.C.

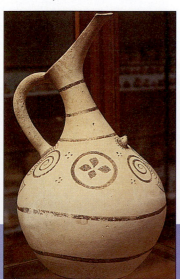

Yokes of Egyptian paste ornaments, as depicted in hieroglyphs, were used to hold up women's garments; c. 2000 B.C.

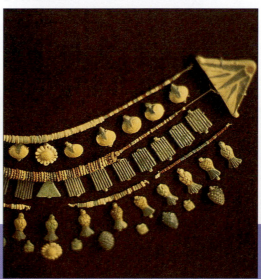

Amlash stylized animal, burnished and bonfired, from Luristan, Persia (Iran); 1500 B.C.

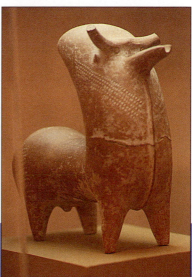

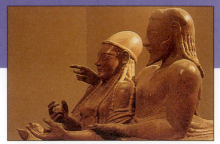

The Etruscans, ancient pre-Roman people of Italy, buried their dead in clay sarcophagi of vast scale topped with representational life-sized figures; 700 B.C.

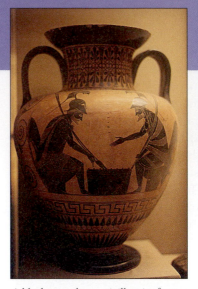

A black on red terra sigillata jar from Attica, mainland Greece, produced during the so-called Golden Age of ceramics, 500 B.C.

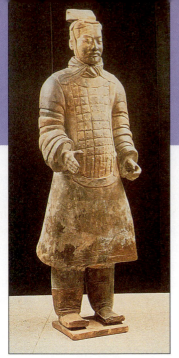

Xian soldier, one of 6,000 life-size figures buried with the Chinese Emperor Ch'in Shih Huang Ti; 200 B.C.

35,000 years ago, during the Ice Age; clay animals and figures emerge, modeled in the round as well as carved in clay floors and walls. Ruins of prehistoric kilns have also been found dating from this period. Native American Indians were burning clay pots in bonfires 25,000 years ago; to this day they do not use kilns. This long and varied history of ceramic art changed directions many times, dropped out of sight, moved forward or stood still, then cropped up again in other pockets of time and space as civilization progressed; it is still continuing.

Although new ways have been adopted by whole cultures, evolutionary stages of clay art have more often originated with individuals. In contrast to the large body of anonymous folk artists, these innovative individuals have often been known by name. Some even reached a stage where they created economic gain for their societies.

Wonderful, spirited engobe decoration characterized Chinese Tz'u-chou dynasty pots; A.D. 600–1100

The mysterious Mimbres North American Indians (A.D. 900–1300) disappeared inexplicably, but left us with exquisite stylized designs on ceremonial pots. When used as a funerary vessel and placed over the face the ho allowed the dead person's spirit to be released

Pottery in the Chinese Tang dynasty was noted for its lead-based polychrome glazes – grass-green, amber yellow, and cobalt blue – and for its technically masterful hollow-built horses, camels, and warriors; A.D. 600–900

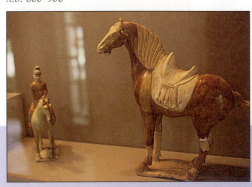

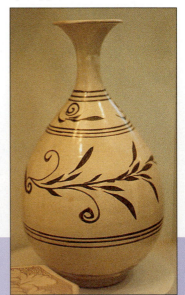

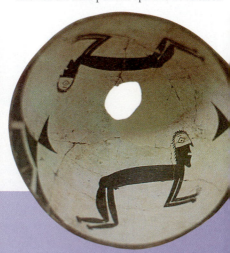

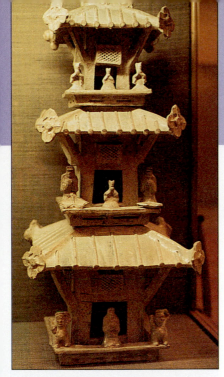

During the Han dynasty in China, seemingly thousands of figures and dwellings were created, depicting with wonderful movement and grace the daily life of the people; 200 B.C.–A.D. 200

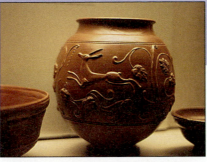

The slick sheen characteristic of Roman pots was accomplished by the use of iron-colored terra sigillata, often over relief designs; A.D. 100–200

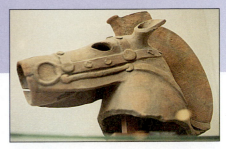

Stylized hollow-built Haniwa figures of warriors and animals were set into the ground around Japanese tombs; A.D. 400

In modern culture the break with tradition initiated by contemporary clay artists in their search for new ways has liberated claywork, sending it storming into the art world, and allowing not only space-age applications but also such non-traditional uses of clay as unfired clay art and site-specific installations.

In the pictorial time-line that comprises this chapter we indicate some of the highlights in the lengthy development of ceramics. The dates given are approximate. This overview is based on our own observations in museums and at archaeological digs in various parts of the world. In the 19th and 20th centuries some of the greatest painters and sculptors of our time have been enamored of the plastic qualities of clay and have chosen to experiment seriously with the medium. We all need to be aware of the magnetism that history holds for our own involvement with clay.

The Chinese Sung dynasty is thought of as the greatest age in ceramics. It combined the highest technical ability with simplicity of form. The outstanding contribution was the discovery of reduction atmosphere, which produced celadons and oxblood red glazes. Porcelain, celadon-glazed ewer, A.D. 900–1200

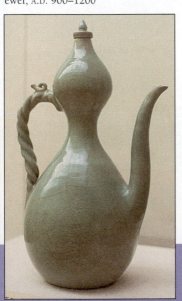

The Persians developed a scintillating luster technique, achieved by painting copper sulfate over a glaze and reducing it on the cooling cycle of a firing at 1300° F (700° C); A.D. 900–1300

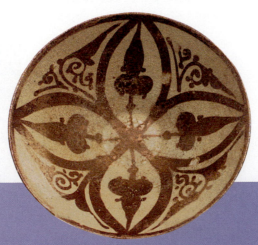

Pre-Columbian pottery from South America is represented by this Zapotec stoneware figure of a god, A.D. 900

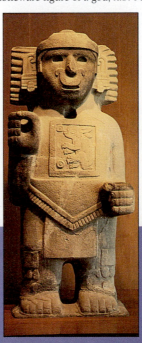

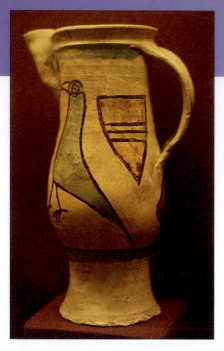

This medieval French jug is an example of the exuberant functional wares that were being produced all over Europe; c. A.D. 1100

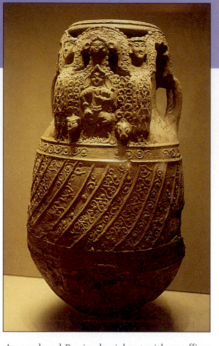

An unglazed Persian burial pot with an effigy; c. A.D. 1150

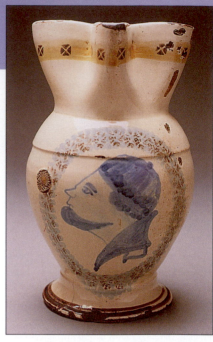

Early Italian majolica overglaze decoration on a tin opacified glazed pitcher; c. A.D. 1400

The famous Persian blue was produced by copper in a high-alkaline glaze. This ewer is decorated with engobe under the transparent glaze; c. A.D. 1600

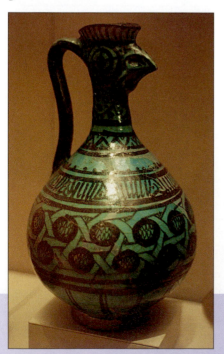

The long history of Turkish ceramics culminated in the 15th and 16th centuries in the beautifully overglazed Iznik vessels and tiles

The important Imari porcelain factory in Arita, Japan, produced spectacular overglaze enameled and gold lustered wares such as this platter; c. A.D. 1600

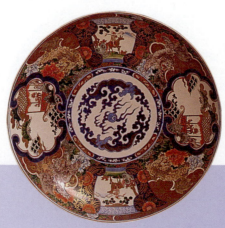

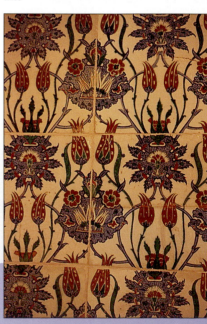

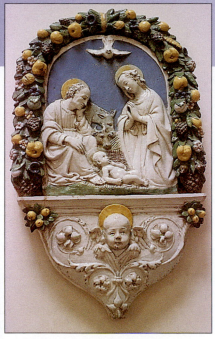

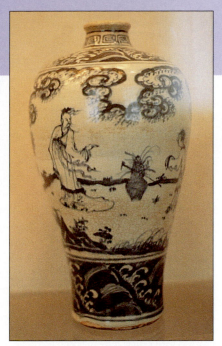

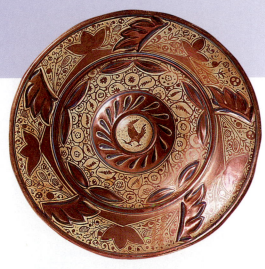

The luster technique that the Persians developed spread across Europe, but was perfected in Valencia, Spain, which was a center of lusterware production in the 1500s A.D.

For several generations the Della Robbia family in Italy produced architectural ceramics for interiors and exteriors, usually in carved white clay body with colorful majolica brushings; c. A.D. 1480

In China, potters of the Ming dynasty imported cobalt from Persia for blue-painted decorations on their clear-glazed white porcelain bodies. The dynasty also gave us the Ming colors of yellow, apple-green, and lavender that have never been duplicated; c. A.D. 1500

In France, King Louis XV instituted a state porcelain factory at Sèvres, where unusually fine overglaze painting was practiced on rather extravagant forms. Floor vase, c. A.D. 1750

The Dutch settlers, originally from German-speaking Switzerland, who came to Pennsylvania in the 1700s brought the peasant style of engobes on redware under clear glaze

Early in the 18th century, a porcelain body was developed at Meissen, Germany; porcelain centerpiece, c. A.D. 1750

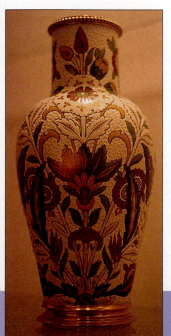

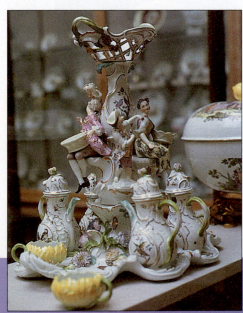

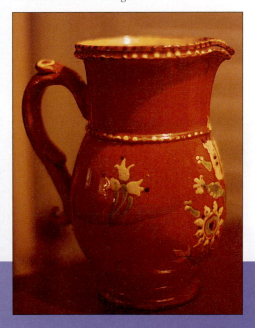

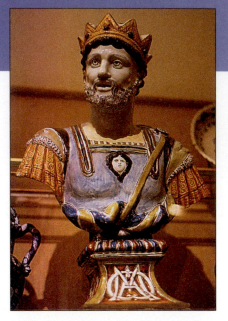

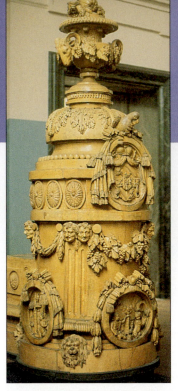

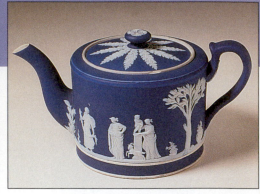

Josiah Wedgwood developed a porcelain clay body at Stoke-on-Trent, England, in 1760. The white porcelain body was colored with cobalt blue, chrome green, or basalt black, with added relief carvings in white porcelain superimposed; teapot, unglazed, c. A.D. 1800

Besides functional porcelain dinnerware, large portrait sculptures were produced all over Europe, such as this one from the 18th-century St-Cloud factory in France

In Switzerland and northern Europe, clay was used exuberantly to fashion sculptural stoves as room-warmers; c. A.D. 1800

Maija Grotell was a Finn who worked in the U.S.A. at about the same time as Adelaide Robineau; both women were influential. The work Grotell did in the 40s and 50s initiated an early modern style in ceramics

Adelaide Robineau made elaborate porcelain carvings early in the 20th century and founded the Ceramic Museum in Syracuse, New York

Platter by Joan Miró (1893–1983)

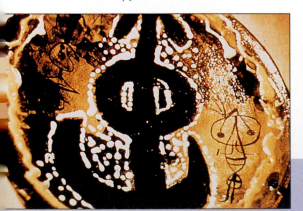

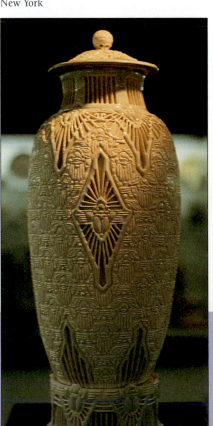

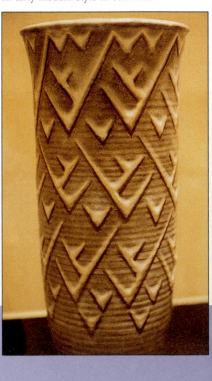

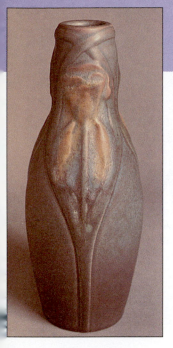

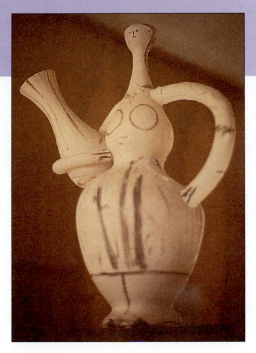

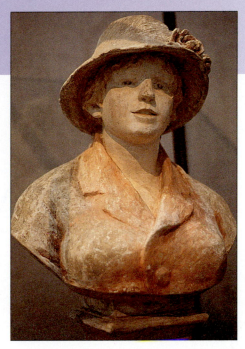

European ceramists who had worked in the state-subsidized porcelain factories settled in Ohio where there were good clay deposits, and founded the Rookwood factory, which closed in 1900. This subtly colored vase was one of this firm's many individually produced designs

European painters who were inspired by the vigor of folk pottery began to use ceramics as an art medium; most notably, Pablo Picasso (1881–1973) carried clay into museum sophistication, as exemplified in this vase. The contribution of many of these artists – Braque, Giacometti, Chagall, Léger, Rouault, Matisse, Gauguin, among others – elevated the status of clay as an art form

Bust by Pierre-Auguste Renoir (1841–1919)

Fine French china from the Limoges factory, overglaze hand-painted in contemporary designs, 1990s

Mai Järmut (Estonia), *Hopeful*, 2000

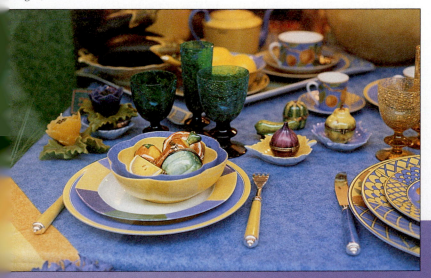

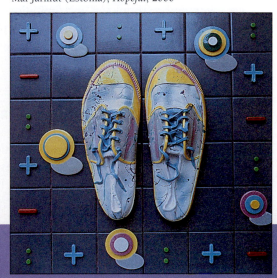

COMPENDIUM

1. SUGGESTED PROJECTS FOR INDIVIDUAL WORK

Decide on general procedure

Choose an abstract or functional piece to begin

1. Determine method of production to be used: hand-building; throwing; coil or slab or both; casting in a mold, or other.
2. Always consider size, proportion, shape, and color in relation to function.
3. Design in terms of the characteristics of your production method.
4. Remember shrinkage and limitations of your clay.
5. Structure of the shape is implicit in the design.
6. Color, textures, type of glaze or clay surface, must relate to the shape and function.

I. OVEN OR SERVING CONTAINER FOR HOT FOODS:

a. *Casserole* – design container for particular foods. What shape? What type lid? Handles necessary? Slant of sides? Easy to clean? Can it be used at table? What volume? Is color pleasing? Easy to store?

b. *Individual casseroles* – same as above.

c. *Soup tureen* – How big? How carried? Does ladle rest in tureen? Designed to keep soup hot? Color?

d. *Chafing dish* – Size? Handle? Where and how does it get heat?

II. BEVERAGE CONTAINER OR DISPENSER:

a. *Pitcher* – Do size and shape correspond to contents? Hot or cold liquid? Easy to grasp or hold? Pleasant and easily cleaned surfaces? Is handle attached near maximum weight? Is handle close to pot for leverage? Does spout provide guide to the liquid? Will spout drip? Does the pitcher have a substantial base?

b. *Mugs* – Large enough? Hot or cold liquids? Easy to grasp or hold, especially if hot? Pleasant lip to drink from?
If members of a set, do they hold correct amount in proportion to size of pitcher?

c. *Teapot* – Size? Spout pours well? Balance of handle? Is lid secure when teapot is tilted? Lid easy to grasp? Relationship of teapot body, handle, spout, and lid? Is there means of straining tea? Spout placed high enough so pot can be filled up?

d. *Cups and saucers* – Cup easy to hold and drink from? Does shape retain heat? Does saucer need a "well"? Relation of cup to saucer?

e. *Wine or liqueur bottle* – Size? Shape? How picked up? Will it pour? Visual appeal for this type of liquid?

f. *Coffee pot* – Large enough? Pouring facility? Lift? Will it keep coffee hot?

g. *Creamer and sugar* – Size? Pouring facility? Pouring

lip? Handles or not? Lid for sugar?

h. *Punch bowl* – Size? Room for ice? Ladle? Cups?

i. *Water cooler or party keg* – Size and shape? How is liquid dispensed?

III. KITCHEN AND TABLEWARE

a. *Mixing bowls* – Different sizes? Can they be measuring bowls? Are they substantial? Reinforced lip? Really designed for *mixing*?

b. *Canisters* – Sized for contents? Shaped for storage? Type of lid? Rugged construction?

c. *Butter dish* – For both serving and storage? Size and shape?

d. *Salt and pepper* – Easy to load? What shape and size? Difference between salt and pepper? Easily cleaned?

e. *Salad bowl* – Shape? Color? Size?

f. *Jello/jelly molds* – Shaped for easy release of contents?

g. *Soufflé dish* – Size? Straight sides?

h. *Fruit bowl* – To hold what kind of fruit? What shape best? Can it have a tall foot?

i. *Cookie/biscuit jar* – How much does it hold? Will it keep contents dry/moist? Large enough opening for hand to go in easily?

j. *Miscellaneous* – Condiment trays, snack servers, cruets, tile hot-pads or trivets, batter bowl, jam pot, garlic pot, herb jars, colanders, etc.

IV. LAMP BASE

Size? Shape? For what purpose – reading, decoration, or light? Type of shade? Fixture? What happens to cord? Proportion of base to size of shade to light fixture? Simplicity, good substantial form, important.

V. PLANT AND FLOWER CONTAINERS

a. What type plant, as to size, color, culture? Should pot be porous? Must it provide drainage? Does it need a stand? Is there enough root area?

b. Cut flowers, what kind? Short or long stems, graceful or stiff? Design container for maximum water at base of stem.

c. Florist-type flower container, possible for mass production, low cost.

VI. OUTDOOR ACCESSORIES

a. *Brazier* – Size? Depth? Stand? Type and placement

of grill? Porous clay body essential.

b. *Planter or decorative garden pot* – Glazed or not? Textured? Root room? Drainage?

c. *Space divider* – Such as could be made from ovals cut from thrown cylinder shapes, or slab constructions, etc.; or from many assembled clay shapes.

d. *Garden sculpture* – Withstand the elements? Where will it be used – among plants, on brick, free-standing? Interesting clay body important asset.

e. *Barbecue cooking accessories* – Large salt and pepper, basting pot, oversized salad container, condiment jars, etc.

VII. INTERIOR ACCESSORIES

a. *Wall decoration* – Flat tiles, relief sculpture, etc. How will it hang? Does it retain clay quality? Movable or permanent?

b. *Tobacco humidor* – Size? Shape? Lid? Means of retaining moisture?

c. *Tile table-top or tile trays* – How are tiles mounted? Spaces between? Continuity? Decorative or functional?

d. *Miscellaneous* – Door knobs, bells, tree or patio decorations, table centerpiece, clock, candle-holders, boxes, mirror frames, branch vases, hanging lights, porch lights, thrown or hand-built sculptures for interior or exterior spaces.

2. SUGGESTED PROJECTS FOR BEGINNING HAND-BUILDING

TEXTURE   Experiment with objects pushed into clay to make patterns: tools, nails, bolts, buttons, seed pods, bark, etc. Glaze or stain to emphasize the texture.

COIL   Round form with coils exposed and textured, or round form with coil building method concealed by smoothing the clay inside and out.

SLAB   Build box or rectangular form with slab

bottoms and sides, or cut *two* patterns and put them together in an asymmetrical shape. Glaze to enhance the main directional line.

HUMP OR SLING

Hump: rock or clay form.

Sling: hammock, draped in box or between four table legs, made of cloth. This is a good method for making simple, flat, low, open forms. You can add a foot or feet, or a top, or spouts, or put two humps or slings together, etc.

HISTORICAL POT OR FIGURE

Not copy, but grasp the same "flavor" as something from ceramic history. Suggestions: Tang, Sung, Haniwa, Jomon, Harappa, Syrian, medieval English, pre-Columbian, Native American, Egyptian, early Greek, Pennsylvania Dutch, etc. (See Bibliography for help in finding historical illustrations.)

POT OR CONTAINER FOR DRIED BRANCHES

Find the grasses, stalks, or branches, then design the pot. This can be designed to hang free, hang against, stand alone, or be a group. Glaze only partially so the vegetation will relate to some "natural" clay surface.

PATIO LAMP

Light, lantern, or candle container, for outdoor use. Most important: light pattern, cut holes designed for shadows.

---

3. PROGRESSION OF INDIVIDUAL STEPS IN THROWING

1. Learn to *center* ball of clay. Try progressively larger balls, up to 10 or 15 lb (5 or 7.5 kg).
2. *Pull cylinder* with even cross-section. Get clay *up* from bat. Cylinder walls should be heavier at base, gradually thinner toward the top.
3. Throw *bowl* shape, low and wide.
4. Pull *tall* cylinder, work up to 13 inches (33 cm) high, even wall-thickness.
5. *Collar* in small neck of cylinder, for bottle.
6. Throw *pitcher* and pull lip. Sharpen pitcher lip-edge so it will not drip. Pull and attach handle.
7. Throw *mug* and add handle.
8. *Pot with lid* to fit. Practice making flange on either pot or lid.
9. *Teapot*, watch size, proportion, balance, height of spout, type of handle.
10. Set of four or six *all alike*.
11. *Set*, one large container and several small ones, according to size and volume. Make enough small ones to hold the contents of large pot, no more, no less.
    - *Watch structure*, learn to prevent warping, slumping. Engineer cross-section and profile for greatest support.
    - *Watch foot shape* and size: should relate appropriately to profile-line of pot, and be similar thickness to the lip of the pot.
    - *Signature of potter* should finish design, not hurt it.
    - *Lip of pot* should end the shape. Try different ways of making and finishing feet and lips – bevels, sharp edges, soft rolls, beads, etc.

If you master the steps above, try these:

1. Try larger lumps of clay, perhaps twice larger at each stage, and do again the beginner projects.
2. Combine wheel-thrown shapes into larger pots or sculptural forms, putting them together wet, squashing or paddling the thrown pieces, adding texture, etc.
3. Large decorative plates
4. Planters
5. Lamps or lights
6. Hanging units: bells, mobiles, planters
7. Tea- and coffee-pots
8. Sets, alike or not, of anything
9. Closed forms
10. Footed compote

4. SUGGESTED PROJECTS FOR CLAY, GLAZE, AND DECORATION EXPERIMENTS

Body and glaze development

1. Learn properties of raw materials by experimental testing.
2. Set up standards for a particular type of clay body, color, firing properties, working qualities. Fit composition together, mix a batch, and run tests.
3. Set up standards for developing glazes to fit this clay body. Determine composition of raw materials, mix a batch, test, make necessary correction, try colorants.
4. Set up standards for any specific type of glaze – surface texture, temperature, color, viscosity. Mix and test.
5. Develop casting slip for specific temperature, type, color.

This can go on indefinitely!

Decoration

1. **Engobe:** brush, trail, dip, sgraffito; add flux to make engobe more vitreous; add more color to make it bleed through glaze.
2. **Underglaze:** decoration with stains or oxides on bisque. Practice varieties of brush-strokes. Vary shading by spraying.
3. **Majolica:** decoration with stains or oxides over an unfired opaque glaze. Lines will fuse and feather. Freer than underglaze technique; use "washes" and other watercolor techniques.
4. **Glaze on glaze:** learn characteristics of various types of glazes. Watch color combinations. Spray, dip, over-dip, brush.
5. **Sgraffito:** draw lines through engobe or glaze or scrape away areas. Glaze should be non-fluid so lines will remain clear-cut in firing.
6. **Wax resist:** brush decoration with paraffin or wax emulsion on bisque, engobe or glaze over, or wax

between two glazes.
7. **Stencil:** spray colored areas through stencil with underglaze, majolica, or over-spray techniques; or brush or sponge color using stencil pattern.

Exploit characteristic effects by analyzing your results, and making more tests.

Design standards to keep in mind

1. Proportion, size relationship, weight, balance, volume.
2. Placement of appendages.
3. Function and utility of shape.
4. Definite changes of plane make more vital form.
5. Keep character and freedom of the clay and its production process.

---

5. EXPERIMENTING WITH MATERIAL ADDITIONS TO A BASE GLAZE

Bisque a number of tiles for making tests: (a) test individual glaze materials mixed with water and applied to tiles; fire at cone 04, 5, and 10 to see the separate melts.

(b) Batch glaze for testing – one you already know or want to try. Mix it dry, well. Divide it into 100-gram amounts and add the proper material additions (see below). Mix each one wet and apply to tile with spatula, or by pouring or dipping. Fire.

Note: It is interesting to try the test at each of the above temperatures to see how it varies, but if you can't do that, just use the one temperature (cone) at which you usually fire.

Code back of each test-tile with cobalt, or black stain, and water, or use a commercial ceramic pencil.

TEST TILES: BASE GLAZE PLUS ADDITIONS. Take a known glaze and test it with additions:

Flint 20%	Flint 30%	Kaolin 20%	Kaolin 30%	Talc 20%
Dolomite 20%	Nephelene syenite 20%	Barium carbonate 20%	Zinc oxide 20%	Whiting 20%
Magnesium carbonate 20%	Calcium borate 20%	Rutile 20%	Wood ash 20%	Base glaze 100%

Make a second test, replacing the 20% with 30% additions and 30% with 40%, to see the limits. Make color tests with oxide additions.

6. GLAZE IMPROVIZATIONS

Everybody, even children of elementary school-age, enjoys doing individual raw material experiments. Always use parts of 100, or parts of 10, that is, keep the "base" adding up to 100 or to 10. Add test materials to the base in percentage amounts to make changes. For example:

MAKE
- 10%–20% additions of all the raw materials on your shelves to many base glazes, your own batches or taken from books;
- or additions of natural raw organic plant materials (wood ash, flowers, volcanic ash, seaweed, etc.) to a base glaze;
- or additions of low-temperature common surface clay (found in the desert or near creek beds);
- or organic ash 50–50 with a glaze, or to glaze batches starting with 10%;
- or crushed, pulverized, ground rock used by itself, or added to other base glazes.

Test these sample experimental glazes on tiles or pots and fire at the temperature you normally use.

Seeing the results of standard glaze materials or of additions such as wood ash, etc., *as they melt by themselves (or don't melt) at various temperatures* can be a fascinating experience for students, and an absolute necessity for the potter; then, make more compositions from these results.

7. GLAZE "LINE-BLEND" TEST

This involves making all possible 50–50 combinations of some basic colors on your favorite glaze, at your favorite temperature.

1. Make 15 tiles for one test. (If you want more tests, add more top-members to the test.)
2. Mix 100 grams glaze for every top-member – in this case there are five, so measure 500 dry grams

of glaze, mix well, and divide equally into five sandwich bags.

3. Add appropriate colorant to each sack and mix well:

For instance: sack #1 = 2% cobalt carbonate; sack #2 = 4% copper carbonate; sack #3 = 10% rutile; sack #4 = 5% iron oxide; sack #5 = 10% zircopax
– or make your own top-member list.

4. The line blend looks like this:

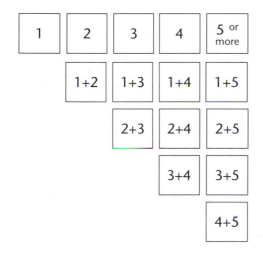

Take a measuring spoon of dry glaze from each of the five sacks, mix it with water and apply each color to the first five tiles. Then each successive tile is a 50–50 blend of the top-members. Take a measuring spoon of dry glaze from each of two sacks, mix together with water and apply to tiles (e.g., ½ #1 & ½ #2; ½ #1 & ½ #3, etc.).
Mark back of tile with code number and fire.

8. SPECIAL LOW-FIRE INFORMATION

Egyptian paste

White Batch Formula (Self-glazing clay/glaze composition similar to that used several thousand years ago by the Egyptians)

Fire cone 010 to cone 04
(1800° to 1900° F, 980° to 1040° C)

Nepheline syenite	342 grams
Silica	342 grams
Ball clay	133 grams
Soda ash	53 grams
Baking soda	<u>53 grams</u>
Total	923 grams

(makes about 2 lb./1 kg.)

Keep wet batch wrapped in damp cloth and stored in airtight container.

Colors for Egyptian paste

(Try adding one of these to the base batch above)

Turquoise – copper carbonate		3% (light)
	or	4% (darker)
	or	6% (black)
Dark blue – cobalt oxide		1–2%
Yellow-green – yellow-green stain		5%
Purple – manganese dioxide		2%
Yellow – yellow stain		8%
Dark green – chrome oxide		5%

Experiment with other metallic oxides and stains for color;
12% color addition is maximum.

Use Egyptian paste for beads, pins, buttons, jewelry.
Fire on ni-chrome (nickel-chrome) wire in regular bisque firing.

Mosaic cement

(Use for setting ceramic or glass mosaic pieces)
Mix: magnasite and magnesium chloride together into paste form, 50–50.

Low-fire engobe

For cone 04: Use dry low-fire clay body for base white batch for firing at cone 04 or lower.

Add colors:

Blue – cobalt blue	20%
Orange – rutile	40%
Green – chrome oxide	40%

Violet brown – manganese dioxide	12%
Black – black stain	10%, plus
iron oxide	10%, plus
manganese dioxide	10%

(start with red clay, if possible)

or mix your own low-fire base white engobe as
  follows:

Talc	70%
Ball clay	30%

(See "Engobes," page 102, for example of a high-fire
  engobe.)

9. EXAMPLE OF A POTTERY STUDIO

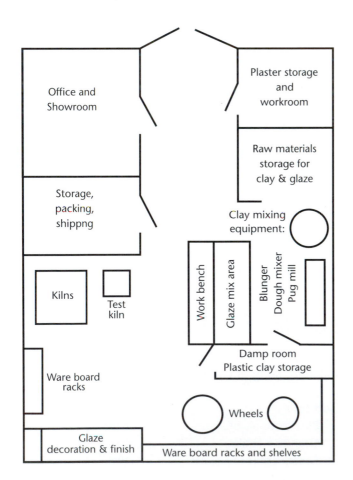

10. TERMS EASILY MIXED UP

Some terms are confusing because they have several meanings.
The list below gives them all or their alternatives.

bat – wheel head; movable work surface of any shape, usually
  plaster but also wood or fiberboard

bisque – biscuit; any unglazed ware at any temperature; an initial
  firing without glaze

calcium spar – Cornwall stone, or any spar high in calcium oxide

china – any white ceramic ware; term for any tableware, usually
  porcelain

china clay – kaolin

china paint – enamel; luster; very low-fire glaze applied over a
  fired glaze

crackle – craze; fine line matrix decoration; fault of glaze chemistry

deflocculant – Darvan; sodium silicate; soda ash; tea

enamel – room-temperature paint; fired-on paint at 300° F (150° C);
  porcelain enamel on signs or refrigerators; low-fire glaze

ferric oxide – iron oxide, usually red but can be black

flux – anything that lowers the temperature of a material or a
  mixture, or that melts at low temperature by itself

frit – ground glass; pre-melted chemical mixture you make yourself
  or buy, numbered according to composition

gum – gum tragacanth; gum arabic; synthetic gum (CMC, methyl
  cellulose)

model – maquette; something to work from; to work clay with
  fingers or a tool

plastic, plasticity – workability of clay; material to cover ware to
  keep it damp

potash spar – Kingman; Custer; G-200, or any spar higher in
  potassium oxide than in sodium oxide

pottery – ceramic; low-fired claywork; any claywork

raw – unfired, greenware (green as in "fresh")

refractory – anything that resists heat or raises the temperature of
  another material, or that fires at high temperature by itself

resist – stencil; latex; wax; paper; metal template

silica – sand; flint; quartz

slip – engobe (liquid clay for decoration); casting slip; slip glaze

slurry – slurpy-wet clay; any liquid mess; plaster not yet hard

soda spar – nepheline syenite; Kona A4, or any spar higher in
  sodium oxide than in potassium oxide

spar – short for feldspar, the mineral

stain – metallic coloring oxide and other chemicals in stable
  combinations; wash; commercially sold or home-made
  pigment mixture; waterbased room-temperature paint thinly
  applied

suspension agent – bentonite; epsom salts; magnesium carbonate

terra cotta – a color; low-fire red clay; art historian's term for
  redware of all kinds

volcanic ash – pumice, found in lumber yards; pumice is purer
  than volcanic ash, and both are natural materials

wax – water-soluble commercial product such as "Ceremul A";
  melted paraffin; crayon

TEMPERATURE EQUIVALENTS OF ORTON CONES

Remember that cone temperatures are approximate – it is always best to watch the cones.

CONE NO.	68°F	20°C	CONE NO.	212°F	100°C	CONE NO.	1112°F	600°C
022	1085	585	23	2876	1580	39	3389	1865
021	1103	595	26	2903	1595	40	3425	1885
020	1157	625	27	2921	1605	41	3578	1970
019	1166	630	28	2939	1615	42	3659	2015
018	1238	670	29	2984	1640			
017	1328	720	30	3002	1650			
016	1355	735	31	3056	1680			
015	1418	770	32	3092	1700			
014	1463	795	32½	3137	1725			
013	1517	825	33	3173	1745			
012	1544	840	34	3200	1760			
011	1607	875	35	3245	1785			
010	1634	890	36	3290	1810			
09	1706	930	37	3308	1820			
08	1733	945	38	3335	1835			
07	1787	975						
06	1841	1005						
05	1886	1030						
04	1922	1050						
03	1976	1080						
02	2003	1095						
01	2030	1110						
1	2057	1125						
2	2075	1135						
3	2093	1145						
4	2129	1165						
5	2156	1180						
6	2174	1190						
7	2210	1210						
8	2237	1225						
9	2282	1250						
10	2300	1260						
11	2345	1285						
12	2390	1310						
13	2462	1350						
14	2534	1390						
15	2570	1410						
16	2642	1450						
17	2669	1465						
18	2705	1485						
19	2759	1515						
20	2768	1520						

TEMPERATURE EQUIVALENTS OF SEGER CONES

CONE NO.	MELTING POINT		CONE NO.	MELTING POINT		CONE NO.	MELTING POINT	
	°F	°C		°F	°C		°F	°C
021	1202	650	01a	1976	1080	20	2786	1530
020	1238	670	1a	2012	1100	*26	2876	1580
019	1274	690	2a	2048	1120	27	2930	1610
018	1310	710	3a	2084	1140	28	2966	1630
017	1346	730	4a	2120	1160	29	3002	1650
016	1382	750	5a	2156	1180	30	3038	1670
015a	1454	790	6a	2192	1200	31	3074	1690
014a	1499	815	7	2246	1230	32	3110	1710
013a	1535	835	8	2282	1250	33	3146	1730
012a	1590	866	9	2336	1280	34	3182	1750
011a	1616	880	10	2372	1300	35	3218	1770
010a	1652	900	11	2408	1320	36	3254	1790
09a	1688	920	12	2462	1350	37	3317	1825
08a	1724	940	13	2516	1380	38	3362	1850
07a	1760	960	14	2570	1410	39	3416	1880
06a	1796	980	15	2615	1435	40	3488	1920
05a	1832	1000	16	2660	1460	41	3560	1960
04a	1868	1020	17	2696	1480	42	3632	2000
03a	1904	1040	18	2732	1500	* Numbers 21 to 25 are obsolete		
02a	1940	1060	19	2768	1520			

GLOSSARY

Anagama Tube-like single chamber hill kiln; predecessor of *noborigama*, a multi-chambered hill kiln of Oriental style.

Ash The residue made by burning tree, plant, or vegetable material; can be used alone or with other materials for glaze; volcanic ash can also be used.

Ball Clay Highly plastic refractory clay that fires off-white; workable, fine-grained sedimentary clay used in white bodies, engobes, and glazes.

Bat Any slab used as a base for throwing or hand-building clay; also applies to a trough used to dry slurry clay to the plastic state; usually made of plaster, press board, plywood, or other porous material.

Batch A mixture of glaze or engobe ingredients calculated by parts or weight.

Bisque, Biscuit Unglazed, but fired ware, usually accomplished in a low temperature firing prior to a glaze fire; also applies to unglazed ware fired high, as in porcelain bisque.

Blistering Bubbles formed in the glaze during the firing due to liberation of gases caused by firing that is too fast; or caused deliberately by putting into the glaze a material such as trisodium phosphate, which will promote decorative bloats.

Blunger A mechanical machine for mixing liquid or slurry clay.

Body A combination of natural clays and non-plastics, especially formulated to have certain workability and firing characteristics.

Bone China Porcelain of high translucency made with bone ash as the flux, produced mainly in England and Japan.

Burnishing Polishing with a smooth stone or tool on leather-hard clay or slip to make a surface sheen; the surface will not stay shiny at temperatures above 2000° F (1100° C).

Casting Process of forming shapes by pouring deflocculated liquid clay slip into plaster molds for repetitive production.

Celadon Glaze Sea-green glaze with a small percentage of iron as the colorant; fired in a reduced oxygen atmosphere, usually a stoneware or porcelain glaze, first used in the Orient.

Centering Pushing a mass of clay toward the center with the centrifugal motion of a potter's wheel.

Ceramics Art and science of forming objects from earth materials containing or combined with silica, produced with the aid of heat treatment at 1300° F (700° C) or more.

China (1) A porcelain clay body, with up to 1% absorption, usually translucent. (2) Whiteware, vitreous and hard, sometimes translucent. (3) A general term used in trade when discussing any kind of tableware.

China Clay Primary or secondary kaolin, refractory, not very plastic, white-burning, rare in the world; used in the blending of all whiteware and porcelain bodies.

Clay Theoretically Al_2O_3–$2SiO_2$–$6H_2O$; earth materials formed by the decomposition of igneous rock; when combined with water, clay is plastic enough to be shaped; when subject to red heat or above, it becomes dense and rock-like.

Coiling, Coil Building Age-old method of constructing hollow forms by rolling and attaching ropes of soft clay.

Cones Pyrometric cones, Orton or Seger brand; pyramids made of clay and glaze constituents that bend at specific temperature. Cones are placed in the kiln during firing to indicate the final heat; they are classified by numbers coded to their softening point.

Core The interior of a piece, or a framing or the stuffing on or over which work can be supported; combustible core materials burn out in the kiln; rigid cores should be removed before the clay shrinks.

Crackle Decorative and intentional fissures netting the surface of a glaze due to a variation of expansion and contraction of the glaze and the clay body.

Crawling Glaze that has separated into mounds on the clay surface during firing, generally caused by fluffy or high-shrink materials in raw glazes.

Crystalline Glazes Large crystals grown on the glaze surface during firing and cooling, primarily induced by high zinc oxide and low alumina content in glazes.

Damper Adjustable shutter to control draft at the kiln flue.

Decal Ceramic pigments photo-screened or pattern-screened onto flexible decal paper for transfer to bisque or over glaze; can be bought or made.

Deflocculation The addition of a catalyst to a clay and water slip to reduce the amount of water required to about 40% by weight.

Downdraft Kiln Kiln with fire entering at the side or base, where heat is forced around, up, and down through the ware, and exits via a flue at the back of the chamber.

Dry Foot No glaze on the foot rim; used for stoneware and porcelain, rather than the stilt method used for earthenware; stilts would warp the piece when fired to these higher densities.

Earthenware All ware with a permeable or porous body after firing; by definition earthenware has 10% to 15% absorption.

Enamel (1) Applied to pottery: low-temperature glazes applied over other glazes. (2) Applied to metals: glaze that melts lower than steel, copper, silver, or gold, on which enamel is used, fired about 1300° F (700° C).

Engobe [*pronounced on-gobe*] A liquid clay slip colored with metallic earth oxides or glaze stains applied to wet or leather-hard ware for decoration. Engobe can be covered by glaze or used alone.

Extrusion Forcing plastic clay through an auger or form, mechanically or by hand, to change its shape; can be solid or hollow.

Faience A general art-historian's word covering low-fire colored clay bodies, such as Egyptian paste.

Feldspar Mineral found in granite which

melts around 2300° F (1260° C), used as a flux in clay bodies and glazes.

Fire Box The chamber of certain kilns into which the fuel is fed and in which the initial combustion takes place.

Fire Clay Secondary clay that withstands high temperature and has a varying amount of free silica in addition to the clay molecule.

Firing (1) Heating in a kiln to the required temperature for clay or glaze, at least to red heat, 1300° F (700° C). (2) Bonfiring in a pit or on the ground.

Firing Curve The track made by firing points on a graph, showing the relationship between change in temperature and firing time.

Flue (1) The passageway for flames in kilns – essentially the combustion space; the flue is the area around the stacking space. (2) The place of escape for the products of combustion from the kiln chamber.

Flux A material or mixture having a low melting point or lowering the melting point of other materials. One of the three main components of glaze; also used to increase density in clay bodies; examples include lead, borax, lime, feldspar, and frit.

Foot Base or bottom of a piece.

Frit Mixture melted at high temperature, quenched, and ground to a fine powder. Fritting renders soluble glaze ingredients, such as soda ash, insoluble, and poisonous materials, such as lead, nonpoisonous.

Glaze Glassy melted coating developed by chemicals and heat on a clay or metal surface. Glaze provides decoration and color, prevents some penetration of liquids or acids, and yields a matt or glossy, functional surface.

Glaze Stains Fabricated ceramic colorants from metallic oxides mixed in combination with other elements to widen the glaze decorating palette; sold by code number, color, and company.

Greenware Finished leather-hard or bone-dry clay pieces not yet fired; raw ware.

Grog Crushed or ground-up fired clay, purchased commercially or made by the potter; used to reduce shrinkage, it yields texture; aids in even drying and firing.

Hollow Casting Pouring liquid clay slip into a hollow plaster mold to create a shell of a specific shape.

Intaglio Depressed surface decoration, the reverse of bas-relief.

Jiggering A mechanical method of producing many of the same shapes with a plaster mold and a metal template.

Kaki Glaze Traditional glaze from the village of Mashiko, Japan. Created by grinding local rock; according to Shoji Hamada it was named for the color that a persimmon is on October 24.

Kaolin Anglicized form of the Chinese word for china clay. Pure kaolin is a white-burning, high-firing natural clay that is the essential component of porcelain bodies and an ingredient in many glazes.

Kick Wheel A potter's machine for working clay with a centrifugal motion propelled by kicking.

Kiln Furnace for firing clay, slumping glass, or melting enamels; studio kilns can achieve temperatures up to 2500° F (1370° C). They can be fueled carbonaceously, organically, or electrically.

Kiln Furniture Refractory slabs, posts, supports (called setters) for holding ware in the kiln, handmade or purchased.

Kiln Wash Half clay, half silica, mixed with water to coat kiln shelves.

Leather-hard Cheese-hard stage which clay reaches before being bone-dry; stiff enough to support itself, but still can be altered.

Luster A brilliant, iridescent metallic film on glaze, formed from certain metallic salts at a specific temperature in a reduced atmosphere, usually on the cooling side of the firing cycle.

Luting A method of putting together coils, slabs, or other clay forms in the wet or leather-hard stage by cross-hatching and moistening; the same as scoring.

Majolica The decorative application of coloring oxides and stains over an unfired glaze that fuses into the base glaze during the firing, leaving fuzzy edges. The term comes from the Balearic island of Majorca.

Majolica Glaze An opaque glaze with a glossy surface, usually white, generally opacified by tin oxide; a base for

colored stain or overglaze decoration.

Matt Dull, non-reflective surface; in the case of glaze, due to deliberate composition or immature firing.

Mesh Holes per square inch in any screen, used for screening clay or glaze.

Millefiore A traditional technique in glass and clay where several, or many, slabs of color are combined in patterns, and cut through in cross-section to make other forms.

Mishima Carved decoration in leather-hard clay, covered with engobe and rubbed off when drier, leaving engobe inlaid in the carving.

Mold Usually a plaster form, single or multi-pieced, which will be used to reproduce any number of accurate copies of the original model in clay or plaster.

Neutral Atmosphere An atmosphere in a kiln that is neither completely oxidizing nor completely reducing.

Off-the-Hump Method of throwing small forms consecutively from one large mound of clay.

Once-firing Glazing leather-hard or bone-dry ware and firing to maturing temperature (this skips the first bisquing); frequently used in commercial production; often the method in salt or wood firing.

Oxidation, Oxidizing Fire Opposite of a reducing fire; the firing of a kiln where combustion of the fuel is complete.

Peephole A view or observation hole in the wall or door of a kiln; it should be large enough to see into the kiln easily during the firing; also used for pulling draw trials and tests during the firing.

Pinching Moving and shaping clay with the fingers.

Plaster The mineral gypsum, with the chemical composition of calcium sulfate, used for clay/mold reproduction and as a work surface.

Plasticity Workability; clay is the only mineral having real plasticity, meaning the ability to form into any shape, and to get progressively harder in the same shape on being fired to 1300° F (700° C) and above. Other materials, such as talc, can be said to have claylike plasticity.

Porcelain Mechanically strong, hard, frequently translucent, fired clay body with 0% absorption; the strongest of all clay bodies unless very thin.

Pottery A loosely used term; often means earthenware or just any clay piece that has been fired.

Pressing Forming plastic clay in a plaster mold or other form, by laying it against the mold face.

Profile Line Outside or inside line; the line formed when shape bisects space.

Pyrometer A calibrating instrument on the outside of a kiln, used with a thermocouple inside the kiln to measure temperature during the firing.

Raku A firing or a type of ware; porous, groggy ware, with or without a glaze, put into and pulled out of a hot fire and sometimes smoked. Developed in Japan in the 1600s.

Raw Glaze Unfired glaze.

Reduction, Reducing Fire Opposite of an oxidation fire; the firing of a kiln with an atmosphere of reduced oxygen, where combustion of the fuel is incomplete. Copper in reduction is oxblood red, in oxidation green; iron in reduction is celadon, in oxidation amber yellow, or brown.

Refractory Resistant to melting or fusion; a substance that raises the melting point of another material. Refractory materials are the basis of high-temperature ceramics.

Resist Wax, varnish, latex, or other substance applied in pattern on a clay or glaze surface to cover an area while the background is treated by another material or color.

Sagger An enclosure for firing pots to achieve various effects.

Salt Firing Rock salt is thrown into the fire at the maturing temperature of the clay until an "orange-peel" clear glaze appears on the ware.

Sawdust Firing Firing with sawdust to reduce oxygen and blacken the ware.

Scoring A cross-hatch and moistening method of putting together coils and slabs in the wet or leather-hard; the same as luting.

Sgraffito A design scratched through one surface to another.

Shards Fragments of pottery; the state in which many clay works are found.

Shrinkage Contraction of clays or bodies in drying and firing, caused by the loss of physical and chemical water and the achieving of molecular density.

Silica Oxide of silicon, SiO_2; found abundantly in nature as quartz, sand, and flint; the most essential oxide in ceramics; the glass-forming oxide.

Slab Flat piece of clay from which shapes can be fabricated.

Slip A suspension of ceramic materials in water; generally refers to casting slip for molds; can mean a liquid clay engobe for decorating or a glaze slip.

Slurry Thick suspension of one or more ceramic materials in water; usually refers to slushy clay.

Spiral Wedging Kneading clay with a pivoting motion to remove air pockets and make the clay mix homogeneous, ready to work.

Stain Watercolor wash on bisque with metallic coloring oxides or commercial glaze stains; also a term referring to "stain" colors.

Stoneware Hard, dense, and durable ware generally fired to 2150° F (1180° C) or above; a body with 0 to 5% absorption, regardless of firing temperature.

Tenmoku Japanese name for a type of glaze used especially by the Chinese during the Sung Dynasty; glaze whose rich black appearance is caused by an overabundance of iron oxide.

Terra cotta Term used to describe rust-red clays; an art historian's term for low-fired, unglazed, generally red-colored ware; a color.

Terra Sigillata Low-fired clay work with sheen resulting from burnishing; an extraordinarily fine-ground clay suspension in water that shines when applied as a coating. It is always fired at low temperature to preserve the shine. It is also the surface on Attic Greek wares.

Thermocouple A pair of wires of different metals (platinum and rhodium or, for low temperature, chrome-alumel) twisted together and sealed at one end. The sealed end registers the temperature; the reading is transmitted through the wires to a connector and thence via insulated wiring to the pyrometer, where the reading is measured in degrees.

Throwing The process of forming pieces on a revolving potter's wheel from solid lumps of clay into hollow forms.

Trailing A method of decorating with engobe or glaze squeezed out of a bulb from a small orifice or poured from a narrow lip.

Translucency Ability to transmit scattered light, not quite transparent.

Transparent Clear, like window glass; can be colored or colorless. Texture or decoration instantly shows through a transparent glaze.

Underglaze or G.S. Pigments designated as underglaze stains, overglaze stains, and body stains, according to usage. Also a name used by commercial manufacturers for a glaze product that stays put and does not melt.

Updraft Kiln Kiln in which the fire is underneath or at the low end of the tube or chamber; heat moves up through the ware and out of a flue at the top.

Viscosity Property of a flow; a highly viscous glaze is "stiff" and does not flow much during firing. A glaze of low viscosity is fluid, and can cause running or glaze decoration to become fluid in firing.

Vitreous Glass-like, hard, dense.

Wax Melted paraffin wax (which is not water-soluble), mixed with kerosene or benzine for ease of application, used for resist techniques; also commercially produced water-soluble waxes such as Ceremul A.

Wedging Kneading clay to expel air and make the mass homogeneous for hand processes.

Whiteware All ware with a white or ivory clay body after firing; industrial term.

LIST OF ARTISTS

*Artists' countries are indicated in the captions, except for American artists
which are the majority.*

INFORMATION SOURCES

Most countries have a Craft Council or similar organization; some have a museum or gallery associated with the organization, such as the American Craft Council and the American Craft Museum in New York City, USA, and the British Crafts Council and the Crafts Council Gallery in Pentonville Road, London. Also in London is the Craft Potters' Association and its shop and gallery in Marshall Street. Generally these craft organizations provide resource materials such as slides, movies, videos, and publications.

The International Academy of Ceramics (IAC) headquarters are in Geneva, Switzerland, at the Ariana Museum.

There are a number of ceramic residency opportunities in the world where clay artists can be invited and subsidized to work for short periods, or where less well-known or beginning clayworkers can pay to work. A few of the most important are: The Clay Studio, Philadelphia, Pennsylvania, the Bemis Foundation, Omaha, Nebraska, the Joe L. Evins Center for Appalachian Craft, Smithville, Tennessee, in USA; European Ceramic Center, Den Bosch, the Netherlands; the Ceramic Center, Shigaraki, Japan; the Artigas Foundation, Spain; the Banff Center, Canada.

Suppliers of ceramic materials and companies that manufacture ceramic equipment are fixtures in most countries. Their catalogs and data books give necessary information about their products. Clay mines, frit and stain manufacturers provide important technical brochures. Finally, commercially prepared clay bodies, under- and overglaze pigments, and ready-to-use glazes, as well as helpful information bulletins, are supplied universally by these corporations.

Ceramics magazines around the world include:

AUSTRALIA
Ceramics: Art and Perception
and *Ceramics Technical*
35 William Street
Paddington, Sydney, NSW
2021

Crafts Art Magazine
P.O. Box 363
Neutral Bay Junction, NSW
2089

Pottery in Australia
2/68 Alexander Street
Crow's Nest, NSW 2065

CHINA
Chinese Potters' Newsletter
Box 100600–9025
International Post Office
Beijing

FRANCE
L'Atelier, Société Nouvelle des Editions Créativité
41 rue Barrault
75013 Paris

La Céramique Moderne
22 rue Le Brun
75013 Paris

La Revue de la Céramique et du Verre
61 rue Marconi
62880 Vendin-le-Vieil

GERMANY
Keramik Magazin
(editorial) Bensheimer Strasse 4a
D-64653 Lorsch
(distribution)
Verlagsgesellschaft Ritterbach mbH
Rudolf-Diesel-Strasse 5-7
D-50226 Frechen

Neue Keramik
Unter den Eichen 90
D-1000 Berlin 45

GREECE
Keramiki Techni
P.O. Box 80653
185 10 Piraeus

ITALY
Ceramica Italiana Nell'Edilizia
Via Firenze 276
48018 Faenza

NETHERLANDS
Foundation COSA
P.O. Box 2413
3000 CK Rotterdam

Kerameik
Kintgenskuun 3
3512 GX Utrecht

SPAIN
Bulleti Informatiu de Ceramica
Sant Honorat 7
Barcelona 08002

Ceramica
Paseo de las Acacias 9
Madrid 5

TAIWAN
Ceramic Art
P.O. Box 47-74
Taipei

UK
Ceramic Review
21 Carnaby Street
London W1V 1PH

USA
American Ceramics
9 East 45 Street
New York, NY 10017-2403

American Ceramic Society Journal
757 Brooksedge Plaza Drive
Westerville, OH 43081-6136

American Craft Magazine
72 Spring Street
New York, NY 10012

Ceramic Industry
5900 Harper Road, Suite 109
Solon, OH 44139

Ceramics Monthly
735 Ceramic Place
P.O. Box 6012
Westerville, OH 43086

Clay Times
P.O. Box 365
Waterford, VA 20197–0365

Studio Potter
P.O. Box 65
Goffstown, NH 03045

BIBLIOGRAPHY

Public libraries, museum libraries, university and college libraries are filled with books on ceramic art, history and technology. Please make yourself aware of these great repositories at some point in your study. New treatises are continuously being added to the long list of in and out of print ceramic books – visit your local book stores often.

The following books will serve as a basic introduction to the general subject. We have tried to recommend only books that are currently in print; libraries will give you access to previously well known volumes.

Books of general interest:
American Ceramics, The Collection of the Everson Museum, Barbara Perry, Rizzoli, New York, 1989

American Ceramics, 1896 to the Present, revised edition, Garth Clark, Abbeville, 1987

Art Deco and Modernist Ceramics, Karen McCready, Thames and Hudson, London, 1995

Ceramics of the World, ed. Lorenzo Camusso and Sandra Bortone, Harry N. Abrams, New York, 1992

Chinese Ceramics, A New Survey by the Asian Art Museum of San Francisco, Rizzoli International, 1996

Chinese Pottery and Porcelain, S. J. Vainker, British Museum Press, London, 1991

Color and Fire, Defining Moments in Studio Ceramics, 1950–2000, Jo Lauria et al., Rizzoli International, 2000

The Craft and Art of Clay, Susan Peterson, Prentice Hall, New Jersey; Overlook Press, New York; Laurence King, London, third edition 1998

The History of American Ceramics, Elaine Levin, Harry N. Abrams, New York, 1988

Illustrated Dictionary of Practical Pottery, Robert Fournier, A. & C. Black, London, revised edition 1992

Iznik, The Pottery of Ottoman Turkey, Nurhan Atasoy and Julian Raby, Laurence King, London, 1994

Modern Pots, the Lisa Sainsbury Collection, Cyril Frankel, Thames and Hudson, London, 2000

Pioneer Pottery, Michael Cardew, revised edition, Oxford University Press, New York, 1989

The Potter's Art, A Complete History of Pottery in Britain, Garth Clark, Phaidon, London, 1995

Pottery by American Indian Women, Susan Peterson, Abbeville Press, New York, 1997

Revolutionary Ceramics, Soviet Porcelain 1917–1927, Nina Lobanov-Rostovsky, Cassell, London, 1990

Smashing Pots, Works of Clay from Africa, Nigel Barley, Smithsonian Institution Press, Washington D.C., 1994

Teapots Transformed, Leslie Ferrin, Guild Publishing, 2000

Traditional Pottery of India, Jane Perryman, A.& C. Black, London, 2000

Turners and Burners, The Folk Potters of North Carolina, Charles Zug, University of North Carolina Press, Raleigh-Durham, 1986

The Unknown Craftsman, Yanagi Soestsu, Kodansha International, New York, revised edition 1986

World Ceramics, Robert J. Charleston, Hamlyn, London, 1968

Monographs
The Art of Peter Voulkos, Rose Slivka, Karen Tsujimoto, Kodansha International, New York, 1995

Bernard Leach, Hamada, and Their Circle, Tony Birks and Cornelia Wingfield, Phaidon, London, 1990

Beyond YiXing, the Ceramic Art of Ah Leon, Purple Sands Publishers, Taiwan, 1998

Ettore Sottsass, Ceramics, Bruno Bischofberger, Thames and Hudson, London

Hans Coper, Tony Birks, Icon Editions, Harper & Row, 1983

Howard Kottler, Patricia Failing, University of Washington Press, Seattle, 1995

Jun Kaneko, Susan Peterson, Laurence King Publishing, London, 2001

The Living Tradition of Maria Martinez, Susan Peterson, Kodansha International, New York, revised edition 1996

Lucie Rie, Tony Birks, Chilton, Radnor, 1989

Lucy M. Lewis, American Indian Potter, Susan Peterson, Kodansha International, New York, 1984

The Mad Potter of Biloxi: The Art and Life of George Ohr, Garth Clark, Abbeville Press, New York, 1989

Maija Grotell, Jeff Schlanger and Toshiko Takaezu, Washington Press, Seattle, 1995

Shoji Hamada, A Potter's Way and

Work, Susan Peterson, revised edition, Weatherhill Press, New York, 1996

Warren MacKenzie, David Lewis, Kodansha International, New York, 1991

Technical Books

Ash Glazes, Phil Rogers, A. & C. Black, London; Krause Publications, USA, 1991

Ceramic Glazes, C. W. Parmelee, C. G. Harmon, Cahners Books, Boston, second edition 1973

Ceramic Masterpieces, Art, Structure, Technology, W. David Kingery, Pamela B. Vandiver, The Free Press/Macmillan Inc., New York, 1986

The Ceramic Spectrum, Robin Hopper, 2nd edition, Krause Publications, USA, 2001

Clay and Glazes for the Potter, Daniel Rhodes, revised by Robin Hopper, Krause Publications, USA, 2000

Finding One's Way with Clay, Paulus Berensohn, Simon & Schuster, New York, 1997

Glazes and Glazing Techniques, Greg Daly, Kangaroos Press, Australia, 1996

Hands in Clay, Charlotte Speight, Mayfield Press, CA, revised edition 1995

The Kiln Book, Frederick L. Olsen, A. & C. Black, London; Krause Publications, USA, 2001

Luster-ware, Alan Cager-Smith, Faber and Faber, London, 1985

Mold Making for Ceramics, Donald Frith, Chilton, Radnor, 1985

Out of the Earth into the Fire, Mimi Obstler, The American Ceramic Society, Westerville, Ohio, 1996

A Potter's Dictionary of Materials and Techniques, Frank and Janet Hamer, Pittman/Watson-Guptill, revised edition 1986; A. & C. Black, London, 1990

Raku, A Practical Approach, Steve Braunfman, Chilton, Radnor, 1991

Smashing Glazes, Susan Peterson, Guild Publishing, 2000

Smoke Fired Pottery, Jane Perryman, A. & C. Black, London, 1995

PHOTO CREDITS

A considerable number of the photographs in this book were taken by the authors. They are specially grateful to Craig Smith, Phoenix, AZ, who took the process photographs and others. Among other photographers, to whom the authors and the publishers would like to express sincere thanks, are:

Vanessa Adams, Noel Allum, Anders Bergersen, R. de la Cruz, John Cummings, Anthony Cunha, Susan Einstein, V. France, Takashi Hatakeyama, Ole Haupt (Denmark), Tom Holt, Paula Jansen, Kelley Kirkpatrick, Vineet Kracker, Bernd Kuhnert (Berlin), Peter Lee, Mahatta, Gail Reynolds

Matzler, Lee Milne, Hiromu Narita, Richard Nicol, Steven Ogawa, Brian Oglesbee, Rick Paulson, Renwick/Smithsonian, Hugh Sainsbury, Joshua Schreier, Bill Scott, Mike Short, Bernd Sinterhauf (Berlin), Gakuji Tanaka, John Tsantes, Van Tuil, Olga L. Valle, Malcolm Varon, Paul Warchol, Neil Winter.

Galleries and other institutions which kindly supplied photographs are listed below:

Garth Clark, New York City, NY; Charles Cowles, New York City, NY; Habitat, Minneapolis, MN; Materia Gallery,

Scottsdale, AZ; Paul Klein, Chicago, IL; LA Louver, Los Angeles, CA; Leedy-Voulkos, Kansas City, MO; Frank Lloyd, Los Angeles, CA; Lu Xiao-Ping; Nancy Margolis, New York City, NY; John Natsoulas, Davis, CA; Netherlands Ceramic Institute; Perimeter, Chicago, IL; Schopplein Studio; Shigaraki Ceramic Cultural Park, Japan.

Special thanks are also due to Cyril Frankel and Ben Williams in London; to Jim Scutt of Scutt Kilns, Portland, OR; Georgies Ceramic Supply, Portland, OR; Laguna Clay, for supplying the variety of fire clays; Paul Soldner for the picture of the Soldner Clay Mixer.

INDEX